Guided Imagery And Other Approaches To Healing

Rubin Battino, M.S.
Department of Human Resources
Wright State University

Crown House Publishing Limited
www.crownhouse.co.uk

First published in the UK by
Crown House Publishing Limited
Crown Buildings, Bancyfelin, Carmarthen, UK, SA33 5ND.
www.crownhouse.co.uk

© 2000 by Rubin Battino

First published 2000.

Permissions to quote from the following sources are gratefully
acknowledged:
Oldways Preservation & Exchange Trust for the traditional
Mediterranean diet pyramid.

British Library of Cataloguing-in-Publication Data
A catalogue entry for this book is available from the British
Library.

ISBN 1899836446

Printed and bound in Wales by
WBC Book Manufacturers,
Waterton Industrial Estate,
Bridgend, Mid Glamorgan.

Dedication

This book is dedicated to the brave people
who have let me share in their lives on
my journey to become a healer. Their
courage and hugs and laughter and living
in the present were and continue to be
what teaches me and sustains me.
Thank you, friends.

Table of Contents

Preface

One of the things I do as I drive is to listen to audiotapes on hypnosis, psychotherapy, and guided imagery. This practice is not dangerous because I am listening to the tapes analytically, i.e., critically taking apart their use of language and delivery styles. My training in Ericksonian hypnosis and hypnotherapy has made me acutely sensitive to language. My experiences in community theater have sensitized my ear to modes of delivery. There are some tapes with excellent content, but the voice characteristics of the speaker feel to me like chalk screeching on a blackboard. There are occasionally good speakers with trained voices presenting nonsense. Many tapes use music that is not background and is intrusively loud; other tapes use music that is just not my style. The field of guided imagery has exploded, but the quality of available tapes is not very high. So, part of my motivation for writing this book was to give professionals a step-by-step approach in doing quality guided imagery work. In that sense, this is a primer or text on guided imagery.

However, the book deals with much more than guided imagery. It is also a systematic presentation of all of the other things I do to help people who have life-challenging diseases. In the early drafts of this book I used the word "threatening" rather than "challenging"—the former is too scary and negative—challenges can be met and overcome. "Threatening" induces a passive reaction, "challenging" an active one. The differences between these two words are not subtle, particularly since this book is about the very careful use of language. My approach to helping people is multi-faceted since the disease itself is but one factor affecting the health of a person. As Viktor Frankl has pointed out, a human being is body *and* mind *and* spirit. *All three* need to be considered to help a person to health. The primary goal of guided imagery work is to diminish or cure the disease, the physical things wrong in the body. The entire second part of this book covers ways to help the client deal with the unfinished business and garbage in their lives. This work typically leads to a peace of mind and clarity, although physical improvement is not uncommon. I do not deal directly with spirit (or soul or inner sense of being), but rather let the words of other healers speak to this issue at the end of the book.

Part One is a systematic development of the structure of a guided imagery session. It starts with a review of the scientific evidence for the effectiveness of mind/body work. After an overview of guided imagery, there is a long chapter on the placebo effect. The client's belief system is central to both the effectiveness of guided imagery and placebos. There is also an extended exploration of prayer under the heading of "Prayer as a Placebo Effect?" Since guided imagery sessions begin with a relaxation component, Chapter 5 explores various relaxation methods. All interpersonal work depends on first establishing rapport with your client— Chapter 6 is on rapport building skills. The importance of the skillful use of language is highlighted in a separate chapter (7) on language for guided imagery. My training in hypnosis is the foundation for the way I work. Indeed, I consider it important for all professionals who do guided imagery work to have approved training in hypnosis, and I urge you to get such training. I have chosen to continue the development by next doing a detailed analysis of several published guided imagery scripts (Chapter 8). This chapter applies all of the preceding materials to actual scripts. A two-column format is used for this analysis, with recommended usage in italics. Chapter 9 contains three of my general guided imagery scripts, and two specific ones that were developed for two special people. Part One ends with an entire chapter on preparing someone for surgery. The end of this chapter is a surgery preparation script I developed for a friend with breast cancer.

The second part of the book is concerned with adjunct psychotherapy-based approaches to healing. Most of these approaches require the skill of a professional trained in counseling or psychotherapy, and should not be attempted by neophytes. After some introductory material, Chapter 12 discusses support groups. Chapter 13 presents a variety of approaches and methods that I have found to be useful in helping clients work through unfinished business, and for the elimination of the garbage in their lives. The last chapter in Part Two gives details and scripts for two approaches (bonding for healing, and fusion for healing) that I have developed, and which appear to be quite effective.

Continuing my emphasis on a multi-modal approach to healing, Part Three deals with related alternative approaches. Chapters 15 and 16 are written for *both* the lay person who has a disease, and the professional helping them. Chapter 15 discusses a number of things like journaling and ceremonies. A special feature of this chapter is Section 15.3 on structured writing with a workbook for people who have cancer. Section 15.4 has a workbook on grieving, and Section 15.5 has a workbook for care-givers. The heart of Part Three is Chapter 16 on coping which details the many practical ways that people can cope with a serious disease in a variety of settings. There are two specialist written chapters in Part Three. The first is by H. Ira Fritz, Ph.D., on nutrition. Professor Fritz has done research on nutrition and taught the nutrition courses at Wright State University for nurses and doctors for over three decades. Helena Sheehan, Ph.D., is a Native American and a healer. Her chapter is on native American healing traditions and her own experiences as a healer. Part Three ends with "some beginning words," a collection of inspirational words by healers who have influenced my life and my style.

Finally, there are appendices with useful special information, and a full list of references. Comments on the book and its contents are always welcome. My email address is:

rubin.battino@wright.edu

This book is a personal statement and was deliberately written in the first person. The book has grown out of my years of working as a facilitator in groups for people who have life-challenging diseases, and those who support them. The content is based in large part on a course I teach in the Department of Human Services at Wright State University.

I wish to give especial thanks to the three people who helped with the typing of this book: Connie Niles, Ruba Vignesaran, and Ann Yoxtheimer. I also appreciate the many helpful comments made by the classes I taught on this subject at Wright State University. Patricia Brooks, Rose Corner, Helena Sheehan, and Nicholas Piediscalzi all read the book in its entirety in draft form. Their comments and suggestions and advice were most welcome. Several members of the Charlie Brown Exceptional Patient Support Group of Dayton have read and commented on the *Workbook for People Who Have Cancer*, the *Workbook for Grieving*, and the *Workbook for Care-givers*—their feedback was most useful. In addition, three members of the Charlie Brown Group read the chapter on coping—their suggestions and experience were most helpful. They are Carolyn Mlinac, Clarissa (Chris) Crooks, and Mary Dyer. I also thank my friends in the Charlie Brown Exceptional Patient Support Group for all they have taught me about living in the moment, and about loving.

Rubin Battino
Yellow Springs, Ohio

Foreword

This new volume on guided imagery by Rubin Battino is being created at the crossroads between psychology, biology and physics. It is a work that is still very much a creative process. Rubin Battino brings his professional background as a professor of chemistry and researcher in thermodynamics to the leading edge of the theory and practice of the new mind-body chemistry of psychoneuroimmunology and healing.

Readers will appreciate the lucid manner with which Battino reviews just enough of the current scientific data to lay the foundation for his unified approach to the practical daily work of psychotherapists. His enthusiasm for developing creative, highly individualized approaches to healing is inspiring. The integrity of Battino's approach is evident in his careful scrutiny and exploration of the most useful attitudes, words and scripts of the pioneers and current practitioners in this field. Battino introduces the tools that a new generation of workers will need to carry on the ancient alchemical ideal of using mind and spirit to develop practical approaches to healing that the individual can actually use. He shows us how the medical profession and therapists of all schools need to carefully integrate the best of modern research and statistical documentation with positive healing attitudes and traditional rituals to facilitate well-being. In all of this he helps readers of a wide variety of backgrounds to construct a solid foundation for the therapeutic arts in the new millennium.

Ernest Lawrence Rossi, Ph.D.

Contributors

Rubin Battino, M.S.

He has a private practice in Yellow Springs, and also teaches courses for the Department of Human Services at Wright State University where he holds the rank of Adjunct Professor. This book is based on one of those courses. He has over seven years of experience as a volunteer facilitator in a Bernie Siegel style support group for people who have life-challenging diseases and those who support them. Also, he has many years of experience in individual work with people who have life-challenging diseases. He is President of the Milton H. Erickson Society of Dayton, and co-author with T.L. South, Ph.D. of *Ericksonian Approaches: A Comprehensive Manual*, a basic text on Ericksonian hypnotherapy and psychotherapy. He is currently Professor Emeritus of chemistry at Wright State University.

H. Ira Fritz, Ph.D.

He received his B.A. in Zoology and his Ph.D. in Nutrition from the University of California at Davis. He was an NIH Postdoctoral Fellow at the University of Pennsylvania. He has taught nutrition at the University of Pennsylvania and at Wright State University. His 34 years of teaching experience have included undergraduate, graduate, nursing, veterinary, and medical students. He is currently Professor Emeritus in the Department of Biochemistry and Molecular Biology at Wright State University. He is also Core Faculty Professor at the Union Institute in Cincinnati, Ohio.

Helena Sheehan, Ph.D.

She is a Native American from Oklahoma who attended high school in Oklahoma and did her undergraduate work in California. Her graduate degrees in Counseling are from Ohio State University. She has taught undergraduate courses in psychotherapy, tests and measurement, social psychology, abnormal psychology, theories of psychology, and also courses in counseling and hypnosis. She has a private practice using hypnotherapy and healing. In addition, she has worked as a counselor and teacher for over 24 years in secondary education. She is a member and officer of the Milton H. Erickson Society of Dayton.

Part One

Guided Imagery for Healing

Chapter 1

Introduction

1.1 Introduction

The purpose of this book is to share with helping professionals the approaches that I have found to be useful in working with people who have life-challenging diseases. Part One is designed to systematically teach how to do guided imagery work. Part Two details the psychotherapy-based approaches which I consider to be necessary for comprehensive work in healing. Part Three is concerned with related approaches.

A broad definition of guided imagery for healing might be: any internal work that you do that involves thoughts (uses the "mind") and has a positive effect on health. This can range from "thinking positive" to elaborately structured processes involving relaxation, meditation, and body postures. It can include biofeedback and various enhancements of mood via music, electrical or vibrating stimulation, massage, acupuncture, magnetic (or other) fields, or ingested supplements of drugs and herbs. The common denominator is thoughts, and their effects on body function. There is currently a great deal of evidence for this assertion. Scientific evidence is presented in the first part of the book. There is then a systematic presentation about the theory and practice of guided imagery, with an emphasis on the "how to." The latter will involve excursions into rapport building and hypnotic language forms. The overall intent of the book is to provide practical methods in such a way that workers in the field can use them with their own clients. Exercises will be introduced where appropriate. One example of this approach is the detailed linguistic analysis of transcripts of guided imagery. Examples of recommended language usage and the design of guided imagery are also provided. Finally, the audiotapes accompanying this book contain examples of generic and specific guided imagery sessions.

Welcome!

1.2 A Personal Note

I have spent most of my professional life as a professor of chemistry, dividing my interest between chemical education and "hard" research in the area of the thermodynamics of solutions, which I continue in retirement. This has been a rewarding career, and includes two co-authored books on thermodynamics and many technical publications.

A number of years ago I was in treatment with a Gestalt Therapist. After I completed my significant personal work with him, I approached him about doing some more group work. Instead, he invited me to join a training group in Gestalt Therapy. I did so, and was the only lay person in training. This involvement led me to obtain a master's degree in mental health counseling in 1978. I have had a small private practice specializing in very brief therapy since that time. (I am licensed in Ohio and a national board certified counselor.) In addition to Gestalt Therapy, I have had training in bioenergetic analysis, Neuro-Linguistic Programming (NLP), Ericksonian hypnosis and hypnotherapy, and solution-oriented approaches among other modalities. T.L. South and I recently (1999) have had published *Ericksonian Approaches: A Comprehensive Manual*. For over fifteen years I have taught specialty workshops for the Department of Human Services (counseling) at Wright State University as an Adjunct Professor. This book is based on one of those courses.

How, then, did I become interested in healing and working with people who have life-challenging diseases? About seven years ago I read Bernie Siegel's first book (1986)—*Love, Medicine & Miracles*—and afterward asked myself the question, "With your skills and training, why aren't you working with the kinds of people Bernie describes?" A phone call to ECaP (Exceptional Cancer Patients, 522 Jackson Park Drive, Meadville, PA 16355: (814) 337-8192) put me in touch with the Charlie Brown Exceptional Patient Support Group of Dayton. They kindly let me sit in on their semi-monthly sessions. With what I learned from them, I started a support group in the village of Yellow Springs. This group ran for two years while I continued to attend meetings of the Dayton group. Eventually, I became one of the facilitators of the Dayton group. (The way the Dayton group functions is described later for those interested in establishing similar groups.)

It has been my practice to "adopt" two or three members of the support group for more intensive follow-up and individualized work. (All of this is done as a volunteer.) The individual work involves teaching guided imagery, information, and the clearing up of unfinished business. My personal philosophy can be summarized in two statements, "I always have hope" and "I believe in miracles." Certainly, some miracles have occurred. In some ways, this book is about facilitating miracles.

Is this work wearing and depressing? Most emphatically NO! There is always laughter and joy in our support group. Of course, there is also some sadness and crying and depression. But, the overall mood of these exceptional people is one of hope and unconditional love. I invariably leave a meeting feeling renewed and inspired by their incredible courage. It sounds paradoxical, but everyone I know who has a life-challenging disease has said at some time that their disease was a *blessing*. For most of them, life was pretty routine, even dull, up to that point. Now, every day, every hour, every minute is important—they are really living in the here-and-now, experiencing life, moment by moment, with an unprecedented intensity. Someone pointed out that the "present" is called that because it is indeed a *gift*. To be alive *now,* rather than dwell in the past or the future, is what my friends have taught me.

Through the very nature of this work many of my friends have died. Yet, I would not trade getting to know them and being part of their lives for anything—they have all become part of me.

1.3 Disease/Cure and Illness/Healing
Despite the ancient adage of "sticks and stones can break your bones, but words can never hurt you" words can have powerful positive *and* negative effects on the human mind and body. Since this book is primarily about the careful use of words to help people (see Chapter 7), it is important to define certain words carefully. We will start this process with a few significant words.

It is popular in some quarters to write the word "disease" as dis-ease, implying that it describes a state which is the opposite of being at ease, in comfort, or relaxed. In this book we define a *disease* as something that is physically wrong with the body. That is, a disease is the pathology itself. Examples are: cancer, infections, hormonal imbalances, diverticulitis, ulcers, strokes, myocardial infarctions and insufficiencies, and broken bones. The reversing or fixing of a disease (in Western societies) typically involves a "mechanical" intervention of some sort: surgery, chemotherapy, radiation, antibiotics, supplements, dieting changes, physical rehabilitation, and drugs. When the disease is fixed or has gone away, the person is said to be "cured." So, a *cure* is the reversal of a disease, the disappearance of its physical manifestations, and a return to normal healthy functioning. We are fortunate that there are a great many diseases that can be cured in a straightforward manner.

The title of this book uses the word "healing." How is healing different from curing? To clarify this, we first need to make a distinction between an illness and a disease. We define *illness* to be the *meaning* that you personally attribute to the disease. These meanings are unique to you and are determined by your history, culture, religion, ethnicity, belief system, intellectual predilection, upbringing, heritage, philosophy of life. Siblings are more likely to interpret a given disease in the same way than people from different cultures. Yet, due to different life experiences, sisters may react in very different ways to a preliminary diagnosis of breast cancer. *Healing* applies to the *meaning* of the disease, i.e., the illness. The root of healing signifies "to make whole." Healing is more related to internal feeling states than physical states.

For example, when I was growing up in the Bronx in a Greek-Jewish subculture, the word "cancer" was rarely mentioned, or spoken in only a whisper. There was a belief that saying the word out loud (or even *thinking* it!) would catch the attention of the "Evil One" and you would then be more susceptible to getting cancer. Evil Ones or devils were part of the belief system of my relatives. This reaction to a word colored all of our thinking and responses. A person who had CANCER was doomed to a horrible death, but it also bore connotations of shame and pity. The *illness* was worse than the disease; it led to a helplessness and hopelessness on the part of the afflicted person, as well as care-givers and well-wishers. Thankfully, many of our attitudes towards cancer-the-disease have changed. Bernie Siegel sums it up best by saying, "Cancer is not a sentence, it is just a word."

Healing deals with attitudes and meaning. When a person is healed, they become whole again, and can be at peace with themself, the disease, and the world at large. Healing is involved with the spirit, the soul, and one's essence. For some, a healing experience may be described as a religious experience, perhaps even a religious transformation. To become whole, to be in harmony, to be centered, to find one's true self, to be at peace with yourself and the world—all of these are manifestations of healing.

Remarkably, although healing is an end in itself, healing is often accompanied by some degree of curing, if not complete cures, with sufficient frequency to be taken seriously. The goal of healing work is not a cure—the cure is a by-product of healing. In fact, if the sole motivation for healing work is a cure, then the healing work becomes contaminated and side-tracked. Healing invariably involves a search for meaning, a spiritual quest. What does it all mean? Why am I alive at this moment in time? Are there things that are meant for me to do in the rest of my life? About two thousand years ago Rabbi Hillel was once asked to summarize his lifelong wisdom. He responded with the following three questions:

> If I am not for myself, who will be?
> If I am only for myself, what am I?
> If not now, when?

We might say that healing an illness involves the honest answering of these questions.

A related linguistic pairing to the subject of this section is in the words "patient" and "client." My unabridged dictionary has a number of meanings for patient. Its origins are in the Latin word for *suffer*. As an adjective, the two main definitions are: 1. Bearing or enduring pains, trials, or the like, without complaint or with equanimity; having, exercising, or manifesting the power to endure physical or mental affliction; as, a *patient* invalid, sufferer, victim. 2. Exercising or manifesting forbearance or self-control under provocation from others; indulgent to the shortcomings or offenses of others; long suffering; as, a *patient* nurse, guardian, teacher. As a noun: 1. A sufferer; one who endures. 2. A sick person, now commonly, one under treatment or care, as by a physician or surgeon, or in a hospital; hence a client of a physician, hospital, or the like. So, the root of "patient" is in suffering and, in seeking healing, we suffer through to a resolution. In this sense, there is an *active* suffering, rather than a *victim* suffering. In modern usage the medical establishment uses the word "patient" rather than "client." Perhaps this is because in so many medical settings a person has to be *patient* in *waiting* for a treatment. For me the word "patient" implies a one-down position, superior/inferior, an unequal status. For many reasons I prefer to use the word "client" which implies providing a professional service for a fee. *Clients* "hire" professionals to carry out a specific function such as: write a will, set a bone, fix a leak, and identify and cure an infection. These are contracted services and the professional *works for you*. Which professionals routinely keep you waiting for the service for which you pay them? It is almost as if your time is not as valuable as that of the physician. Occasional waits for medical services would be reasonable due to unforeseen circumstances. But, waiting seems to be the rule rather than the exception. I had a dentist in Chicago who always had me in the chair at the appointed time. He had an emergency repair at one of these sessions and asked my permission to take care of that client first. He treated his clients with respect, just as I responded to his request with respect. In the patient position, procedures are generally *done to you*. As a client, there would be more cooperation in what happens. In relation to medical practices it is wise, and even healing, to be a client rather than a patient.

1.4 Complementary and Nontraditional Approaches; Alternative Medicine and Therapies

Bernie Siegel rightly insists that your healing/curing journey needs to be done in *partnership* with traditional medicine. After all, there are a great many diseases that can be competently and effectively treated by modern medicine. These range from fractures to by-pass surgery (where needed, since there is evidence that this procedure is over-prescribed), (most) infections, hernias, allergies, and cataract surgery. While it is true that the most significant contributor to the increase in longevity since 1900 has been public sanitation, the armamentarium and skills and contributions of present-day allopathic physicians are indisputable. One would be foolish, indeed, to not avail themself of such proven services. Yet, somehow, parallel with the advances of medicine we find increasing interest in nontraditional approaches to health and health care. Why is this?

Although great progress has been made in many areas, there are still many diseases like cancer, AIDS, and the common cold which continue to defy modern medicine. Since hope springs eternal and your Aunt Mary had this tonic that always worked in your family, why not try it? There are many folk remedies and traditional Chinese herbal medicines that have been used for centuries. There is *occasional* scientific evidence, such as double-blind studies, for some of these substances. But, mostly, the evidence for efficaciousness is historical and anecdotal. One advantage of most of these substances is that side-effects appear to be minimal. "Above all, cause no harm to your patients."

There is a small problem in labeling non-modern-medicine (allopathic) approaches. They have been called "complementary," "nontraditional," and "alternative." Each of these words has advantages and disadvantages, but since they all convey the sense of being different from standard traditional Western medicine I think they can be used interchangeably—let your preference guide you. Another way to describe these approaches is *transpersonal medicine* (Lawlis, 1997).

Historically, scientific Western medicine is quite young. It can probably be dated from Semmelweis' introduction of antiseptic practices, Pasteur's germ theory of disease, and Morton's use of diethyl ether for anesthesia. This makes modern medicine a little over one century old. Until this time, the medicine that was practiced worldwide was based on historical traditions in each culture. Native Americans have a rich lore of natural products, as well as various healing rites. This is also true in China, Africa, South America, India, and even in Europe. The 19th century apothecary in London, Vienna, and Philadelphia contained many of the same substances, almost all of them "natural." Trial and error was the "scientific" basis proving the efficacy of these materials.

Before the development of western medicine, practitioners relied on giving patients many of the same natural or synthetic materials that are in use today. Their primitive surgical methods were sometimes successful. But, the advent of scientific medicine led to an emphasis on "mechanical" interventions (surgery and drugs) and ignored the mental, spiritual, belief, and meaning sides of both healing and curing. To be sure, physicians had to be aware of exceptional patients who got well without their help. A scientist understands cause and effect: splinting a broken bone leads to its proper knitting together; a by-pass operation improves heart capacity; an antibiotic rids the body of an infection. But, where does an AIDS or cancer patient who becomes symptom free fit in? How do you explain Norman Cousins' cure from ankylosing spondilitis? How can sand paintings and psychosurgery help? By what mechanisms do acupuncture and hypnosis let patients undergo major operations pain free?

Western medicine has separated the mind from the body. The much older, traditional medicines made no such distinctions— man was a whole: integrated mind, body *and* spirit. Viktor Frankl (1959, 1962) repeatedly stated in his lectures that physicians treat only the body, psychologists and psychiatrists the mind, and that both ignore the third dimension of the spirit or soul. In Frankl's sense, you can't really be a healer if you deal with only one aspect of the mind/body/spirit continuum. They are inseparable. There may be times when, for convenience, you deal with just one part, but that is done for whose convenience? Native healers, shamans and witch doctors have always dealt with the whole person—how can you be in *harmony* with yourself and nature as isolated parts?

Organized and personal religion have used prayer as a method to attain healing and cures. Prayer has been basically used in four ways. The *first* is simply a person talking to God, supreme being or spirit: a way to communicate with something or someone beyond themselves—a sharing of their inner thoughts with this external presence. The *second* is to ask this external and knowledgeable and powerful entity for help in a specific concern. These concerns range from mundane specific items (winning the lottery, passing an exam, appropriate weather) to the correction of physical ailments to attain cures. In some way, the justice of your cause or plea is recognized and the all-powerful all-knowing being or entity directly intercedes in your behalf. The *third* form of prayer is more spiritual, and is a kind of meditation whose result is some degree of fusion with, or knowledge of, the universal spirit. When someone has a life-challenging disease, the second type of prayer appears to be the most common. There have been double-blind style studies where people pray for the improved health of a person whose name they know or picture they've seen, but the patient does not know of this prayer. A *fourth* form of prayer is the simple "thank you" that is part of saying grace or just a way of showing appreciation. (There will be more on the subject of prayer later when Larry Dossey's work and others are discussed in Section 4.6.)

Belief systems can have powerful influences on our lives. Many people who consider themselves to be hard-headed rationalists still react in nonrational ways in particular circumstances. These may be automatic learned responses that they learned in childhood. For example, is the power of prayer correlated with the depth of your belief? Is belief the core of the placebo effect wherein an inert substance or neutral intervention results in a profound physical change? (See Chapter 4 for a more detailed account of the placebo effect.) Bandler and Grinder (the founders of NLP) coined the word "psychotheology," and indicated that if your client *believed* in your brand of psychotheology that you could probably help them. Are all alternative therapies psychotheologies?

The search for meaning drives many people. When a person functions with that meaning directing their life, there can be profound physical and psychological effects. This quest has been expressed in different ways: (1) Viktor Frankl as a search for meaning; (2) Joseph Campbell as finding and following your bliss; and (3) Lawrence LeShan as discovering and singing your own unique song. The quest involves identifying your hopes, dreams, and unfulfilled desires. What is it that you've always wanted to do or be? Bernie Siegel cites the story of a lawyer who had "terminal" cancer. This man became a lawyer to please his father. Faced with a limited life, he gave up his law practice and returned to his first love of playing the violin. Somehow, the cancer disappeared and he found a new career as a professional musician. Will this always be the case? Of course not. Yet, at the minimum, finding and singing your own unique song can lead to a healing. Why wait for a diagnosis of something like cancer to send you on your quest?

The lawyer's story is "anecdotal evidence" of the power of the mind, the spirit. As such, it is inadmissible in the court of modern medicine. Yet, every physician (if pushed!) could tell you such stories about their own patients, i.e., people who underwent, for no scientifically known reason, complete remission or cures. How many such anecdotes are needed before the scientific establishment starts a serious hunt for their causes? The National Center for Complementary and Alternative Medicine (NCCAM) of the National Institutes of Health (NIH) is currently funding such research activities. The study of exceptions has led to many discoveries.

Lawrence LeShan (1989) in the introductory chapter to *Cancer as a Turning Point* cites many sources prior to 1900 which connect cancer to hopelessness and deep anxiety and disappointment. These observations recognized mental state as a major contributor to the onset of cancer. Based on his studies LeShan wrote (p. 14)

> … The profound hopelessness was, in many of the people I saw, followed by the appearance of cancer. Over and over again I found that the person I was working with reminded me of the poet W.H. Auden's definition of cancer. He called it "a failed creative fire."

> As this pattern became clearer, I also began to work with *control groups*, people without cancer to whom I gave the same personality tests and worked with in the same way psychologically. Over a period of many years, I found this pattern of loss of hope in between 70 to 80 percent of my cancer patients and in only 10 percent or so of the control group.

Hopelessness is certainly a factor in cancer, but it is only one factor. Knowledge of this factor was the basis for LeShan's approach to working with people who have cancer, to have them find and sing their own "unique song." The importance of hope and meaning in life is a central theme of Bernie Siegel's work. It is a major part of my work. Appendix A lists LeShan's 31 significant questions (1989, pp. 161–165) as a guide to his work and yours.

Bernie Siegel has frequently stated, "What's wrong with hope?" In the face of all of the evidence of mind/body interaction and exceptions, is it still necessary for physicians to baldly state, "Statistics show in your case a four month longevity"? The *hopeful* statement would be, "While your prognosis is not good, perhaps a few months, there have been many remarkable recoveries. Let's continue to work together. Would it be okay if we prayed together? And, I could certainly do with a hug before you leave." Which statement is more honest? Pancreatic cancer has a high mortality rate; typically people rarely survive three months beyond diagnosis. But, studies have shown that one per cent are still alive five years after diagnosis! Are we "percentiles" or unique human beings with amazing potentials? Even though hope cannot be quantified, it seems to have only positive side effects. Hope depends on the *way* you say things.

An excellent book on alternative treatment for cancer is the one by Michael Lerner (1996). This book is based to a large extent on a governmental study (U.S. Congress Office of Technology Assessment, Unconventional Cancer Therapies, 1990). *All* of the alternative treatments that Lerner writes about have in fact helped *some* people. The outcomes are neither consistent nor predictable. People are unique and vary in characteristics—this is what the Bell curve or the Gaussian distribution of probabilities is all about. The pharmacopeias can give you the dose for the *average* person of a given body weight, but, this will be an overdose for some people and ineffectively low for others. Lerner's book does give balanced and well-researched guidelines to alternative/complementary treatments for cancer.

The psychiatrist, David Spiegel (1989, et seq.) has now provided definitive proof that a psychotherapeutic support group has been effective for last stage breast cancer. The women in the support group lived about twice as long beyond the start of the study as the women in the control group. It is not clear why the support group had this effect, although the original study has been replicated.

1.5 Summary

Hopes are dreams, and without dreams we are doomed to a humdrum existence. The remarkable people I work with are dreamers—along with whatever travails the capriciousness of life has brought to them, they continue to hope, to dream, to be, and to be more alive in the moment than the rest of us. This book is a tribute to what they have taught me about living, about being alive. From time to time they can benefit from the guidance of a professional helper. This book is a guide for such professionals.

Chapter 2

Scientific Evidence

2.1 Introduction

For some people the word "scientific" in relation to alternative therapies is a contradiction in terms. Yet, these same people may have a favorite remedy inherited from their parents or grandparents. I have spent most of my life as a "hard" scientist working in physical chemistry and chemical thermodynamics. But, when I have an upset stomach, nothing seems to settle it like strong chamomile tea and several slices of wholegrain toast. This is what my mother gave me as a child. Does drinking the tea and eating the toast regress me to an earlier time when I was comforted by her care and love? Probably. On the other hand, chamomile tea has been a folk remedy for millennia for stomach distress, and dry toast is nourishing and bland. None of these "facts" connect to the special effect of tea and toast for me.

We begin our exploration of the extant scientific evidence with a study of psychoneuroimmunology (PNI), which implies not only a mind/body interaction, but an involvement of that interaction with the immune system. The field of PNI is considered to be the mainstay of proof for mind/body healing.

2.2 Psychoneuroimmunology (PNI)

For years physicians have accepted the idea of psychosomatic illnesses. That is, stress has been noted as a factor in migraine headaches, ulcers, spastic colon, lower back pain, tension headaches, allergic reactions, and autoimmune disorders. A cynic might say that the medical establishment accepts the idea that mental factors can cause physical problems because they make money from the results. In addition, some physicians may have difficulty with mental attitudes leading to the diminution or curing of diseases since that happened without their participation. Not being a cynic, I think that one reason that alternative therapies are not accepted is that cause/effect relationships cannot be demonstrated consistently. Also, while some cause/effect relationships have been shown, the *mechanism* connecting the cause to the effect is itself unknown. For example, it is well-known and demon-strable that antibiotics disrupt and destroy bacteria. But, how does hypnosis or acupuncture control pain, and by what possible "mechanism(s)" can guided imagery or support groups lead to the disappearance of a tumor mass?

The brain was once considered to be accurately described as a complex telephone switchboard, and more recently as some kind of computer. It is, of course, known that the brain controls a host of functions within the body and, like a computerized industrial process, that it uses sensors of various types and feedback controls to maintain homeostasis and normal body functions. This version of a brain describes a passive-mechanical-biophysiological proces-sor. The autonomic nervous system maintains and regulates the internal environment; and is considered to be involuntary, i.e., beyond voluntary control. It has been known for a long time that some individuals can control involuntary functions like heart rate, blood pressure, and the temperature of particular body parts like fingers. People can also be "trained" via biofeedback to control these functions. (Since the pain of headaches is caused by the dila-tion of blood vessels in the brain, increasing the volume of the blood system by creating warm hands through biofeedback fre-quently gives symptomatic relief.) The beginning steps in reinte-grating (conceptually) the mind and the body are the many examples of "mind" control over some autonomic nervous system functions.

The next step may be found in the work of Candace Pert (she was then at NIH) and others who showed that the brain is not just this passive regulating blob, but also is capable of synthesizing many specialty molecules. You may wish to read the interesting dialogue between Pert and Ornish in the latter's book (1997, pp. 216–220) that contains much up-to-date information on PNI research. To date, dozens and dozens of such biochemicals have been identi-fied and their methods of interaction elucidated. There are opiate receptors in the brain that can produce a class of compounds col-lectively called endorphins that have opiate-like properties. These endorphins have been shown to provide relief from pain via the placebo effect (Levine et al., 1978). Enkephalins, brain molecules, have a role in modifying the immune system. So, here we have two groups of brain-synthesized molecules which are involved in pain control and the immune system. These biochemicals are sometimes referred to as neurotransmitters and, in modern terminology, as "messenger molecules." Rossi (1993) likes to think about these mind/body processes being exercises in *information transduction*. After all, it is well known that the surface of individual cells contain thousands of specialized receptors, each fitting a particular molecule (like a key in a lock). With the development of PNI over the past twenty years (see, e.g., Ader, 1981) we have the scientific basis for mind/body interactions, i.e., a rationale for Norman Cousins' cure.

Human cancers can be considered to be caused by a breakdown in the automatic functioning of the immune system. One theory of how cancers develop starts with the idea that, for whatever reason, aberrant cells are continually produced in the body. These cells may be the product of radiation (x-rays, cosmic), known and unknown chemical carcinogens, genetic predisposition, or just random events that occur because of the billions of cells the body produces. Normally, the immune system can identify such abnormal cells and eliminate them. For most of us, this is the ongoing automatic outside-of-awareness process that keeps us cancer-free as well as protects us from various viral and bacterial invasions. In some people, the immune system functions less effectively over a particular period of time, and a certain kind of cancer cell proliferates as a small or large mass, or in several locations. It is known that certain cancers are "clever" in the sense that they can fool the immune system into ignoring them. Whether the immune system has been tricked or overwhelmed, these aberrant cells can multiply to the point of detection by their size or by their effects on normal body functions.

Some treatments for cancer involve enhancing and strengthening the immune system. Traditional medical interventions such as surgery, radiation, and chemotherapy serve to eliminate and destroy cancer cells to give the immune system a helping hand. The surgical removal of a well-defined and encapsulated tumor (some of these can be grapefruit size) may be all that is needed to become cancer free. Once a cancer has metastasized or spread from its initial site(s), only the systemic treatments like chemotherapy and bone marrow transplants seem to work. Dr. O. Carl Simonton emphasizes in his lectures that aberrant cancer cells are typically *weaker* and less capable of survival than normal cells. Since we now know from all the PNI studies (among others) that the mind and mental processes can have profound physiological and psychological effects, how can this information be utilized to strengthen the immune system?

Ader and co-workers, and others (1981), have shown that the immune system is trainable. In a classic study with rats they found that pairing an immunosuppressive agent (something that destroys white blood cells and otherwise suppresses the immune system) with a harmless stimulus such as saccharin resulted in the *saccharin alone* having the same effect. In a study of allergic reactions an artificial rose was found to trigger the allergy—an immune response—and even *thinking* about the allergen can bring on the allergic reaction. This shows how powerful the mind is. It is a strange phenomenon that most people have a sense that "they can make themselves sick," but then need to go to a physician to get well. And yet they do not pay attention to the obverse of the statement in quotes. Glaser (1985) and Kiecolt-Glaser (1984) have demonstrated the effect that stress has on the immune system— basically, stress serves to weaken the immune system. The death of a spouse is one of the most stressful things that can happen to a person. It is not unusual for the surviving partner to come down with some life-challenging or severe disease within 12 to 18 months after this death.

If stress can suppress the immune system, will the opposite emotional states such as joy, happiness, peace of mind, and relaxation strengthen the immune system? Can thinking happy thoughts heal? Norman Cousins (1981) with the cooperation of his physician apparently laughed himself to health. If *one* human being is capable of a documented "spontaneous remission," i.e., the disappearance of the disease due to non-physician related interventions, that means that we *all have the potential* for such happenings. After all, we all have the same wiring and physiology. The important word above is "potential." Norman Cousins did it, but will the next person who tries laughter achieve the same results? What percentage of cures attributable to laughter and happy living is needed before this becomes a standard treatment like the chemotherapy agents taxol and cis-platin? This is an important question because many of the chemotherapy agents that are in present-day use have effectiveness ratings (via the usual double-blind studies) of significantly less than 50%. Is it preferable to try chemical X because your oncologist can cite studies that *prove* that it is 33% effective, versus an alternative therapy with an anecdotal helping rate of 25% (or whatever percentage)?

Green and Green (1977) examined four hundred reported cases of spontaneous remission and found that the only common factor was a change of attitude from despair and hopelessness to hope and positive feelings before the remission occurred. While changing your attitude does not guarantee a remission, neither does taking chemotherapy; the major difference is that the former has no physical side effects. These spontaneous remission patients can all be classified as being *exceptional*. In addition to positive attitudes, life expectancy is increased by being more creative and receptive to new ideas, and to being flexible and argumentative. A certain amount of orneriness appears to help. Denial is commonly considered to be a bad idea, but when it is denying being a victim rather than denial of the existence of the disease, it can be a force for health. Many of these exceptional people turn outward for an external source to give them extra strength. They are fighters, and were fighters before the onset of the disease.

Let me add a few words about the word "victim" since it is still common usage to refer to people who have cancer as cancer victims. Victim comes from the Latin *victima* which means to consecrate. Thus, the first dictionary definition states: 1. A living being sacrificed to some deity, or in the performance of a religious rite; a creature immolated, or made an offering of. The second definition is: 2. A person or living creature injured, destroyed, or sacrificed, in the pursuit of an object, in the gratification of a passion, from disease, accident, or the like. The third definition is: 3. Hence, one who is duped or cheated. Is a "cancer victim" someone who is being sacrificed due to sins they have committed, or because of some manner of improper living, or at the whim of some powerful person or force? There is a fateful helplessness involved in being a victim. The opposite stance is probably that of the hero or heroine, a person who takes action, and who has some control over their life. Survivors, people who beat serious diseases, are more like heroes and heroines than victims.

Lawrence LeShan, a psychologist, has worked with terminal cancer patients for several decades (1974, 1977, 1982, 1989). He has indicated three reasons that a person typically gives for not wanting to die: (1) they fear the circumstances of death or dying, i.e., pain, the unknown, the helplessness; (2) they want to live for others, helping the others attain their goals; and (3) they want to live their own life, to be able to sing their own unique song. Of these reasons LeShan states (1982, p. 139):

> For reasons I do not fully understand, the body will not mobilize its resources for either or both of the first two reasons. Only for the third will the self-healing and self-recuperative abilities of the individual come strongly into play. When individuals with cancer understand this and begin to search for and fight for their own special music in ways of being, relating, working, creating, they tend to begin to respond much more positively….

LeShan's conclusion ties in with the importance of hopes and dreams, and dealing with unfinished business in healing. It was LeShan's finding that psychotherapy invariably led to some level of *healing* for terminal cancer patients. He was probably not surprised to find some remissions and increased longevity. Does psychotherapy work through some psychoneurological/ immunological process? Probably. There will be more on this later in this chapter.

Rossi's book (1993) on the psychobiology of mind/body healing, gives an excellent summary of the research in this area. Rossi started his career as a Jungian analyst, and through his work with Milton H. Erickson, M.D., has gone on to pioneer new directions in hypnosis and hypnotherapy. For example, his recent book (1996) attempts in part to provide a theoretical basis for hypnotherapy in nonlinear dynamics or chaos theory. Part of the 1993 book deals with hypnotherapeutic techniques for healing. I am a practicing Ericksonian hypnotherapist, and much of the material in this book is based on that perspective. Using words to lead a person into a relaxation and guided imagery session is not unlike an hypnotic induction. One of the themes of Rossi's 1993 book is "state dependent learning and behavior" (SDLB). This simply means that a stimulus in the present calls forth in all dimensions the experiences from your past which were triggered by that stimulus. This means that you have to be an astute reader of body language when delivering a guided image. You may find being at a beach relaxing, but a beach setting may have been the site of a severe sunburn or a near drowning for your client. The SDLB theory states that just words can be a sufficient trigger to recall past events, and as a therapist you have to be prepared in case those events were traumatic.

Dean Ornish (1997) provides an excellent summary in his recent book of the scientific basis for the healing power of intimacy. In fact there are ten pages of references for his chapter 2 on this scientific basis. Chapter 6 is a long chapter wherein he holds dialogues with many of the people in the field, asking them to comment on their experiences and research on the healing power of intimacy. The question he asks them is, "Why do you think love and intimacy are such powerful factors in affecting diseases and premature death from virtually all causes?" Their responses should convince the most skeptical. Ornish's multi-faceted program for reversing heart disease (1991) is considered in some detail in Chapter 17 of this book.

Finally, we report on some recent studies that show that new nerve cells can be formed in the adult human brain. In a popular article, Kempermann and Gage (1999) cite the evidence for this interesting phenomenon. Factors that enhance the growth of new nerve cells are an enriched environment by which the brain is challenged with new information, and novel experiences and puzzles to be solved, and by physical exercise. Research is continuing in this area for its potential for better treatments for neurological diseases, but this work also emphasizes the importance of mind/body/environment interactions.

The bottom line is that research in PNI and related areas have provided the missing scientific foundation for mind/body healing. If miserable and stressful thoughts can harm the body, then relaxation and happy thoughts can both heal and cure the body. This idea has long been a tenet of folk wisdom.

2.3 The Pioneering Work of the Simontons

It is now over twenty years that Simonton et al.'s book (1978) enti-tled *Getting Well Again* appeared. O. Carl Simonton is an oncolo-gist and his (then) wife Stephanie is a psychologist. They reasoned that a combination of relaxation and guided imagery would have a healing effect, if not also a curing one. They began their work before PNI had been established. In the early stages of develop-ment the relaxation and guided imagery were done with groups of patients. The imagery, which was for everyone in the group, typi-cally involved some scavenging or fierce animal like a shark or a wolf who would be inside them and destroy cancer cells, much as a lion eats a deer. The method was slowly refined and the images tailored to the person in individual work. A shark is not a proper anti-cancer agent to use for a Quaker or a pacifist. An angel might be more appropriate.

The not-so-surprising results from a modern perspective showed that there was increased longevity (beyond medical predictions) for a significant number of patients using imagery. Also, a number (again, beyond medical prediction) of patients using imagery went into remission. Their book opened an entire new field for ways of working with people who have serious diseases. Stephanie Simonton continues to work in this area in Texas, and O. Carl Simonton has a clinic based on his principles in California (Simonton Cancer Center, P.O. Box 890, Pacific Palisades, CA 90272; (800) 459-3424).

2.4 Michael Lerner's Guide

Michael Lerner's *Choices in Healing* (1996) is a wonderful resource compiled by the director of the Commonweal Cancer Help Program (P.O. Box 316, Bolinas, CA 94924; (415) 868-0970). Commonweal is a place where people who have cancer can visit for one week at a time and be in a healing milieu involving: nutri-tion, massage, group sessions, information on alternative treat-ments, and staff consultations. Lerner's book is based in part on a government study (1990) on alternative treatments, and gives much detail on the history, the practitioners, the treatments them-selves, and the results of any scientific or other studies on out-comes. Each of the treatments discussed has helped some people to cures; however, the scientific evidence from carefully controlled studies is missing. Some of the practitioners use substances and methods which they consider to be proprietary, and will divulge no information as to composition. Other practitioners openly published such details. Without controlled studies, Lerner could not recommend any of the described treatments.

However, Lerner indicated that there was sufficient evidence to suggest the efficacy of a few approaches. The following were not recommended, but rather the reader was encouraged to investigate them seriously for potential benefit. The first of these was psychotherapy and psychotherapeutic support groups. (See Section 2.7 below on David Spiegel's work.) In addition to individual psychotherapy along the lines of LeShan's work and that described in Part Two of this book, the benefits of support groups was discussed. People are often actively discouraged by friends and relatives to discuss openly their feelings about having cancer or the trials and tribulations of various treatments. Such personal statements are encouraged and respectfully attended to in support groups. One caveat here is that support groups are highly variable, and you need to attend several before making a choice.

A second area to explore for potential benefit is guided imagery, the primary concern of this book. From the Simontons' early work to Jeanne Achterberg's ground-breaking book (1985) to *Rituals of Healing* by Achterberg et al. (1994) (which contains healing imagery transcripts for many conditions), there are many choices and much evidence for help.

Hypnosis has proven to be effective for helping people who have life-challenging diseases in many ways. It has proven to be useful for controlling pain, and for such side effects of chemotherapy as nausea. Hypnosis has been useful in preparing people for surgery and other interventions—for these purposes the main modality is a dissociation triggered via a posthypnotic suggestion. Guided imagery may be considered to be a form of hypnosis. The American Society of Clinical Hypnosis (2200 East Devon Avenue, Suite 291, Des Plaines, IL 60018-4534. (847) 297-3317) has a rigorous set of standards for certifying hypnotists. There are many studies showing the efficacy of hypnotism for pain control and for helping patients with life-challenging diseases (see the special issue of the American Journal of Clinical Hypnosis, 1982–1983).

Traditional Chinese medicine has a very long history. A chapter (pp. 369–396) of Lerner's book (1996) is devoted to this subject. Lerner summarizes the research that has been carried on in traditional Chinese medicine which consists of four major treatment approaches: (1) *acupuncture*—a way of restoring energy balance, although in the West it is known primarily as a method for pain control; (2) *acupressure*—a system of massage in which finger pressure on the acupuncture points (used in place of needles) is used for diagnosis and treatment; (3) *herbal medicines*—the principal mode of treatment with a two millennia history of practice and development; and (4) *Qigong*—this is "energy medicine" which is difficult to describe, but involves "energy" movement and control. One major difference between Chinese and (most) Western physicians is that the former directs their attention to the *complete* physiological and psychological individual rather than narrowly focusing on a particular symptom. Lerner ends his chapter with this conclusion (1996, p. 393):

> Traditional Chinese medicine is, in my judgment, one of the most intriguing of the adjunctive therapies for cancer. There is considerable evidence for its benefits in pain control and in alleviating the side effects of chemotherapy and radiation therapy. Patients frequently report these benefits as well. There are also some reasons to believe that traditional Chinese medicine may help in the battle to extend life with cancer and to lower the risk of recurrence of cancer.

In addition to Lerner's book, the reader may wish to consult Fink (1997), an annotated compilation of alternative treatments for cancer with phone numbers and fees and brief descriptions of treatment approaches.

Acupuncture has a long history in the Far East and in China, in particular. It has been used for pain control and anesthesia, as well as for many ailments. (See Lerner, 1996, pp. 375–80.) Until Reston's emergency appendectomy in China with acupuncture as the sole anesthetic, it was generally ignored by western medicine. To the westerner there were two problems: lack of controlled testing, and the lack of a mechanism for attaining its results. There still appears to be little scientific controlled evidence as to acupuncture's efficacy. Yet, centuries of experience cannot be ignored.

The mechanism side is still troubling, but a study by Melzack et. al. (1977) has provided some evidence. Acupuncture works by stimulating specific points in the body which lie along meridians connecting the points to each other and body parts. Melzack and co-workers found a 71% correspondence between standard acupuncture points and anatomically known nerve trigger points or concentrations. Melzack and Wall (1983, p. 325) state:

> This close correlation suggests that trigger points and acupuncture points for pain, though discovered independently and labeled differently, represent the same phenomenon and can be explained in terms of similar underlying neural mechanisms. A comparable study (Liu et al., 1975) investigated the relationship between motor points and acupuncture loci and also found a remarkably high correspondence.

These studies demonstrated a connection between acupuncture points and significant structures in the nervous system. How the stimulation of these points results in anesthesia or other effects is not known. Also not known is the mechanism(s) for change involved in electrical stimulation using acupuncture needles. On the other hand, side effects to the use of acupuncture (with the modern usage of sterile needles) are essentially nonexistent.

2.5 David Spiegel's Research

The title of Spiegel et al.'s landmark paper (1989) is *Effect of psychosocial treatment on survival of patients with metastatic breast cancer*. In the introduction they state:

> Our objective was to assess whether group therapy in patients with metastatic breast cancer had any effect in survival.... We started with the belief that positive psychological and symptomatic effects could occur without affecting the course of the disease: we expected to improve the quality of life without affecting its quantity.

Their surprising results can be ascertained from the *summary* in their article. (SD = standard deviation)

The effect of psychosocial intervention on survival of 86 patients with metastatic breast cancer was studied prospectively. The 1 year intervention consisted of weekly supportive group therapy with self-hypnosis for pain. Both the treatment (N=50) and control groups (N=36) had routine oncological care. At 10 year follow-up, only 3 of the patients were alive, and death records were obtained for the other 83. Survival from time of randomization and onset of intervention was a mean 36.6 (SD 37.6) months in the intervention group compared with 18.9 (SD 10.8) months in the control group, a significant difference. Survival plots indicated that divergence in survival began at 20 months after entry, or 8 months after intervention ended.

Another way of examining their results is to reproduce their Table III (Spiegel et al. 1989) on survival in months with given Mean (SD):

	Control	Intervention
Survival from:		
Study entry to death	18.9 (10.8)	36.6 (37.6)
Initial medical visit to death	81.2 (53.9)	94.6 (61.0)
First metastasis to death	43.2 (20.5)	85.4 (45.4)

Each of these categories is interesting in its own way. Perhaps the middle entry is most significant, indicating an almost 7 year period from the initial medical visit to death for everyone in the control group, and that members of the intervention group survived 13 months longer on average. Most surprising may be the fact that 3 members of the intervention group were alive at the 10 year follow-up. Despite criticism of the research (1989, Letters to the Editor, two citations), the research was solidly based and was the first real evidence of the effectiveness of psychosocial interventions. (This work has since been replicated by Spiegel and co-workers and others.)

It is also worth quoting here, in its entirety, the nature of the intervention:

The intervention lasted for a whole year while both control and treatment groups received their routine oncological care.

The three intervention groups met weekly for 90 minutes, led by a psychiatrist or social worker with a therapist who had breast cancer in remission. The groups were structured to encourage discussion of how to cope with cancer, but at no time were patients led to believe that participation would affect the course of disease. Group therapy patients were encouraged to come regularly and express their feelings about the illness and its effect on their lives. Physical problems, including side-effects of chemotherapy or radiotherapy, were discussed and a self-hypnosis strategy was taught for pain control (Spiegel 1985). Social isolation was countered by developing strong relations among members. Members encouraged one another to be more assertive with doctors. Patients focused on how to extract meaning from tragedy by using their experience to help other patients and their families. One major function of the leaders was to keep the group directed toward facing the grieving losses.

The emphasis of this program was on "living as fully as possible, improving communication with family members and doctors, facing and mastering fears about death and dying, and controlling pain and other symptoms."

It is hard not to overemphasize the significance of Spiegel and co-workers' work. Here was the first significant evidence that "mind" oriented interventions could have physical effects on disease. Recall that *all* of the women in the study had metastatic breast cancer, and they all continued to receive standard oncologic treatment. The control group was very closely paired with the intervention group on many factors. The only difference appeared to be the psychosocial intervention. So, despite the initial thesis of the researchers, mind can and does have a significant effect on the progress of disease.

2.6 Conclusions

Even a sceptic like myself, a physical chemist, has to acknowledge that there is now sufficient evidence for mind/body interactions helping people to better health to warrant the serious study of ways to do this. This book is the result of my conviction of the efficacy of mind/body healing. Although guided imagery is emphasized, my approach is multi-modal.

Chapter 3

An Overview of Guided Imagery

3.1 What is Guided Imagery?

The term "guided imagery" has been in use since the pioneering work of the Simontons (Simonton, Simonton, and Creighton, 1980) with people who have cancer. In this early work, groups of patients were first given suggestions for relaxation and then *guided* through visualizing healing images. The emphasis was on the visual component and seeing sharks or wolves or other entities move through the body, seeking out and destroying cancerous cells. As you will read later, people tend to have a preferred way of representing the world to themselves in language. The three significant representational systems are: auditory (having to do with sound and hearing), visual (having to do with seeing), and kinesthetic (having to do with physical sensations and feeling). A person whose primary representational system is auditory or kinesthetic will (generally) find it difficult to visualize, i.e., see pictures in their head. So, healing language that involves only seeing or visualizing will not connect or be understood by perhaps two-thirds of the population.

We now use the word "imagery" to represent *all* of the senses. That is, you can "visualize" by using the senses of hearing or touch or proprioception. The important factor is to *guide* your client to enhance their own natural healing processes via paths and sensations that are unique to them. Although it is possible to produce "generic" healing imagery tapes (there will be transcripts of such tapes later), it is best to tailor a guided imagery session to exactly match your client's way(s) of representing and interacting with the world. There will be many specific examples of this later in this book.

Another concern has to do with the nature of the imagery. One woman I worked with was quite religious and of a generally pacific nature. She had a personal angel and we developed imagery in which the angel would gently persuade cancer cells that their time was up and it was okay for them to be eliminated. The angel would swathe more recalcitrant cancer cells in a cocoon of love and escort them from the body. One day my friend said that she wanted something stronger—so we developed a tribe of fierce Indians who would ruthlessly track down and ambush cancer cells and then kill them. In our sessions together, following her lead, we would sometimes use the angel, sometimes the Indian tribe, and sometimes both. The closer the guided imagery work matches your unique client's ways of being in the world, the more effective the work.

In this preliminary chapter we will present some of the basic background for the structure of guided imagery work. In subsequent chapters there will be a systematic development of its components.

3.2 Some Different Forms of Imagery

The typology for imagery that is presented here is based on the detailed descriptions given in Achterberg, Dossey, and Kolkmeier (1994). These types of imagery are involved in various aspects of using imagery for healing. Again, it is emphasized that the word "imagery" is used in a *general* way that includes visual pictures as well as all of the other senses.

Images that just appear or spontaneously form in the conscious mind may be termed *receptive imagery*, i.e., being received in the moment rather than being created. Dreams are more in the realm of being received, for example, than being created. Receptive images just "pop up." These kinds of images are most likely to occur in the hypnagogic state—that in-between time when you are falling asleep—or the hypnopompic state—when you are waking up or half-awake.

By contrast, *active imagery* involves a conscious and deliberate effort in constructing the image. In this process you literally call up the image from memory or construct a new one. The active image is volitional and you can choose an image for a specific purpose such as a bone break healing faster, or the destruction or elimination of cancer cells. In a sense, then, you can "speak" to your body through active imagery. This imagery may be symbolic or realistic. Some practitioners feel that using realistic images such as macrophages or T-cells to destroy cancer cells are more powerful than symbolic images such as Pac Man or predatory animals. It is probably more important to follow the client's lead in terms of what *they* know (in an inner sense) will be most effective for them. The body seems to respond better to images than it does to words, i.e., a high pressure hose flushing out cancer cells versus repeating the phrase "you're going to be flushed away."

Concrete imagery for healing is really *biologically correct imagery*. For cancer, you would use accurate knowledge of the way the immune system works via white blood cells (leucocytes), neutrophils, macrophage, the lymphocytes (killer T-cells and the B-cells), and natural killer cells. For bone healing you would use knowledge of how bones knit and new bone tissue is laid down. Whether you use concrete or symbolic imagery, most people find it useful to have some knowledge about the actual biological processes which are involved in curing their disease. To this end O. Carl Simonton likes to emphasize on his audio tapes that cancer cells are *weaker* than healthy cells, and that they are more easily eliminated than healthy cells via traditional procedures such as chemotherapy and radiation.

In *symbolic imagery* you use some image which is of especial sig-nificance to you to represent a healing/curing power or force. Personal symbols can be very powerful since they are uniquely yours, i.e., they embody the deeper levels of your body/mind with all of your somatic, verbal, conscious, and unconscious memories. If you tell me that your healing/curing image is an eagle or a cat-fish, I must go into *my* experience and *my* memory banks to dis-cover just what those images mean to *me*, and how they are represented. There is no way that I can experience an eagle or a catfish or a healing light the way that you do. The power in a per-sonally chosen symbol lies in that person's unique history. It is for you, the facilitator, to help your client find symbol(s) that work for them.

Process imagery is the *mechanics* of how an image works or is used, that is, the steps for implementing the activity of the image. Suppose that your image for eliminating breast cancer cells is a personal angel named Gloria. After attaining a relaxed state (see Chapter 4), you call up Gloria's presence. You may do this by sim-ply calling her, or listening for her musical voice, or sensing the fluttering of her wings, or hearing her happy laughter. Once she is present, you can give her instructions of what you would like her to do during her visit. Then you imagine her shrinking to a size where she can freely move through your body to wherever her ministrations are needed. Or, you may have her place her healing hands or lips in contact with the areas of your body containing the cancer cells. Gloria may also instruct your own healing mechanisms as to how to work more effectively and efficiently, so that the healing work will continue after she departs to help others in need. Gloria may let you know just where she is working by a sense of warmth or coolness or a tingling. When her work for this visit is over, you thank her, and she departs with some loving words or a caress or laughter or a song. This process will be discussed in more detail later.

End state imagery is an image of you in your healed state, where the disease (or condition) has been completely eliminated, or eliminated to your satisfaction. The power of the image of the final healed state cannot be over-estimated. This is the goal, the dream, *and* the reality. This healed state has to be visualized/known in *sufficient detail* to be both realistic and realizable. A fuzzy representation needs to be sharpened by removing whatever hindrances there are; frequently these hindrances are connected to unfinished business. Of course, you always need to be sensitive to your clients' desires—do not try to impress *your* end state image for them on them. They may have made their peace, for example, and accept their condition and its progress. When doing art therapy for healing with clients, it is useful to ask for four drawings: (1) present physical condition; (2) the treatment(s); (3) the final, healed state; and (4) how you got from (1) to (3).

Healing images may be *general* or *generic imagery*. Some that are commonly used are: (1) a healing light or energy from some potent source; (2) hands whose touch is healing; (3) warmth or coolness; (4) a healing guru, wise person, outer or inner guide, guardian, religious figure or healing presence (unspecified)—a trek to such a person is often part of the image; (5) a journey or trek or pilgrimage to some healing object or location, sometimes involving a substance whose possession or ingestion is healing; and (6) a "power" animal or totem or fetish with curative and/or restorative capabilities. These images may be made part of a generalized guided imagery session for a group, being careful to use nonspecific language so that everyone can fill in their own unique details.

Individual cultures and subcultures have adopted certain general images. For example, Christians may use Jesus or Mary; Native Americans may use power animals. (Transcripts for some general guided imagery work will be presented *after* detailed information on structure and language for this work.)

Naparstek (1994, pp. 47–71) in a book entitled *Staying Well With Guided Imagery* describes another classification of guided imagery. *Cellular imagery* focuses on what is happening at the microscopic level in the cells—this is also called *physiological imagery*. *Metaphoric imagery* uses symbols for what is happening physically or psychologically. *Psychological imagery* is designed to change a person's way of thinking about or looking at themselves. *Feeling-state imagery* is concentrated on changing mood or emotional tone broadly. *Energetic imagery* focuses on the physics of our electro-magnetic fields. With *end-state imagery* the highlight is on realistic concrete short-term goals and are like the "carrot" that motivates. The idea of *spiritual imagery* may encompass all of the above, but is concerned with universal, global, non-ordinary dimensions of reality—this may include religious experience, transpersonal phenomena, or a search for meaning.

3.3 Duration of a Guided Imagery Session

Guided imagery sessions are in two main parts: (1) orientation and relaxation; and (2) delivery (by someone external or by internal talking) of the guided image itself. It is generally recommended that a session be 15 to 20 minutes in duration and that they be done daily. Some professionals recommend 2 to 3 sessions per day, but be careful about making this a "prescription" rather than a choice on the part of your client. I prefer to say, "Once each day is recommended. If you feel two to three times are helpful, then please do so. It is okay occasionally to skip a session."

Why do we start the process with a period of relaxation? (Methods of attaining a relaxed state are the subject of Chapter 5.) The answer is simple—there is considerable evidence that the body's immune system and native healing processes are *enhanced* when you are relaxed. We know that significant healing goes on while you are asleep—a state of deep relaxation. During the waking state most of your attention is on conscious activities, the mind/body system is preoccupied. Some of the evidence for relaxation enhancing the immune system derives from the opposite effect of stress, tension, and anxiety depressing the immune system. Mind and body are integrated and changes in one can affect the other. A sprained ankle or a headache has mood effects; happiness, joy, and laughter have measurable physiological effects. A folk observation is that laughter helps digestion. Another is that an engrossing movie cures headaches. Relaxation enhances healing.

How relaxed do you need to be, and for how long? Achterberg found that people reach their maximum state of relaxation (using a standardized relaxation method) in 10 ± 2 minutes. The depth of relaxation was determined by various physiological markers, including blood samples. Continuing the suggestions for relaxation beyond about ten minutes did not deepen the state. Of course, people experienced in meditation and self-hypnosis could quickly get to their deepest state of relaxation, but additional time did not deepen the state. This means that it is not necessary to go beyond 8 to 12 minutes for the relaxation portion of a guided imagery session.

How long should the over-all session be? To answer this question, we will first discuss the concept of *ultradian rhythms* (Rossi and Nimmons, 1991). Life is replete with many cycles and rhythms with a wide range of periods: neural—0.1 to 10 sec.; cardiac—1 sec.; respiration—4 to 5 sec.; biochemical—1 to 20 min.; enzyme and protein level—20 to 90 min.; hunger—90 to 120 min.; circadian (sleep/wake)—24 hr.; and human ovarian—28 days. Rossi and Nimmons (1991) made a detailed study of human ultradian rhythms which last 90 to 120 min. During the sleeping state the REM (rapid eye movement) cycles occur every 90 to 120 min. Rossi and others have found that the REM cycles of alertness and calm continue throughout the waking state and these are called *ultradian rhythms*. The troughs and peaks last about 20 minutes each. If you do not allow yourself a break of some kind every 90 to 120 minutes, then you may experience "ultradian stress." (See Rossi and Nimmons 1991 for more on ultradian stress.) Rossi learned about these rhythms by observing the great hypnotherapist Milton H. Erickson, M.D. Erickson could recognize when a client was in the trough region, which means the client was more susceptible to an hypnotic induction, at which point he would start his hypnotic work. Guided imagery sessions work best by matching them to your client's own natural ultradian rhythm rather than forcing them into a pre-designated time. However, the start of an ultradian cycle can be influenced.

To answer the question that opened the previous paragraph we refer to another study by Rossi and Lippincott (1993). They studied people who were adept at self-hypnosis and found that the self-hypnosis session lasted about 20 min., but with a large standard deviation of 17 min. The 20 min. duration was also found to be the most common time for experienced meditators and relaxers. This suggests that about 20 min. is the optimum time for a guided imagery session. That is, 10 ± 2 min. for relaxation and 10 ± 2 min. for directed guided imagery work. Bernie Siegel's guided imagery tapes typically use 15 min. for the entire session. In my tapes I tend to use 5 to 7 min. for the relaxation portion, and 8 to 10 min. for the guided imagery portion. People who have cancer, for instance, may find it difficult to concentrate for long periods of time. The shorter (less than 10 min.) relaxation works because the client becomes conditioned to your voice and the tape and rapidly relaxes. Before I make a tape, there will be one or more sessions spent on introductory material and training in relaxation. Also, with 15 min. sessions, it is easier for the client to make time for this work.

Chapter 4

The Placebo Effect

4.1 Introduction and Definitions

In the first outline of this book a discussion of the placebo effect was incorporated as part of the previous chapter. Then, I researched the subject and found an extensive literature of literally thousands of papers, and a number of very good books. Since the effectiveness of guided imagery work may be largely due to the placebo effect, it made sense to devote an entire chapter to the subject. *All* of the alternative treatments for cancer, for example have helped *some* people. These treatments do not hold up to the modern standard of double-blind studies, but they have had *some* success. Is it possible that the common denominator is the placebo effect? Read on.

There are several important books that this chapter is based upon. A. K. Shapiro was perhaps the most consistent and long-term student of the placebo effect. His wife, E. Shapiro, completed their book (Shapiro & Shapiro, 1997) after his death. We will write more about his contributions later, but a major one can be summarized as "*... until recently the history of medical treatment was essentially the history of the placebo effect.*" [emphasis added] (Shapiro & Shapiro, 1997, p.2). White, Tursky and Schwartz (1985) are the editors of a book on the placebo effect whose contributors emphasize theory, research, and mechanisms. Harrington (1997) is the editor of papers contributed by participants at a symposium on the placebo effect—this book includes as a last section an edited discussion. Spiro's book (1986) is a good introduction. A popular article by Brown was recently published (1998).

Shapiro and Shapiro's preferred definitions with regard to placebos follow (1997, p. 41)

- A *placebo* is any therapy (or that component of any therapy) that is intentionally or knowingly used for nonspecific, psychological, or psychophysiological, therapeutic effect, or that is used for a presumed therapeutic effect on a patient, symptom, or illness but is without specific activity for the condition being treated.

- A *placebo* when used as a control in experimental studies, is a substance or procedure that is without specific activity for the condition being treated.
- The *placebo effect* is the nonspecific psychological or psychophysiological therapeutic effect produced by a placebo.

They state earlier (p. 31): "According to its original definition and the definition used during most of its history, the word placebo describes a medication often commonly in use, knowingly prescribed by a physician 'to please a patient' rather than for its specific effect on a symptom or illness."

The following etymological history of the word "placebo" is based on Spiro (1986, pp. 10–11). Apparently, the first use of *placebo* literally meant "I shall please." One illustration of early use is from the *Oxford English Dictionary*, "He earned a miserable livelihood ... By singing placebos and dirges." From this beginning the word "declined" and took on connotations of flattery and of being a sycophant. A. K. Shapiro has written that the first medically related use of the word was in 1785 where it meant "commonplace method or medicine." The modern use of placebo came into use first in 1811 as "all medicine prescribed more to please the patient than for its therapeutic effectiveness." (How many of us find it difficult to leave our doctor's office without a prescription?) Spiro further states (1986, p. 75): "Fisher distinguishes the placebo *response*, which is the behavioral change in the subject receiving the pill from the placebo *effect*, that part of the change which can be attributed to the *symbolic* effect of being given a medication. As the placebo affects the patient, and not the disease, it is very important to distinguish response from effect."

Benson (with Stark, 1996) recommends the use of the phrase "remembered wellness" rather than the placebo effect. His book has an entire chapter (pp. 25–45) on this topic. He states (p. 32) that there are three components to *remembered wellness*: (1) belief and expectancy on the part of the patient; (2) belief and expectancy on the part of the caregiver; and (3) belief and expectancies generated by a relationship between the patient and the caregiver. In fact (p. 32), "Belief in or expectation of a good outcome can have formidable restorative power, whether the positive expectations are on the part of the patient, the doctor or caregiver, or both." He quotes

(p. 34) the 19th century French physician Armand Trousseau as saying, "You should treat as many patients as possible with the new drugs while they still have the power to heal." Benson's phrase adds an interesting perspective, but will probably not replace the placebo effect. Later in this book (p. 206) Benson states, "We are beginning to be able to explain the way that physiologic mechanisms transmit and materialize faith to produce healing. This leaves us to ponder the truly remarkable fact that our brains/bodies are so equipped. And rather than thinking that science debunks miracles, I choose to believe that science underscores the awesome, and perhaps even miraculous, design of the human body."

Sometimes the language that people use in their writing implies that the person is separate from the disease. This misses the point that somehow *within* the placebo effect a person has the capability of using one part of their mind/body continuum to affect another part. The placebo effect cannot be separated from the totality of the human being.

You will note as you read this chapter that I decided to treat the subject by incorporating many quotations from the original literature. There is a separate section (4.5) on the related nocebo effect. Since the effectiveness of prayer may be due to the placebo effect, there is also a separate section (4.6) on prayer.

4.2 The Placebo through History
Shapiro and Shapiro (1997, p. 2) categorically state: "The great lesson, then, of medical history is that the placebo has always been the norm of medical practice ... *until recently the history of medical treatment was essentially the history of the placebo effect.*" (emphasis added). In their first chapter (pp. 1–27) they give examples of the placebo throughout history. The following are a sample:

- The Ebers Papyrus ... about 1500 B.C. ... contains 842 prescriptions and mentions more than 700 drugs of mineral, vegetable, and animal origin—all, with a few possible exceptions, worthless. (p. 4)
- The ancient Egyptian healers were fond of dung, recommending excrement from humans and eighteen other creatures. (p. 4)

- Bloodletting began in Egypt in 1000 B.C. Disease was viewed as a curse cast on an individual by an evil spirit, and bloodletting was used to purify the body of evil spirits. The ancient Egyptians were obsessed with the anus, referred to in 82 prescriptions. (p. 4)
- It has been suggested that the symbol used on prescriptions, the Rx, represents one of the restored eyes, Rx xR, or Horus. (p. 5)
- Asclepius surpassed all other healers and later became a god ... his daughters Hygeia, who represented health, and Panacea, who represented healing were the personification of all earthly remedies. (p. 5)
- [concerning the four humors] ... the basic elements of matter were earth, air, fire, and water. Similar constituents in humans are the four humors: blood (secreted by the liver), phlegm (secreted by the lungs), yellow bile (secreted by the gall bladder), and black bile (secreted by the spleen), with the brain secreting only mucus. (p .6)
- ... The mixture of the humors, affected by diet, weather, and climate, determines the basic condition, temperament, health, and disease. (p. 7)
- Hippocrates strongly emphasized diet but discouraged vegetables and fruits, a practice that probably resulted in vitamin deficiencies, especially among the rich. Frequent references are made to purgatives, sudorifics [cause or increase sweat], emetics, and enemas, consistent with Hippocratic theory requiring the purification of the body from disease-producing humors. (p. 7)
- ... Hippocratic precepts guided medicine for more than two thousand years. (p. 8)
- [with respect to Chinese medicine] ... everything was made of five elements: water, fire, wood, metal, and earth; as well as the legendary sixty-four combinations of yin and yang ... Simple diseases were treated with five tastes (vinegar, wine, honey, ginger, and salt), five kinds of grain, five kinds of drugs (herbs, trees, insects, stones, and grains), and five flavors (pungent, sour, sweet, bitter, and salty). (p. 8)
- Although acupuncture is used in many countries ... adequately controlled studies have failed to confirm its effectiveness. Moreover, it is likely that acupuncture in the past killed many more people than it helped, since the use of

unsterilized needles probably was responsible for homologous serum jaundice, which was endemic in China for centuries. (p. 9)

■ The cornerstone of ancient Indian treatment was the use of mantras, dieting, drugs, and withdrawal of the mind from injurious and harmful thoughts ... there is no record that the use of six hundred or so drugs known in early India was effective. (p.9)

The drug named theriac has been in use for well over two thousand years in many formulations—the number of ingredients is about one hundred. We give here in the first quote just the first ten from Galen's *electuarium thericale magnum*—the list was given in Greek verse so they could be remembered:

■ Root of Florentine iris, licorice, 12 ounces each; of Arabian costus, Pontic rhubarb, cinquefoil, 6 ounces each; of ligustricum meum, rhubarb, gentian, 4 ounces each; of birthwort, 2 ounces; herb of scordium, 12 ounces ... (p. 11)

■ Galen's therapy was based on the principle of opposites: if a drug causes or is thought to cause fever, it can be used to treat chills ... Galen's pharmacopoeia of 540 vegetable, 180 animal, and 100 mineral substances—a total of 820 placebo substances—dominated treatment for fifteen hundred years. (p. 18)

■ [Galen also wrote:] *He cures most in whom most are confident.* (emphasis added) (p. 18)

■ Clysterization (the purification, purging, or removal of evil bowel contents), currently called enema, ... was used in most periods of history. Voltaire advised every young man to secure a wife who could give an enema pleasantly and quickly to keep the passages open. Despite their extensive use, *enemas cause dehydration ... making them potentially lethal.* (emphasis added) (p. 13)

■ Powdered Egyptian mummy, resembling and tasting like rosin, was believed to heal wounds and to be an almost universal remedy. (p. 16)

■ The laying on of hands is one of the oldest and most persistent treatments. (p. 17)

■ James Lind's simple and straightforward study of the efficacy of lemons and oranges in prevention of scurvy, a result not accepted by physicians for another 160 years and not fully appreciated by Lind himself. (p. 24)

A hallmark in medicine occurred in the 17th century with the introduction of cinchona bark which worked for fevers of malarial origins and *not* for other fevers. Thus, cinchona may be considered to be the first drug that was not a placebo, i.e., it was the first drug that showed a way of distinguishing between placebo and non-placebo. It is important to understand that the judgment that the medications used in the past were placebos is that of *hindsight from the present* and not that of the physicians who prescribed the medications (see Galen's statement above). Placebo-medicine was finally put in perspective in the 1950s when controlled clinical trials, double-blind procedures, and statistical analyses began which were accepted as proof of the efficacy of medications (and other treatments). A curious aspect (side-effect?) of double-blind testing is that not only can it unambiguously show the efficacy of a particular treatment (versus a control), but that such testing equally demonstrates the efficacy of placebos (versus the same controls)! Indeed, the distinction between placebo and medicament is not very sharp.

Before discussing factors that contribute to the placebo effect and other related matters, we will continue with some additional historical observations.

The Shapiros (1997, p. 43) point out that, "The word *quack* is a shortened version of *quacksalver*, meaning one who boasts ("quacks") about the virtues of salves and ointments. When mercury became a fad in Europe, causing more toxic poisoning than benefit, nonphysicians began to use it. They were known as *quacksalvers*." (An interesting aside is that a common name for mercury is "quicksilver.") They further comment (p. 44)

- The U.S. Food and Drug Administration estimated [1993] that 38 to 40 million Americans spent $30 billion annually for fraudulent treatment, with 10 percent of the users suffering side effects…. Although quackery is a particularly malignant form of the placebo effect, its omnipresence and massive use is another manifestation of the ubiquity of that effect.

The concept of *catharsis* defined as a cleaning/purification, or purging of the body, the mind, or the soul is a common "curative" factor underlying the history of essentially all treatment. The removal of the supposed bad, evil, or diseased component via the endlessly creative methods developed by our ancestors served to reassure the patient, increase hope, and make them feel better. After all, there was the physical and fairly repulsive evidence of what had been removed/purged from their bodies.

There were very few substances used in the past that had proven efficacy (there were no controlled studies). Among other factors, there was no quality control as to source, purity, and processing of the ingredients. This meant that dosages were highly variable. Also, most of these medicaments were used as mixtures—isolating one component for a particular effect being essentially impossible. The Shapiros state (1997, p. 64) "... the poppy, or opium, is the earliest effective and most consistently used ancient drug.... Opium's usefulness tends to be exaggerated." Malachite and honey were used for wound healing in Egypt and later in other countries. Copper salts and honey *do* weakly inhibit certain bacteria found in wounds. In ancient Chinese medicine *mahuang* (ephedrine) was one of the drugs that could be cited as effective. But, note that these few effective medicines (uncontrolled) are rather rare exceptions.

With respect to the physician's role the Shapiros write (1997, p. 55)

- The tendency for healers to overvalue the verity of their clinical diagnosis and treatment is a major factor contributing to the placebo effect and is so powerful that it can cause physicians to reject effective treatment....

Further (p. 59)

- The history of medicine is characterized by the introduction of new placebos by successive generations of physicians.... The strong beliefs of physicians, objectively unjustified, suggest that they have been as defensive about their treatments throughout medical history as they are today.

With respect to mental treatments (Shapiro & Shapiro, 1997, p. 231): "Psychiatry and psychology are rife with placebo effects ... although psychotherapy has been reported to be more effective than placebo, its efficacy has yet to be proven." They suggest that the treatments offered by all types of psychotherapists may work to some extent, not due to theories of behavior and etiology, but more to the placebo effect. An important observation directly related to this book is (pp. 232–233)

■ Another reflection of the placebo's popularity is the current interest in mind-body relationships,... Treatments that are nonspecific may reduce the reaction to distress; decrease depression, demoralization, and hopelessness; and promote health-enhancing behavior; and thus secondarily may have a favorable effect on illness. Increase in survival rates, therefore, may be related primarily to psychical intervening variables such as compliance with medical management....

Their crucial observation is (p. 233):

■ We are still beset by the problem that the *mechanism* by which psychological factors, placebos, and psychological therapies may effect physical illness and disease is *unknown*. (emphasis added)

One final set of comments apply to surgery (p. 230)

■ Surgery is not subject to controlled studies, primarily because controlled trials in surgery are technically more difficult to devise and ethically more difficult to justify. The result is that surgery, because it is difficult to subject to clinical trial, is more prone to placebo than medicine. Serious questions about the overuse, effectiveness, safety, and benefit of caesarean sections, hysterectomies, spinal fusions, transplants, and surgery for cardiac problems are documented in the literature.

On the other hand, it is probably the case that the vast majority of surgical procedures are safe, beneficial, and needed.

4.3 Factors Affecting the Placebo Effect

The standard method for evaluating new drugs is to compare them with a placebo and a control group. To be considered to be effective the drug must show more improvement than the placebo. But, with drugs, is it really effectiveness that is being evaluated or the *mechanism* of its action? After all, the effect of the drug itself has both a specific physiological component *and* a nonspecific psychological component. The placebo only has the nonspecific psychological component. It may then be considered that the *total* effectiveness of the drug is a combination of both, or that what is being evaluated is how much the specific physiological component *adds* to the nonspecific psychological component. The analysis of a double-blind study is thus quite complex. An assumption is that physiological and psychological components are independent of each other and involve different mechanisms. It may have been useful in the past to separate mind from body, but there is just too much evidence regarding their inter-relatedness and influence on each other for this dualistic model to hold. For example, we know of the so-called psychosomatic diseases and the physiological effects of stress.

The word "expectancy" frequently crops up in discussions of the placebo effect. The human subject has a sense that the test substance or procedure will bring about a beneficial effect. To what extent does an expectant attitude also result in changes in *motivation*, and how does that contribute to the resultant changes attributed to the test substance or placebo? Evans (1985, p. 219) comments on "suggestibility":

■ ... the few available clinical experimental studies have found no consistently significant relationship between the placebo response and a variety of measures of suggestibility. In addition, the placebo response is uncorrelated to the susceptibility to hypnosis.

Evans (1985, p. 221) comments on anxiety reduction thus:

■ Placebo effects are often attributable to anxiety reduction.... These results, along with other recent studies, suggest that a placebo-induced reduction in suffering can be expected in a context in which anxiety is concomitantly reduced.

And continuing about expectancy/suggestibility (Evans, 1985, p. 224)

- ... the placebo effect is highest in double-blind studies, is lower in single-blind studies, and is lower still in non-blind or open-label studies ... it appears that when the patient as well as the physician *believe* that a powerful drug is being used, a strong placebo effect is obtained in a double-blind administration.... the *conviction of the therapist* about the drug's potency—which presumably communicates itself to the hopeful patient in terms of the feasibility and expectation that it will work, and the consequent reduction of anxiety— seems to be a powerful mediator of therapeutic effectiveness. (emphases added)

Evans (1985, p. 217) has defined an useful *Index of Drug Efficiency* (IDE) as:

$$\text{Index of Drug Efficiency} = \frac{\text{reduction in pain with unknown active drug}}{\text{reduction in pain with known analgesic}}$$

The placebo effect can then be rated against this more realistic IDE when comparing it with a new analgesic. Comparing a placebo against different analgesics for pain levels corresponding to that analgesic's best use showed (Evans, 1985, p. 223):

- ... the effectiveness of a placebo compared to standard doses of different analgesic drugs [morphine, aspirin, darvon, codeine, zomax] under double-blind circumstances seems to be relatively constant... . it appears that placebo is about 55–60% as effective as active medications, irrespective of the potency of these active medications... . For placebo reactors, the likelihood of responding to morphine was 95%; however, for placebo nonreactors, only 55% of patients responded to morphine.

In commenting on this 55% analgesic effect, Tursky (1985, p. 229) points out that there are three dimensions of pain: (1) intensity— how strong the pain is; (2) reactivity—how unpleasant the pain is; and (3) sensation—what the pain feels like. In hypnotic work for pain control it is common to ask a client to rate their pain experience on two scales from zero to ten where zero is perfect comfort. The first scale is the intensity of the pain, and the second scale is about how much the pain "bothers" them. It is not unusual for a severe pain to be well-tolerated, i.e., low on the bother scale, or a mild pain to be very bothersome. Both aspects are important.

Grevert and Goldstein (1985) comment on the mechanism of placebo analgesia as follows [note that naloxone is a narcotic antagonist, i.e., it suppresses the narcotic effect]:

- In summary, when analgesia is produced by an opioid mechanism, as in electrical stimulation of appropriated sites in the brain, naloxone, at adequate dosage, effectively suppresses the analgesic effect. Analgesia produced by acupuncture or transcutaneous electrical stimulation in humans appears to fall in this category. … Hypnosis analgesia is unaffected by naloxone, and this suggests it is not mediated by an opioid system. (p. 336)
- … at the present time there is some experimental evidence suggesting that endogenous opioids mediate placebo analgesia. (p. 348)

Is the placebo effect a conditioned response as in the behavioral conditioning of experimental animals? The classic experiment was carried out by Ader and Cohen (1975) where they paired saccharin-flavored drinking water with injections of cyclophosphamide, an immunosuppressive and nausea-inducing drug. A subgroup of mice who were not given additional injections, but continued to get the saccharin-flavored water, kept dying at high rates, i.e., the saccharin drink by itself triggered the same immunosuppressive effects as cyclophosphamide injections. The immune systems of the mice behaved far from normal in a kind of placebo effect with profound changes in physiological functions. Human reactions like expectation and hope did not play a part in mice reactions. Ader (1997) continues to believe that there is a conditioning component to placebo effects in humans as per the following quotes:

- However, experimental and clinical data clearly indicate that there is a greater placebo effect when placebo medication is given after a period of effective drug treatment than when it is given as the "first" medication. (p. 148)

■ Nonetheless, the observation of prolonged effects when inactive drug follows active (and effective) drug treatment is exactly what one would predict if conditioning occurred during the period of active pharmacology. (p. 147)

■ A conditioned stimulus is neutral only the first time that it is presented; once it has been paired with an unconditioned stimulus, it is no longer neutral! (p. 159)

The mechanism of how the mind/body reacts in these ways is still not understood.

Shapiro and Shapiro (1997) comment on the nature of double-blind studies (p. 21):

■ How blind is blind?... in our review of 27 studies, with a total of 13,082 patients, drug allocation was guessed correctly by clinicians in 67 percent, by patients in 65 percent, and relatives and other staff in 71 percent of the studies.

What are the contributions of expectation and hope to the placebo effect in the face of these percentages? The following are relevant comments about factors involved in the placebo effect:

■ Clinical placebo effects are not correlated with susceptibility to hypnosis, test of suggestibility, or laboratory studies using volunteers, and vary over time. *Placebo stimuli must reflect a credible therapy for the patient.* (emphasis added) (p. 30)

■ A positive placebo effect occurs more frequently in patients with manifest or free-floating anxiety and with the expectation of improvement by patients, doctors, and staff. Expectations of improvement, however, may be independent or overlap such factors as optimism, enthusiasm, hope, faith, belief, motivation, and conditioning. A positive placebo effect occurs more frequently in patients who have minor illnesses, symptoms that spontaneously vary and remit, over time, and primarily affect the reaction to distress. (p. 30)

■ Positive placebo effects increase significantly when the placebo test instructions suggested a favorable response to treatment: "Your evaluation indicated that you should respond favorably to the test drug." (p. 31)

In this contributed paper Shapiro and Shapiro (1997) continue to write that the efficacy of psychoanalysis and psychotherapy have not been proven: "Psychotherapy appears to be an unsystematic myriad of nonspecific elements mixed together in the hope that some will be effective." (p. 23) Quotes from their paper are concluded with three cautionary comments:

- With growing appreciation of the healing power of the placebo, its therapeutic power, as is true of all therapies, has become greatly exaggerated. Faith in the power of the placebo has become a bandwagon effect. (p. 24)
- Another problem is that the mechanism by which psychological factors, placebos, and psychological therapies affect physical illness and disease is unknown. (p. 26)
- However, adequately controlled and replicated studies, as yet, do *not* support the hypothesis that placebos have a direct and permanent physiological effect on medical disorders. (emphasis added) (p. 27)

Spiro (1997) makes some astute observations regarding the placebo effect:

- Doctors look for *cure*, but patients still want *care*. (p. 39)
- … patients who adhere to treatment, even when that treatment is a placebo, have better health outcomes than poorly adherent patients. (p. 42)
- … *participating in a group*, is highly beneficial. (p. 42)
- For most physicians, *disease* is what the doctor sees and finds, *illness* is what the patient feels and suffers. (p. 45)
- Let me assert that placebos help illness, they relieve pain, but they do not cure disease. I have examined the claims for placebos healing cancer and other diseases, but I have found not one placebo that stands up to scrutiny. (p. 46)
- [Placebo] injections are more effective than pills in relieving pain … (p. 48)
- There is a difference between treating cancer with placebos and treating the pain that comes from cancer with them. (pp. 50–51)
- The placebo is powerless without the physician. (p. 52)

Brody (1997) has written about the doctor as therapeutic agent—a theme mentioned and even stressed by other students of the placebo effect. He considers the effect to consist of at least three general components, "... providing an understandable and satisfying explanation of the illness; demonstrating care and concern; and holding out an enhanced promise of mastery or control over the symptoms." (p. 79) Is there, for example, a *neurobiology of meaning*? Brody considers the telling of stories as being a fundamental way of assigning meaning. (Stories and metaphors and myths and legends have long been a part of the structure of change.) Brody agrees with the observation (p. 90): "... that the patient, and not the physician, is in the end the therapeutic agent—the placebo stimulus, whether the physician's behavior or something else, simply uncorks the internal pharmacopeia which all humans possess as a biologically-programmed tool for self-healing."

Price and Fields (1997) have written about the contribution of desire and expectation, to wit:

- ... we propose that two general factors mediate placebo analgesia: (1) *a desire or need for relief of pain* and (2) *an expectation that a given procedure or agent will relieve the pain.* (emphases in the original) (p. 117)
- Human studies also clearly show that prior experience with an effective analgesic drug enhances the analgesic effectiveness of a subsequent placebo.... placebo given as a second treatment acted as an effective analgesic when it followed an effective analgesic; whereas placebo following a placebo continued to have the same slight analgesic effect as the first placebo had. (p. 120) [There is obviously some kind of conditioning effect occurring here, but is it physiological, psychological, or both?]
- ... greater placebo effects are achieved by more believable and more technically convincing agents. Thus, it is claimed that placebo injections are more effective than placebo pills and that placebo morphine is more effective than placebo aspirin. (p. 122)
- Despite the commonly asserted claim that expectation constitutes a critical factor in placebo effects, its role has not been consistently demonstrated in experiments explicitly

designed to assess its relative contribution, particularly in analgesic studies. (p. 124)

Along similar lines Kirsch (1997) has contributed:

- These data [from many studies] convincingly demonstrate that many self-reported placebo effects reflect an actual change in condition. (p. 169)
- Contrary to this prediction, placebo effects can be very long lasting. (p. 174)
- Thus, the effects of expectancy appear to be stronger than the effects of stimulus substitution. (p. 175)
- The popular definition of *placebo* as "nonspecific" treatment is not entirely accurate. Although the ingredients of a placebo preparation may be nonspecific, the effects of the placebo are very specific ... The specific nature of the effects of placebos depends on the information available to the recipient. For example, placebos given as tranquilizers produce very different effects from the same placebos presented as stimulants. (p. 176)
- The effects of placebos generally mimic the effects of the active drugs bearing their label. (p. 177)

Morris (1997) comments on the placebo effect from the perspective of a bicultural model.

- Contrary to the widespread myth that one-third of all patients are placebo responders, the effectiveness of placebo ranges anywhere from 1 percent to 100 percent, depending on the conditions of the trial. (p. 188)
- Godehard Oepen is quoted with respect to placebos: "If you don't believe in them, they don't work." (p. 188)
- Placebos ... place belief and meaning at the center of the therapeutic encounter. ... Why, for example, do injections have a more potent placebo effect than pills, large pills a more potent effect than small pills, and very small pills a more potent effect than average-size pills? (p. 189)
- The ways in which a culture represents pain has much to do with how people will experience it. (p. 191)
- ... psychologists usually agree on the basic point that pain always involves learning.... learning about pain extends to *both* behaviors and beliefs. (p. 195)

And, finally, just a few additional quotes from the discussion section at the end of Harrington (1997).

- Hope is where you have a desire *and* an expectation that are positive, going in the same direction. (p. 222, Price)
- ... wonder whether you can get a placebo response in a situation of absolute informed consent. (p. 237, Stone)
- Back in the 1940s, when I was at Harvard Medical School, there were catalogs of pills you could buy cheaply. And in the catalog, there were several pages of placebos. They came in blue and yellow and green and all the rest, and doctors were perfectly happy to have them. (p. 237, Spiro)

4.4 The Nocebo Phenomenon

The question arises, "If placebos can be used to help people in distress, can the reverse effect be used to harm people?" Hahn (1997) has written about the *nocebo effect*. Again, we will let the expert tell about the phenomenon in his own words.

- The nocebo effect is the causation of sickness (or death) by expectation of sickness (or death) and by associated emotional states. There are two forms of the nocebo effect. In the *specific* form, the subject experiences a particular negative outcome and that outcome consequently occurs.... In the *generic* form, subjects have vague negative expectations. (p. 56)
- Placebo side effects are numerous and common. In the nocebo phenomenon, however, the subject expects sickness to be the outcome, i.e., the expectation is a negative one. Nocebos may also have side effects, that is, when negative expectations produce positive outcomes or outcomes other than those expected. (p. 57)
- In one experiment, 47.5% of asthmatics who were exposed to nebulized saline solution (normally innocuous) and told that they were inhaling irritants or allergens experienced substantially increased airway resistance. (Luparello et al., 1968). The twelve subjects who developed full-blown attacks were relieved by the same saline solution when it was presented therapeutically. Controls who did not have asthma were unaffected by exposure to the same stimulus. (p. 66)

- [explaining nocebos] First, local cultures present traditional ideas of what sickness is and what to expect.... Second, within cultural settings, certain social and/or psychiatric circumstances increase the susceptibility to available nosological conditions.... Third, processes of social interaction and communication powerfully shape attention and perception, suggesting particular experience to be experienced.... Fourth,... language is embodied—not only physically through the sound-producing and receiving capacities—but also symbolically, through the power of words to elicit profound emotional responses. (pp. 69–71)
- The nocebo phenomenon is a little-recognized facet of culture that may be responsible for a substantial variety of pathology throughout the world. However, the extent of the phenomenon is not yet known, and evidence is piecemeal and ambiguous. There is evidence that inner, mental states affect pathological outcomes, independent of other risk factors; that symptoms may spread in communities by being witnessed; and that symptoms may be caused by experimentally induced expectations. (p. 71)

The common examples of the nocebo phenomenon are in "voodoo" deaths and the Australian aborigine practice of "pointing the bone." Many cultures have nocebos in terms of the evil eye and evil spirits. People have been characterized as having (at the extremes) either *nourishing* or *noxious* personalities. When you spend time with nourishing people, you feel better for hours afterward. On the other hand, noxious people can literally "give" you headaches—I had a "friend" like this, until I cut off all connection with him. A sobering study in the medical field by Thomas (1987) found that patients did appreciably less well than a control group if a physician told them, "I am not sure what is the matter with you, and I am not sure the treatment will have an effect."

4.5 Ethics of Placebo Usage

In this era of informed consent, what are the ethics of attempting to use the placebo effect? The very last sentence in the previous section indicates that *what* physicians say, and implies also *how* they say it, can have profound physiological effects on a patient. Surely, the reverse of this observation is also true. Physicians have been traditionally taught about the importance of a good bedside manner. The evidence from earlier parts of this chapter shows the effectiveness of this approach. This means that the attitude of a friendly and caring physician can no longer be considered to be a placebo, that is, the physician's attitude is not an inert factor, but is rather an active ingredient with astonishing potency *vis-à-vis* "proven effective medications." Is this caring-physician-effect reproducible? Certainly, there are certain medications like antibiotics for specific infections that are 100% reproducibly effective across the population. There are many drugs (like anti-hypertensives, insulin for diabetics, and muscle relaxants) that also show very high effectiveness. There are also many drugs whose effectiveness is in the $50 \pm 20\%$ range.

The well-known Native American psychotherapist Terry Tafoya stated in one of his presentations that the only useful thing he learned in graduate school was the existence of the Bell or Gaussian or normal distribution curve. With respect to any intervention, physical or psychological, people's responses fall on a continuum, being bunched around some average value, such that two-thirds fall within one standard deviation of the mean. In such a distribution there are always out-liers, for example, if a "standard" dose of a given drug is 5 mg/kg body weight, then some people will be overdosed at 1 mg/kg and others will be undermedicated at 15 mg/kg. Let us quote Evans (1985, p. 217): "Thus, placebos are effective in reducing severe clinical pain to about half of its original intensity for about a third of suffering patients.... A standard dose of morphine, for example, will successfully reduce pain intensity by half in only about 75% of patients. Even when the dose is increased, 10–15% of patients will not obtain significant relief...." Placebos help one-third, morphine (well-known active drug) helps 75%, and a small number—out-liers—do not get much help at all. This variability in response suggests that individual reactions must always be sought and valued, and that physicians/practitioners need to use every possible ethical method to help people who are suffering.

A dear friend with leukemia was told by her oncologist that the only thing he knew that could help her was a certain chemotherapeutic regimen. He further stated that, in his opinion bolstered by the literature and his experience, the regimen had a one-in-three chance of helping her. My friend's reaction was, "Terrific! Let's do it!" The therapy did put the cancer into a short remission. When it returned, she refused any further treatments. In this circumstance, it would have helped (it certainly couldn't hurt!) if the oncologist initially said, "There's a new chemotherapy regimen we can try. The statistics are so-so, but knowing you, knowing what a battler you are, I wouldn't be surprised if this approach turned out to be extremely helpful for you. Some people have strong side effects, but I expect you will get through the treatment in much comfort."

Scarry (in Harrington, 1997, p. 238) describes a circumstance where a physician has a patient in the ICU who needs medication for pain, but who also has a respiratory problem. The preferred analgesic has a bad effect on respiration. The physician could ethically have given a placebo and said (Scarry's words) the following:

- "I have a choice in prescribing medication for your pain. I can either give you a substance which will interfere with your breathing, and the advantage is I know how this substance works. Or, I can give you another substance that I know will not interfere with your breathing and that I have reason to believe will work equally well, but I don't myself, understand how it works."

Some may feel that this way of helping a patient is dishonest, yet the physician has spoken the truth—they do not know how the placebo analgesic effect works, but they know that it will not affect respiration. In Section 4.6 there is a two-column format which suggests various alternative ways of avoiding medical "hexing." These alternative statements are examples of how linguistically to utilize the placebo effect in communications between the physician and the patient.

Bernie Siegel has been quoted often as saying, "What's wrong with hope?" Placebos *please* the patient; they give hope; and they are surprisingly effective for both physical and psychological problems. I recently had an inguinal hernia surgically repaired— "placebo" surgery (whatever that could be) would not fix the problem. The freely available pain medication was ordinary tylenol (acetaminophen). This is really a rather mild analgesic, yet it was the rare patient this did not help—we all took the proffered pills and told each other how well they worked, and even advised new patients to be sure to take these wonderful pain pills. (This was at the Shouldice Hospital in Toronto which has a deserved worldwide reputation for hernia repair which is their only surgical procedure. The *expectation* of superb care and the reinforcing ambiance made for successful outcomes, which could be characterized as placebo-enhanced.)

I really do not believe there is anything like "false hope"—belief is important and potent. There are ethically proper ways to use the placebo effect. The mechanisms are not known, but how many people drive cars who do not understand the underlying thermodynamic Otto cycle, or use computers and know nothing about binary logic or programming? Certainly, we must use *both* the strengths of modern medicine and the placebo effect. Some would say that placebos should not be used because, for a particular purpose, they were shown to be only 25% or 50% or 70% effective. Yet, many "proven" medicines and chemotherapeutic agents also are significantly less than 100% effective. For example, morphine does not relieve pain for some people, yet it is the analgesic of choice that works for most last stage cancer patients.

4.6 Prayer as a Placebo Effect?

Unless I devote a separate chapter to the effectiveness of prayer in healing and curing, which I am reluctant to do, then the question arises: Where within the framework of this book should I discuss the extensive literature on prayer and healing? Including this discussion at the end of the chapter on the placebo effect seemed to be a logical choice. After reading this section you can decide for yourself whether or not prayer when used for healing incorporates the placebo effect. We also deal with curses, a kind of negative prayer, as being related to the nocebo effect.

Organized and personal religion have used prayer as a method to attain healing and cures. To my mind prayer has been basically used in six ways. The *first* is simply a way of talking to God or a supreme being or spirit: a way to communicate with something or someone beyond—a sharing of inner thoughts with this external entity/presence. The *second* is to ask this external and knowledgeable and powerful entity for help regarding a specific concern. These concerns range from mundane specific items (winning the lottery, passing an exam, appropriate weather), to the correction of physical ailments to attain cures. In some way, the justice of your cause or plea is recognized and the all-powerful all-knowing being or entity directly intercedes in your behalf. This kind of prayer is a *petition* for help for one's self. If you pray for someone else, this *third* form of prayer is an *intercessory prayer*. When someone has a life-challenging disease, petitionary and intercessory prayers appear to be the most commonly used mode. The *fourth* form of prayer is spiritual, and is a kind of meditation whose result is some degree of fusion with, or knowledge of, the universal spirit. A *fifth* form of prayer is the simple "thank you" that is part of saying grace, or just a way of showing appreciation. A *sixth* form of prayer is praising or lauding the universal spirit, saying how wonderful it/He is. Karl Rahner (1985, p. 404) describes seven different aspects of prayer historically recognized in the Christian faith as, "adoration, praise, thanksgiving, penitence, oblation, intercession, and petition." [I had to look up "oblation" which my dictionary defines as: (a) a religious or ritualistic offering, usually of something without life in contrast to a sacrifice of living things. (b) Anything offered or presented in worship or sacred service; an offering; a sacrifice. (c) An offering made to a church, as for the fabric fund, the support of the clergy, or aid for the poor.]

Since our concern is the use of prayer as a vehicle for healing/curing, then the rest of this section will be devoted to the second and third forms of prayer, i.e., for the granting of a petition for yourself or of an intercession. Dossey (in VandeCreek, 1998, p. 10) defines prayer in a deliberately broad and ambiguous way as, "Prayer is communication with the Absolute." Later on the same page he states, "Intercessory prayer is therefore, a go-between—an effort to mediate on behalf of, or plead the case of, someone else. Intercessory prayer is often called 'distant' prayer; because the individual being prayed for is often remote from the person doing the praying." Finally, (same page) he states, "Many researchers shy away from using the word 'prayer' in favor of a more neutral term such as 'distant intentionality'." There is obviously much room for discussion here. Dossey's definition of intercessory prayer is a good working one for the purpose of this section, except that it omits the aspect of asking for an intercession on one's own behalf, i.e., a petition. Intercessory prayer is asking for assistance for another from the "Absolute" to use Dossey's term.

Dossey is the leading expositor and proponent of the effectiveness of intercessory prayer and has lectured and written extensively in the field (1991, 1993, 1996, 1997, and the lead chapter in VandeCreek, 1998). His book *Healing Words. The Power of Prayer and the Practice of Medicine* (1993) contains the best summary of evidence for the effectiveness of prayer in this field. The problem, as with all alternative/complementary approaches, is the elucidation of a *mechanism* for the effectiveness of prayer. *How* does it work? Dossey has recently stated categorically (VandeCreek, 1998, p. 25), "The major criticisms against distant phenomena, including intercessory prayer, have in my opinion been firmly refuted." He cites a variety of sources and studies for this assertion. The mechanism is still elusive, so he wisely states (VandeCreek, 1998, p. 33), *"Although we have focused on the experimental evidence for intercessory prayer, let us recall that prayer does not require science to validate it.* There is no need to hold our breath in anticipation of the next double-blind study on prayer. *People test prayer in their individual lives, and one's life is the most important laboratory of all.* However, self-deception is possible, and science is an effective safeguard against some forms of illusion." [emphases in original] If one's life is the real laboratory and science is not needed for validation, then we are again in the realm of belief systems and the placebo effect.

Dossey's book *Healing Words* (1993) contains the most accessible information about the research evidence for prayer in healing. His Appendix 1 (pp. 293–331) is an extensive listing of 131 controlled trials, their results, and a full citation of references. This appendix is based in large part on a survey by Benor (1990, 1993). Dossey states (p. 293), "Fifty-six of these show statistically significant results at a probability level of < .01 or better ..." The studies include enzymes, bacteria, plants, animals, and human physical problems, amongst others. An assortment of quotes from *Healing Words* will give the reader a sense of the content of the book and Dossey's scholarship (28 pages of notes and references). The page citation is given at the end of each quote.

- Sickly saints and healthy sinners show us that there is no invariable, linear, one-to-one relationship between one's level of spiritual attainment and the degree of one's health. (p. 20)

- Prayer tends to follow instructions laid down by the great religious traditions; prayerfulness does not. It is a feeling of unity with the All, rather than with specific leaders, traditions, or holy books. Intercessory prayer has a tendency to ask for definite outcomes, to structure the future, to "tell God what to do," such as taking the cancer away. Prayerfulness, on the other hand, is accepting without being passive, is grateful without giving up. It is more willing to stand in the mystery, to tolerate ambiguity and the unknown. It honors the rightness of whatever happens, even cancer. (pp. 32–33)

- There are no simple guidelines. Perhaps the Buddhist injunction, "Have good intent," is the best guide.... I would maintain that as long as our efforts are filled with compassion, caring, and love, there is little reason to fear that our prayers for others without their consent are somehow unethical. (p. 111)

- *But there is no evidence whatsoever in any of the experiments on prayer that anything is "sent," or that energy of any kind is involved.* (p. 113) [emphasis in original]

- It is important to bear in mind that *the most important discovery of the Spindrift tests is that prayer works and that both methods are effective.* But in these tests the *non*directed technique appeared quantitatively more effective, frequently yielding results that were twice as great, or more, when compared to the direct approach. (p. 133) [emphases in original; Spindrift address is in the list of references]

- Spindrift believes, on the basis of a large number of tests, that when a nondirected prayer is answered, the outcome is always in the direction of "what's best for the organism." (p. 134)

- ... love is no guarantee of health, longevity, or anything else but paradox and deep mystery. What do we really *know* about the place of love in healing? What can we say without undue fear of contradiction? We can demonstrate experimentally that love, compassion, caring, and empathy catalyze healing events, and that this power operates at a distance and outside of time. But we know also that love is compatible *with* illness—in the same sense that Jesus said, "Love your enemies," not "Don't have any." Love occupies a majestic place in healing. Lying outside space and time, it is a living tissue of reality, a bond that unites us all. (pp. 160–161) [emphases in original]

- Without some change in the legal climate, it is doubtful that most doctors will become courageous enough to intentionally use belief therapeutically, in spite of the fact that they may honor the evidence of its power to heal. (p. 195)
- The scientific evidence suggests—overwhelmingly, in my opinion—that the effects of prayer are not due entirely to placebo effects. *But*, I would ask, *even if they were, what would it matter?* Suppose a cancer disappears and it can be proved beyond doubt that its disappearance was due "just" to placebo effects and suggestion? The cure would be no less real nor less appreciated by the patient. (p. 232) [emphases in original]
- I feel the Byrd [Byrd 1988] experiment is suggestive but inconclusive and inherently ambiguous. It simply contains too many problems that prevent us from drawing firm conclusions about the possible power of prayer. In fact *all* the human prayer studies we have examined so far fall into this category. (p. 258) [emphasis in original]
- If God is included in the "loop," does this increase the overall effect, making prayer more effective than godless imagery? Or does God appear content to work through imagery and visualization without being explicitly acknowledged in the process? These questions have not been answered by any of the research we've looked at. (p. 262)
- The first question anyone suffering from infection, gout, or inflammation asks of any new therapy is not "*How* does it work?" but "*Does* it work?" As history shows, full explanations frequently come later. So it may be with prayer and spiritual healing. (p. 277) [emphases in original]
- [the following are two of Dossey's predictions] The use of prayer will become the standard in scientific medical practice in most medical communities. So pervasive will its use become that not to recommend the use of prayer as an integral part of medical care will one day constitute medical malpractice. (p. 286)

Perhaps a mechanism for "distant intentionality" will someday be found. A mechanism seems to be irrelevant for people who pray. On the other hand, the mind boggles at what must be going on in the space between people on this planet and between them and wherever the Absolute dwells. There may be several hundred million people praying at any one given time—how are these myriad messages sorted and channeled to the right person, entity, or place? Is there any way that they influence each other in terms of canceling or enhancing effects? Are these "practical" matters worthy of any consideration whatsoever? Some quotations from people who have studied these matters may be helpful.

- While God certainly has the wherewithal to heal and reconcile in the absence of our prayer, we presume that God is also content to heal in response to or in concert with our entreaties on behalf of others. (J.T. VanderZee in VandeCreek, 1998, p. 40)
- The theological questions include those about God's omniscience (do we need to tell God someone is in need of healing?), God's beneficence (does God need our appeals to act favorably in someone's behalf?), God's intentionality (why would God heal one person who was prayed for and not another?), and the relative merit of the intentions (should prayer determine the outcome of the championship basketball game for my school's team?). (M. Cutting in VandeCreek, 1998, p. 46)
- It remains open to question whether experiments in "mental intentionality" have anything to do with God. (M. Cutting in VandeCreek, 1998, p. 48)
- … already a century ago Søren Kierkegaard held that to believe that God acts on human beings in an external way is superstition. For him, God acts only on human inwardness; the efficacy of prayer lies in the inner transformation of the one who prays. According to Kierkegaard, prayer is something we do so that God can do something to us that we can see ourselves honestly as we are and thereby be transformed more into God's image. (D.C. Baker citing Kierkegaard in VandeCreek, 1998, p. 98)

Dossey (1991, pp. 128–136) discusses the "tomato effect" and the "snakeroot effect." In North America in the 1700s and the early 1800s the tomato was considered unhealthy since people "knew" it was poisonous, after all it belongs to the "deadly nightshade" family. The tomato was being eaten in Europe without any deleterious health effects at that time. A public demonstration of eating tomatoes without getting sick in 1820 in New Jersey slowly changed attitudes about the tomato. So, the *tomato effect* (named by J.S. and J.M. Goodwin) is described according to Dossey (1991, p. 128) by, "If we encounter therapies that do not fit our preconceived ideas about what an appropriate treatment should be, we may reject them *even if evidence for their effectiveness is staring us in the face ...*" [emphasis in original] By contrast the *snakeroot effect* is the refusal to acknowledge that a treatment or substance you use and believe in is harmful in spite of overwhelming evidence. Both of these effects are pervasive in all cultures and may be considered to be illustrations of the placebo and nocebo effects.

Dossey has commented that when he gives lectures on the power of intercessory prayer for healing he invariably gets a question about the reverse, that is, if prayer is effective for healing, can it not also be effective for harming? This would be the nocebo side of the positive effect of prayer. In fact he has written an entire book about this (1997) which is illuminatingly entitled "Be Careful What You Pray For ... You Just Might Get It." He cites a 1994 Gallup poll which found that 5% of Americans prayed for harm to come to others. Dossey cites (1997, p. 2) Florence Nightingale as saying, "The excellence of God," she said, "is that he is inexorable. If he could be changed by people's praying, we should be at the mercy of those who attempt to change his mind through their prayers." Later (1997, p. 214) he cites C.S. Lewis, "If God had granted all the silly prayers I've made in my life, where should I be now?" Dossey has written this book partly because he felt that denying the dark side of prayer was like ignoring the harmful side-effects of drugs. In the introduction (1997, p. 5) he quotes Dion Fortune's observation, "There is no essential difference between sticking pins into a wax image of an enemy and burning candles in front of a wax image of the Virgin." He also states:

■ For example, if we believe that the world is haunted and con-trolled by the devil, and if our prayers are continually filled with diabolic images, do we run the risk of actually *creating* demons? If I am so fearful of getting cancer that that's all I can think of in my prayers, am I actually creating the prob-lem I want to pray away? Is this one way prayer becomes negative? If images actually create changes in the physical world, we should be careful what we pray for. (p. 91)

- Although murderous thoughts are universal, it is obvious that they do not invariably kill, otherwise no one would be alive. (p. 104)

Dossey considers most negative prayers to be unintentional, as in shouting something like "damn you" when you are angry. When you use imagery to rid your body of cancer cells or an infection, is this not a form of negative prayer since the *intent* is to *kill* those cancer cells and bacteria? In this sense, a "negative" prayer is a healing one! With respect to these kinds of negative healing prayers, Dossey believes that *generalized* instructions to the body (e.g., achieve balance and harmony) are more effective than highly biologically correct specific ones—the body seems to respond to general directions and fills in the details somehow by itself.

Dossey has an entire chapter on "medical hexing" (pp. 53–81). The opening quote is by a Navajo Medicine Man:

- In my practice, when I'm working with the patient, I am very careful of what I say, because any negative words can hurt the patient. So, with Western medicine, a doctor could be treating a patient, and he can mention death, and that is sharper than any needle. Therefore, with the tongue that we have, we have to be very careful of what we say at the time and point we're treating the patient.

The delivery of any serious prognosis can be considered to be a potential curse, so great care must be used by the doctor. In Dossey's opinion, a patient must also be offered some form of *protection* at the same time. He has an entire chapter (pp. 195–217) devoted to methods of protection. He feels that intimidating environments are facilitative to the casting of spells. One such environment is the medical imaging facilities in modern hospitals—special caution should be used in them to provide "protection" for the patient.

The potential for "medical hexing" for inducing harmful mental and physical responses is so important, that we do a two-column treatment with the potential hex on the left and suggested alternative and "protective" statements on the right. (Most of the medical hexes were taken from Dossey.)

Medical Hex	**Alternative Statements**
There is nothing more we can do for you.	At this time I do not have anything new to offer you. But, let's keep working together. There is always hope. I'll keep exploring what is out there for you. You can always rely on me.
It will only get worse.	It may get worse for a time— that's what the books say. Miracles do happen; I've seen them. Let's work together and do whatever we can.
You will just have to live with it.	Sometimes, you just have to live with the condition. We will do whatever we can to make you comfortable, while we continue to explore other ways to deal with this. There is always hope, and I have been surprised many times.
You'll be dead in six months.	You know, the books give all kinds of numbers for your condition. I could quote them to you, but you are a unique person, and I believe you will beat whatever the odds are. I just don't know if you have a few months or a few years left, or much much longer. I enjoy surprises.
You're living on borrowed time.	You know that your condition is a serious one. Let's do whatever we have to do together so that you can get through this period comfortably, and we can turn this thing around.

You are going downhill fast.	On the surface your condition appears to be getting worse. But, there are many things we can do to reverse that so that you can get better. Here are a few of them ...
The next heartbeat may be your last.	Your heart is not in the best condition, but there are many things we can do to strengthen it so that it will last a long time for you.
You can have a heart attack or worse at any minute.	Your heart is not in the best condition, but there are many things we can do to strengthen it so that it will last a long time for you.
The *Malach amoveth* (angel of death) is shadowing you.	Fate has a funny way of doing things that are surprising. Your condition may not improve for a while. But, here are some things we can do together to improve your health ...
You have a time bomb in your chest.	There are some problems with the state of your heart. We can stabilize the condition and do things to strengthen it. Are you game?
Enjoy what's left of your life.	You know, we never know what life has in store for us. We can plan and plan, and there are always surprises. I think the best plan is to always live one day at a time and take life as it goes along, enjoying every minute. That's what I do.

Let's pray you get over this.	[Since the patient who hears this may interpret it as meaning that they haven't a hope of getting well and that only prayer will work, you can use the following.] In addition to whatever medical things we do, some of my patients find that praying together is helpful. Would it be okay with you if we add that and pray together?
There's no hope when it gets this far.	You know, there is always hope. Many of my patients have had remarkable turn-arounds with this disease. There are still some things we can do. I know that you are religious. Would it be okay if we prayed together and I kept you in my prayers?
You have breast cancer.	The test results show that you have breast cancer. There are many things we can do, and most of my patients have a very good prognosis. Let's work together on getting rid of it. My patients do best when the cancer doesn't have them. Cancer is just a word—it is not a sentence.
Get your affairs in order and say your "goodbyes."	I have a will and so does my wife. We also have living wills and durable powers of attorney for health. We just do not know how long we have and we do not want to leave a mess for our children. I don't know how long either of us has—crazy accidents happen. It is always wise to get

> your affairs in order as we have.
> Let's continue to work together
> on this.

You will notice that the alternative statements are always longer. It is easy to "curse" and much harder to be affirmative in terms of helping people. Take whatever time you need. Two of the alternative responses above suggest that the physician offer to pray with and/or for the patient. Much caution should be used here since a patient may take the offer to pray for them as meaning that there is no hope and that only a miracle through prayer will help. If you happen to be given a medical hex, do not believe it, confront your doctor, and explore alternatives. There is always hope.

Rachel Naomi Remen (1996) devoted a short chapter (pp. 270–272) to prayer. Some of her comments (pp. 270-271) are illuminating:

- But prayer is not a way to get what we want to happen, like the remote control that comes with the television set. I think that prayer may be less about asking for things we are attached to than it is about relinquishing our attachments in some way. It can take us beyond fear, which is an attachment, and beyond hope, which is another form of attachment. It can help us remember the nature of the world and the nature of life, not on an intellectual level but in a deep experiential way. When we pray, we don't change our consciousness. We move from an individual, isolated making-things-happen kind of consciousness to a connection on the deepest level with the largest possible reality. And then the question "How did you become well?" becomes more a question about mystery than about efficacy. A very different kind of question.

She also cites the traditional American Indian prayer, "May we be helped to whatever is most right." as a simple way of relinquishing ultimate causality.

Before the end of this section I would like to cite *When Therapy Isn't Enough: The Healing Power of Prayer and Psychotherapy* by S. Menahem (1995). This is a thoughtful book by a psychotherapist relating his connections of spirituality, prayer, psychotherapy and healing.

Dossey has done us a great service by his scholarly approach to the effectiveness of prayer for healing and curing. The jury is still out on this subject. Prayer may be considered to be a form of the placebo (or nocebo) effect, but the placebo effect under any name is real, and it is powerful. You need to follow your own belief system in this matter. If you feel that your personal prayers are helpful to you, then please pray. If you feel that a prayer circle or the prayers of others will help you, then ask for those prayers. Prayer is a personal matter.

My friend and colleague Nicholas Piediscalzi, Professor Emeritus of Religion, has been particularly helpful in his comments on this chapter. In a letter dated 14 October 1999, he had the following clarifying comments to make that are both relevant to this section and this chapter:

> It seems to me that the mechanism of the placebo effect is its ability to help us make contact with our inner healers and the healing powers of nature and communal relationships. Clearly it is an ability that cannot be objectified or quantified, but it is there and it functions effectively. For this reason, I prefer Benson's approach and his calling the placebo effect "remembered wellness." In this context, prayer certainly may be a placebo, but it is a placebo that puts us in touch with our inner healing powers and the powers of nature and communal relationships.

> Siegel, Chopra, Benson, Ornish and many others, point to a realm of healing power that undergirds all life. For them, prayer and meditation are tools that enable individuals to make contact with and to participate in that healing power. Because this is healing power, it is not always curing power. Part of prayer's function, from this perspective, is to assist the individual to live a life of healing rather than curing. I miss this kind of discussion in your presentation on prayer. For this reason, your approach to prayer appears to me a bit dated and anachronistic, removed from some of the cutting edge thinkers on prayer. Also, prayer is a multi-dimensional tool that goes beyond Dossey's categorizations. (I think that Dossey is much too simplistic and somewhat naive in his approach to prayer.) Here are some words from Driver (1991, pp. 95–96) to consider:

As for prayer, its character as transformance may be considered in two different ways. The most familiar version of "the efficacy of prayer" is the idea that the deity, prompted by prayer "works," and so on. There is another, perhaps less obvious, sense in which prayer may be understood to transform a situation. The act of prayer may establish or re-establish relationships— between the people or groups who pray, the deity *to* whom they pray, and the people or circumstances *for* which they pray. Like speech in general, prayer may on occasion have not only, and not mainly, the function of conveying information, but rather that of establishing and consolidating relationship through intensifying the "presence" of one being to another. Hence prayer may transform isolation into community, emptiness into fullness, despair into hope, and so on. I am suggesting that it is not the mere thought of deity that accomplishes this, but rather such thought in conjunction with the physical enactment of prayer in speech or body language—that is, in performance.

This type of "performance" connects or reconnects individuals not only to divine power as some claim, but also and perhaps more importantly to certain healing powers in nature, communal relations and the individuals' own psyches.

4.7 Summary

This chapter is particularly long for several reasons. One is that I am personally fascinated by this as yet unexplained (no known mechanisms) phenomenon. Second, I deliberately flooded the chapter with many quotes by many experts to demonstrate the scope of the placebo effect, the enormous amount of research in this area, and to emphasize its many facets. (The serious student may wish to consult the cited sources.) Finally, it appears to me that the efficacy of guided imagery (and other interventions described in this book) is intrinsically connected to the placebo effect, which is, in essence, a mind/body phenomenon. The words "psychophysiological therapeutic effect" appear prominently in many scholarly papers. To me "psychophysiological" means mind/body interactions. I do not think that it is a problem that the mechanisms for the placebo effect are not known—such mechanisms are not known for many "proven" drugs and treatments. It is also not a problem that placebos are not 100% effective (there are only a few drugs like the antibiotics that approach this figure)— the modern "reliable" pharmacopeia contains many drugs that are partially or mostly effective. Although placebos are sometimes accompanied by anticipated side effects, proper administration can minimize or eliminate such side effects. All in all, guided imagery and mind/body work are inextricably intertwined with the placebo effect—let's use it wisely.

Chapter 5

Relaxation Methods

5.1 Introduction

In previous chapters we discussed the importance of relaxation and its connection with enhancing the immune system. The so-called "relaxation response" hit public awareness with Benson's landmark book (1975) on the subject. Here was a simple, non-invasive meditative technique that (according to the jacket blurb): "… will unlock your hidden asset and help you: relieve inner tensions; deal more effectively with stress; lower blood pressure; (and) improve your physical and emotional health." These may appear on the surface to be the assertions of a snake oil salesman, but Benson cited careful studies demonstrating that these effects are indeed real for the relaxation response. In addition to the above, relaxation also: enhances immune system function, lowers oxygen consumption and the respiratory rate, decreases the heart rate and blood pressure (in those with elevated blood pressure), increases alpha waves, and decreases muscle tension. Relaxation really is beneficial in a variety of ways.

There are many ways to attain a relaxed state. Among the more common are: Transcendental Meditation, Zen practices and yoga, autogenic training, progressive relaxation, and hypnosis. It apparently makes little difference in the final physiological markers as to which technique you use. In what follows, some of these methods will be discussed briefly. My preferred approach (including a transcript) is given at the end of the chapter.

Transcendental Meditation is a school of meditation involving classes and trainers and an individual mantra for repetition. This training is effective. *Zen* meditation is a discipline taught by masters and involves much practice. (See Suzuki, 1964, for more information.) One part of training in *yoga* involves the physical positions (asanas), and another part involves a meditative practice. *Autogenic Training* (Linden, 1990) is based on learning six mental exercises for daily practice until they become almost automatic. *Hypnosis and self-hypnosis* with suggestions for deep relaxation also work well. A common denominator in all approaches is that you get better with practice, i.e., you can attain deeper states more quickly.

5.2 Jacobson's Progressive Relaxation

The Jacobson progressive relaxation method was devised by a University of Chicago physician/physiologist in the 1930s (Jacobson, 1938). The name is descriptive of the process. Typically starting with the feet, you say to yourself (or follow a guide), "Now tense the muscles in your left foot. Then relax them. Now tense the muscles in your right foot. Then relax them (or release the tension)." You then progress, alternating the cycle up your legs to the abdomen, the buttocks, the back, the chest, hands and arms and shoulders, to the neck, and the head. Practitioners differ on the number of muscle groups. The tension is typically held for a few seconds before releasing. A passive attitude while lying down in a quiet room is helpful. The process may end with tensing the entire body before releasing, perhaps with a deep sigh. Progressive relaxation teaches the client to recognize through tension-and-release how to be able to release muscular tensions arising in any part of the body. The procedure is still widely used.

You will notice in Section 5.5 where I present my recommended method for relaxing, that I make no use of the progressive relaxation approach. This comes out of my background in hypnosis where one of the things we point out about language usage is that negation does not exist in the mind. Consider the direction, "Do *not* think about a pink polka-dotted elephant," or to a child, "*Stop* doing that!" The unconscious mind slides by the negation and in the first example will hear, "... think about ..." and in the second, "... do that." Also, you cannot blank out an image of a pink polka-dotted elephant without *first* conjuring up the image. To get compliance with a directive, it is preferable to state what you want in a positive way rather than invoke the negation. What does this have to do with progressive relaxation? If you consider the directions, every other activity involves *tensing* a group of muscles or *tension*. So, at least half of your attention is focused on tense muscles. While you do develop a physical sense of the different sensations for tense and relaxed muscles, the inordinate emphasis on tension stands out and will affect your reactions and feelings. A much better way to do progressive relaxation would be to first experience the sensations of tension and relaxation with *one* group of muscles on both sides of the body—making a fist would be a good starting point. Then, starting with the feet say something like, "Now that your body knows the difference between tension and relaxation, starting with your left foot, just let all the muscles there relax, become soft and comfortable and at ease. Now, relax all of the muscles in your right foot." Continue with these directions, emphasizing comfort and ease and softness and lightness, for all of the other muscle groups, ending with a total body sense of calm and relaxation (perhaps, with an audible sigh). Imagine how you would respond to doing a progressive relaxation in the traditional style versus the way that mentions "tension" only once. As we will discuss later, the careful choice of language can make a big difference.

5.3 Benson's Relaxation Response Method

Benson (1975) found that there were four common components for eliciting the relaxation response, regardless of the approach or cultural source. The *first* is a quiet environment: the phone is disconnected, people are told not to disturb you, and you use a back room away from street noise. The *second* is an object to dwell upon. This may be repeating a sound or word, gazing fixedly at an object, or concentrating upon a particular feeling or sensation. Since there will always be distracting thoughts, you return to your focus over and over again. (With practice, fewer distracting thoughts emerge.) The *third* component is a passive attitude. This, of course, cannot be willed as in the injunction, "Be spontaneous." Benson considers a passive attitude to be the most important component. The quiet environment and object of focus aid in attaining passivity, as does the *fourth* element of a comfortable position. The recommended position is sitting since lying down may lead to sleep, which is okay in itself, but not the goal of learning to attain and use the relaxation response. The process is not complicated, although a teacher can be helpful.

In Benson's 1996 book (with M. Stark) he devotes an entire chapter (pp. 123–148) to the relaxation response. His table 2 (p. 131) gives a comparison between the fight-or-flight response and the relaxation response. It is summarized below.

Physiologic State	Fight-or-Flight Response	Relaxation Response
metabolism	increases	decreases
blood pressure	increases	decreases
heart rate	increases	decreases
rate of breathing	increases	decreases
blood flowing to the muscles of the arms and legs	increases	stable
muscle tension	increases	decreases
slow brain waves	decreases	increases

Benson states that there are only two basic steps to elicit the relaxation response: (1) repeat a word, sound, prayer, phrase, or muscular activity; and (2) passively disregard everyday thoughts that come to mind, and return to your repetition. He states that their research has found that performing a focused exercise activates the relaxation response. Benson teaches the following nine-step generic technique (p. 136) to his patients.

Step 1. Pick a focus word or short phrase that is firmly rooted in your belief system.

Step 2. Sit quietly in a comfortable position.

Step 3. Close your eyes.

Step 4. Relax your muscles.

Step 5. Breathe slowly and naturally, and as you do, repeat your focus word, phrase, or prayer silently to yourself as you exhale.

Step 6. Assume a passive attitude. Don't worry about how well you're doing. When other thoughts come to mind, simply say to yourself, "Oh, well," and gently return to the repetition.

Step 7. Continue for ten to twenty minutes.

Step 8. Do not stand immediately. Continue sitting quietly for a minute or so, allowing other thoughts to return. Then open your eyes and sit for another minute before rising.

Step 9. Practice this technique once or twice daily.

The above is a good and well-founded basic approach to relaxation.

5.4 Meditation

My unabridged dictionary defines "meditate" as both a transitive and intransitive verb. *Transitive*: to contemplate; to keep the mind or attention fixed upon; to watch; to study; to muse upon or over; to ponder. *Intransitive*: to keep the mind in a state of contemplation; to dwell in thought; to muse; cogitate; reflect. The *noun* meditation is: act of meditating; thought; esp., close or continued thought; serious contemplation. Meditations have been part of all religions in some way through all times. Our image of holy persons involves seeing them at their meditations.

At some point in my life I became convinced that meditation would be helpful, yet I did not want to become part of some movement or cult. I learned how to meditate by studying Lawrence LeShan's book (1974), particularly Chapter 8 on "The 'How' of Meditation." (You can now purchase this excellent book with an audiotape and guide.) The meditation of breath counting is the simplest one. LeShan recommends, "you strive to be aware of just your counting and to be as fully aware of it as possible." He also recommends counting the exhalations, going up to four, and then repeating. If you count both inhalation and exhalation, you can add an "and" between each number. He recommends picking a number and a duration before you start. You can begin with 15 minutes of daily practice and slowly move up to 30 minutes. LeShan also discusses other styles of meditation. Meditation is an excellent way to elicit the relaxation response.

5.5 How to Relax

In this section you will be given some detailed directions on how to relax, including a relaxation transcript. The popular notion of relaxing is coming home from work, kicking off your shoes, getting into comfortable clothes, having a drink, and "relaxing" in a comfortable chair with the paper or watching television. This undoubtedly involves getting into an easier, quieter and calmer state of mind, but it is not what we have in mind as the first part of a guided imagery session. The parts of the relaxation process follow:

a. Quiet Space It is important to be undisturbed for the 15 minutes or so you need. A room without a phone or with it unplugged is a beginning. (Remember just unhooking a phone frequently results in that endless beeping signal.) Other people in the house/apartment need to be told about your quiet time and that you are not to be disturbed. A room away from street noise is helpful, particularly if you need to leave the window open. Soft lighting is better than bright lights; some people prefer the dark— you must suit yourself in this regard. When you are experienced at relaxing, you can do this in almost any environment as long as you are not directly disturbed—the environment becomes a kind of "white" noise. (As a student, I used to study in the university cafeteria!)

b. Comfortable Position The literature on meditation generally recommends a sitting posture with a straight back. This prevents falling asleep and promotes easy breathing. Really flexible people may adopt the lotus posture using a cushion or a low stool. My recommendation is to use any chair, couch, bed, or any position in which you will feel comfortable and without any body strain for the time period you have chosen. For example, I typically meditate in the morning lying flat in bed. I occasionally fall asleep. If you are so relaxed that you do fall asleep, then that may be what your mind/body needs most at that time. You are not being graded on how you relax. There is no failure here, just different ways to attain the same goal.

c. Time. Your mind contains a remarkably accurate clock. Tell yourself at the beginning of the session just how long you wish it to last. Your session will end itself within a minute or two of that time. Do not use alarm clocks—their ring or buzz can be startling. If you wish, you can position a clock where you can easily see it by opening your eyes for a second. Earlier we indicated that the optimum duration for a relaxation/imagery session is 15 minutes. As a beginner, 10 to 15 minutes is sufficient. As you become more experienced, you may enjoy longer sessions. There are no rules for duration.

d. Eyes Open or Closed Most people do best to close their eyes during a session. Eye closure greatly reduces the amount of sensory input. Some people are uncomfortable with their eyes closed; staring at an object and/or de-focusing your eyes are just as effective in limiting input. You may even experience "tunnel vision" with defocused eyes. Again, there are no rules—do what is comfortable and normal for you.

e. Object of Focus The relaxation process works most smoothly when there is something to focus your mind on, to contemplate if you will. This can be a physical object such as a spot on the wall, a candle, a picture or part of a picture, or a flower. You may focus on a particular sound you make like "Om," a mantra, or a phrase that is repeated like "God is good," or "God is One", or "Peace", or LeShan's nonsense phrase of "La-de" ("Lah-dee"). I recommend that you focus simply on counting breaths. Although LeShan prefers a count of 4 (and I did this for many years), you may count to any number you wish before returning to 1. To avoid monotony I vary the count, sometimes going as high as 20. You may count the inbreath and the outbreath or both. This is a matter of personal preference. When counting breaths I frequently focus on the end of my nose, sensing the cooler inbreath and the warmer and moister outbreath—this extra point of concentration narrows the field and serves to limit potentially distracting sensory input.

As you become more experienced, there are fewer distracting thoughts. But, there are *always* such random thoughts drifting through your mind. Simply acknowledge the presence of the thought, thank it, and go back to 1. Some days there will be many such temptations to distract you—thank the thought *and* go back to one. If the thoughts become too insistent, this means that this was not a good time for a meditative session, and stop it short. Such an experience is just another way to learn about yourself. *Forcing* yourself to relax is like forcing yourself to be spontaneous....

f. Imagery Work You have now paid attention to the "mechanical" factors involved in relaxing. By whatever method you choose, after 7 to 10 minutes of relaxation you are ready to start on your imagery work. Without looking at a clock you either program your internal clock to let you know it is time to begin or, better, you just know by your physical quietude and the ease and softness of your breathing and a period with no distracting thoughts, that this is imagery time. This inner knowledge of when to start comes with practice—you will find an unique sense of it for yourself.

The imagery work itself incorporates the specific visualizations, words, or sensations that you have an inner sense of really knowing that they are appropriate and helpful for you. This imagery may be developed by you, with a guide, or adapted from the many ritual images presented in Achterberg et al. (1994), or from some other source. Generally, the more vivid and detailed the image, the better it works. That is, it is important for you to be engrossed in your own imagery. For some people, observing the image working in your body from a dissociated perspective is the mode of choice. Also, for some, generalized directions such as, "Okay, immune system, just get in there and do what it takes to get rid of this cancer," are the preferred approach. Again, the imagery work is unique to the individual.

The imagery portion of the session lasts from 7 to 12 minutes, ending at a natural place for you.

g. Re-orientation Loud noises or interruptions while you are in a relaxed state can activate the startle reflex. Re-orient yourself slowly to the waking state. You can give yourself suggestions about ending the session with a few deep breaths, blinking your eyes, stretching, and returning to the present with an inner calm.

5.6 Relaxation Script
Hello! This is a tape designed to help you relax into a comfortable and calm state. Please be sure you are sitting or reclining in a way that is easy for you, and that you are in a quiet place, with nothing to bother you and nothing to disturb you. This is your quiet time, a peaceful one, a special time just for you. If at any time you need to move or adjust your position to be even more comfortable, please do so. I may not be using just the right words for you now, or saying them in just the right way—please feel free to change the words and how you hear them, so that they are just the best for you at this time ...

And, you can continue your relaxation by paying attention to your breathing, noticing each breath in, and each breath out. Slowly and easily, calmly, just breathing in a soft natural way. In, and out. Notice how the cooler air enters and warmer moister air leaves. Simply, softly, breathing. Perhaps, counting your breaths—one ... and ... two ... and ... three ... and ... four ... and ... five ... and, back to one ...two ... three....

If any stray thoughts should wander through your mind, notice them, observe them, thank them, and then go back to ... one ... and ... two ... and ... three.... That's right. Safely moving and drifting with each easy calming breath. Softly. Simply. Naturally. Your time. Your safe secure quiet time. Breathing easily. Enjoying this moment, now; this breath, this peaceful time and place. Softly breathing, such calm, such peace. This breath ... and the next one ... your time ... your quiet time ... a healing space and place ... allowing this peace to fill you. Your peaceful time. Relaxing even more. Yes. Another easy breath. And another. Enjoying.

And within your mind now, you can just drift off to some safe and secure place, one that is uniquely yours. It may be real, or just real within your imagination ... your place ... a special place ... peaceful and calm ... serene.... There may be music ... your music.... You may be alone or with someone special ... or with many ... your time ... your place ... safe and secure and serene ... relaxing even more.... You become so engrossed that time almost stops ... enjoying just being ... your place ... peace.... And, you can return here whenever you wish ... remembering ... taking time for yourself ... a few quiet breaths ... relaxing ... drifting off ... safely....

[*Pause*] And, when you are ready, will you find yourself taking a deep breath or two, stretching, and blinking your eyes? And, you can come back, now, to this room feeling ever so relaxed, so at ease, rested. Yes. Thank you.

The previous example may be spoken to you by someone you know, or you may wish to make a tape of it for yourself. Your quiet time. Thank you.

The next three chapters provide the necessary background in rapport building, language, and analysis of guided imagery scripts to be ready to design guided imagery of your own for a specific client. In particular, since the medium for the delivery of a guided image is language, much space (Chapter 7) will be devoted to language usage.

Chapter 6

Rapport Building Skills

6.1. Introduction[1]

Before you can effectively work with someone, rapport has to be established. Your client must trust you and have confidence in you. There are some people you just automatically trust, and there are others whom you somehow distrust. How can you maximize useful rapport with your clients so that the cooperative work of their getting what they want will be enhanced? *Establishing rapport is something that can be learned.* In this chapter we will teach you the basic skills of rapport building and provide exercises for practicing and honing those skills.

It will always be the case that some people are "naturally" better at rapport building than others. Yet, we all learned those incomparably harder skills of walking, talking, and writing. Remember that the early stages of learning any new skill involve confusion and awkwardness as well as a sense of "something" being just not right. Practice does make perfect. Giving the people you work with the congruent sense of having your "unconditional positive regard," that you are there for them and with them during the session, that they have *your* undivided attention, is the foundation on which *all* change work is based.

We exist and function in the world in terms of our proprioceptive senses and also in terms of language. We function in many different contexts, cultures, subcultures, and even mini-subcultures. When you meet a fellow countryman abroad, there is an automatic feeling of recognition. If the two of you were both white, black or Hispanic, then another level of recognition would occur. If you shared the same religion, region of the country, sex, university, town, relatives, etc., the feeling of comfortableness around each other would increase even more. The closer the match, the greater the sense of rapport, of connection, of existing in the world in the same way.

---

[1] This chapter is adapted from Battino and South (1999) with permission.

Some people may raise an ethical objection here with respect to being "genuine" when you are working with someone. You cannot be other than yourself. If you adapt your behavior for the advantage of your clients, isn't that ethical and responsible behavior? If shifting the way that you phrase your speech to be closer to that of the client helps build rapport, what can be wrong with that? In fact, to not do so would be irresponsible since you should be free to do whatever you ethically can to help people. In this chapter, we will explore ways of shifting your verbal and nonverbal behaviors to establish rapport better.

6.2 Rogerian Approaches

Carl Rogers pioneered the approach of giving the client your "unconditional positive regard." He meant a number of things by this. First and foremost is that your clients should know from your *congruent* behavior that you are there for them, that you are concerned about their well-being, and that you will do whatever is ethically possible for them within the therapeutic context. Almost everyone has something about themself that is likeable, and with which you can make some connection. This also helps to separate the person from their problems or difficulties within your own mind. Clients should have your undivided attention during a session since this is *their* time. There is no place while dealing with clients for imposing your belief systems, your politics, your religion, your sexual preferences, etc., on them. Since you cannot be other than who you are, then somehow or other you must make certain that your personal preferences will not show up in the session. When you deal with significant people in your life, there are some subjects that are just taboo if you wish to maintain that relationship. I know a couple who "somehow" never discuss the subject of abortion—he is adamantly opposed to it and she is not. If your belief system gets in the way of working with a particular client, then you must refer that client to someone else who would be comfortable with them. This "unconditional positive regard" is the foundation for all therapeutic and healing relationships. A surgeon may possess remarkable technical skills, but even those skills can be enhanced by the belief of his/her patient that the surgeon is there for them and the patient is not just another case.

6.3 Gathering Information

How much do you need to know about a client to help them? The answer is "just enough." Healing work via guided imagery and the other modalities described in this book needs to be done in cooperation with the person's physician or with the knowledge that the person is also under conventional medical care. I use the same one-page intake form for guided imagery work that I use for my private psychotherapy clients. This form obtains vital information such as address, phone numbers, family, etc., and then leaves one-half of the page for—"briefly describe your concerns and what I can help you with." A ten to thirty minute discussion will usually provide sufficient information to devise interventions to help the client. Direct inquiry can also be useful.

Some therapists indicate that doing healing work is 95% gathering information and 5% interventions. My philosophy is that since you cannot design a guided image without information, it is important to gather *just enough*. You can always gather more information later, if needed.

Body language is an important channel of information and it is important that you "read" your client. This means being aware of facial expressions, voice quality, posture, movements, and breathing patterns. Of course, this should be done without being obvious. Pay special attention to incongruencies between verbal and nonverbal messages. With practice, you can read bodies automatically and with peripheral vision.

6.4 Representational Systems

We function in the world in terms of language. As we have experiences, we describe those experiences for ourselves in words which are then stored along with other sensory inputs such as images, sounds, sensations, and odors. A number of observers have pointed out that people *tend* to have a *primary* representational system which they favor such as visual, auditory or kinesthetic (bodily sensations). NLP (neuro-linguistic programming) practitioners have done the most with this concept, although the literature appears to be ambivalent about its validity. As with many other ideas in psychotherapy, the concept of representational systems can sometimes be useful. If it works for you with a particular client, then use it.

Language can be limiting if your vocabulary is limited in some way. For example, there are some cultures whose language has words for only the numbers one and two. They can count only: one, two, many ... There are some cultures which have words to describe only a limited number of colors, so they can describe what they see in terms of only those words. The full spectrum of colors may be out there, but if the only words you know are black, white, red, and green, then your reality is circumscribed by those words. The Inuit have an enormous number of words to describe snow and can do so with a fineness of distinction that eludes other people. A linguist might be able to write down all of the Inuit words for snow and what they are told their meanings are, but they would be meaningless for someone not growing up in the Inuit culture and incorporating, along with those words, a *physical* sense of what they represent. The cross-cultural significance of how different peoples use time, space, and language can be found in the works of anthropologists such as E.T. Hall (see Hall, 1959, for example). We are bound by our culture, our words, and our language.

Since the meaning of any communication is the response that you get, it is important to be exquisitely sensitive to how your clients react to what you say and do. You may intend one thing by the content of your language, but your client may be understanding something quite different. When in doubt, ask. Of course, much marital and family discord comes from misunderstandings that arise from habits of hearing in a particular way. Language is important to communication and it is also important in terms of establishing rapport.

Let us assume for the moment that everyone does have a preferred representational system, that is, everyone tends to perceive and record reality primarily in visual, auditory, or kinesthetic terms. The senses of taste and smell are important, but are used less frequently in terms of language than the three mentioned. Table 6.1 lists words and phrases that are typically used by people whose representational system preference is visual, auditory or kinesthetic. In addition, the table shows some words that are generally "neutral" with respect to representational systems.

Visual	Auditory	Kinesthetic	Unspecified
see	say	handle	think
picture	tone	firm	sense
clear	feedback	force	judging
visual	tune	build	assume
imagery	sounds good	handy	allows
point out	talk	push	learn
focus	hear	calm	motivate
eye	tempo	grasp	thought
look	shout	hard	discover
view	scream	reach	aware
draw	rhythm	solid	decide
appear	believe	narrow	agree
perceive	rings a bell	pull	apply
show	tell	feel	believe
movie	sounds like	shape	develop
delight	strike a note	burdened	evaluate
blurred	said	hold	guess
foggy	spoken	measure	realize
keep your eye on it	sound the alarm	go around	process
		take apart	use
		fluid	allow
		grind	know
		thrust	understand
		nail down	many ways
		step by step	internalize
		concrete	

Table 6.1
Typical Words and Phrases used in each
Representational System.

These words are in general predicates or process words—verbs, adjectives, and adverbs that people use for communication. As you practice with representational systems other words will come to mind.

A person tends to stick to one representational system, although within given contexts and normal word usage they may switch around. It is sometimes difficult to figure out a person's primary representational system. When in doubt, be sure that your communication involves the use of *all three* systems. It makes good sense when giving general lectures or presentations to use all three representational systems insofar as possible. By careful observation, you may find that you get stronger responses using one system rather than another.

The usefulness of the idea of representational systems is that it lets you "speak the same language" as your client. You can then "be in touch," "be on the same wavelength," "be in tune," "have the same grasp," "be in step," "see eye to eye," "see things the same way," "have the same image/vision/picture," "be on the same footing," "sound the same," etc. There is therefore something *simpatico* about the way that you speak and exist in the world. You are literally speaking the same language as your clients when you join their representational system (and any shifts in it that occur during the course of a session).

One use of the concept of representational systems is in establishing rapport with your clients. Another is in enlarging their world view. If you have a client who is primarily visual, for example, they may be missing out on two-thirds of the possible ways of experiencing the world. Sex for such a person may be unsatisfactory since they are "seeing" rather than feeling. Music may not be as impactful since they would be *seeing* an orchestra play rather than really experiencing (hearing) the sounds. One way of expanding representational systems is by the process of *overlapping*. You, as therapist, can describe an experience such as walking in the woods by first talking about what it is that you see, and then adding sound and feeling to the description so that the senses "overlap" from one to the other. The other senses are then connected to sight. For example, you might say, "As you look around in the woods and see the trees and leaves and path, you can also be aware of the sounds that your shoes make as you walk over the path and how it feels differently to walk on leaves or dirt or stones. Taking a close look at the bark of a large tree, you can see the various shades of brown and the texture, and running your fingers over the bark, just feel the places where it is rough and smooth, and listen to the scratching noises as your fingers rub on the bark, or your clothing brushes up against it as you look so keenly at the tree."

Representational Systems Exercise
This exercise can be done in dyads or triads. If done in dyads, the *A* person engages the *B* person in conversation, perhaps in the form of an initial interview, and elicits information. In the course of this conversation, *A* attempts to discover *B*'s preferred representational system. Once you think that you know what

that system is, then you *match* the system and observe *B*'s responses. A powerful check on this is to switch to other representational systems and observe *B*'s responses. Does "violating" *B*'s preferred system make *B* appear uncomfortable, pull back, or…? After five minutes, switch roles. When the second person has finished this part of the exercise, then the two people should process what has happened. Ask for each other's experiences during the process. Feedback is important to calibrate what you have done. If you don't know, ask. *A* might say "When I said this, you responded that way. What was going on then?"

When the exercise is done in triads, person *C* has two roles. The first is that of observer of both *A* and *B*. The second is that of adviser to *A*. *C* can whisper comments to *A* or pass notes to *A* about things to try or do or observe. *C* can also take notes. When all three participants in the exercise have had an opportunity to try the three different roles, then they can process what has occurred together.

Identifying representational systems can be difficult and, as in any new learning, requires practice. You can train yourself to be sensitive to representational systems by *listening* to the radio, television, movies, conversations in cafeterias and other public places, and within your family. Once you are aware that people can have a preferred representational system, you will find this phenomenon everywhere. This is also prevalent in books and other writings since authors also have preferred systems. If you look and listen for them, you will find them.

As another exercise, you can practice overlapping in dyads once you know each other's representational systems. Overlapping not only helps enlarge your clients' experience of the world, but in the process of doing this for your clients, *your* world experience will also be enriched. A "blind" walk, a "deaf" walk or a touching with hand-in-glove experience will really emphasize the power of representational systems.

6.5 Pacing and Leading
A good place to observe natural pacing behaviors is in a shopping mall. All you have to do is observe the way people interact with each other. For example, two people walking along together

generally walk with the same stride and rhythm. Two people standing and conversing will generally stand in mirror images of each other. If one of the pair is leaning against a wall, then the other will too. If one has his head slightly cocked to the right, then the other will have her head slightly cocked to the left. If one speaks loudly, softly, rapidly or in a special cadence, then the other is likely to speak in the same pattern. It is a general observation that couples who have been married for a long time (to each other!) tend to "look" alike. What we are perceiving here is that they tend to stand, walk, sit, posture, and use the same, if not similar, facial expressions. We take these similarities to mean that they "look" alike when we are experiencing the way that they fit into the world as a totality of their postures, movements, and expressions. Adopted children grow to "look" like their "parents." These children certainly "sound" like their parents! Since each person fits uniquely and unconsciously into the world in terms of their postures, movements, expressions, and speech, one way of establishing a subtle rapport with them is for you to also fit into the world in the "same way" to communicate this sense of oneness to them. First, we will discuss verbal pacing, then physical pacing, and finally the use of pacing in leading. This will be followed with some exercises.

Some of the characteristics or variations in speech include: tempo, loudness, speed, rhythm or cadence, accenting, regional or cultural accents, and breathiness. It is common knowledge that people from the same culture, subculture, and even mini-subculture, have identical speech patterns. *Verbal pacing* means to match your client's speech patterns in some way so that they feel more comfortable in your presence. Generally, *you need to match in only* **one** *characteristic* such as volume or rhythm for this ease to become apparent. It is important not to mimic or match too exactly since this will be detectable by the client and taken as a manipulation or an insult. *Pacing must be subtle.* Pacing should be done in such a way that it is perceived outside of conscious awareness and not directly in consciousness by the client. If a client speaks rather loudly, you do not have to shout with him, but just *increase* the *normal* volume of your voice. Some people speak exceedingly fast or slow. This may be difficult for you to duplicate directly, but you can duplicate this by *cross-over pacing* by using finger or toe movements or slow head nods to match the rate of speech. These other movements in a different system will be perceived outside of awareness. With verbal pacing, you literally want to "speak" your client's language in some way so that you both fit into the world similarly.

Physical and postural pacing has to do with matching your client's movements or postures in some way. Again, you do not have to match *all* movements and postures. It is only necessary to match the general way the other person is sitting in a chair, or to tilt your head to the right just a bit if they are a head tilter, or to nod your head a bit if they are a nodder, or move one of your feet if they are a foot tapper or wiggler. Exact mirroring can be detected and will be taken as an intrusion or mocking. Physical pacing should be subtle, not exaggerated.

Pacing a client's breathing pattern is perhaps the most effective, and yet the most subtle way of fitting into their world. Breathing is such a basic pattern of existence that matching it is a profound experience. Babies do this automatically when placed on their mother's bosom. *In doing guided imagery work it is important to pace your speech to the breathing patterns of your client.* This is a fundamental axiom for this kind of communication. In some cases it may be necessary to match breathing patterns in a cross-over form. Of course, you should not stare at the bosom of your female client to pick up her breathing pattern, particularly if you are a male therapist. Breathing patterns can be picked up via peripheral vision, or by observing the small movements in clothing, in the shoulders, or in the abdomen. Subtle observation and matching are always better.

Being aware of body language is an important part of the science of being an effective healer since it is not possible to do verbal and physical pacing without reading body language. Knowledge of body language is not only useful to pacing, it is also important in terms of being aware of your client's emotional state and changes in that state. Since the meaning of any communication is the response it gets, be aware of what *you* might be reading into your client's body language. Check out any meaning or interpretation before jumping to conclusions. A smile may not mean happiness. A grimace may not mean pain. A "blank" face may not mean being somewhere else. Gestalt Therapy teaches you to look for incongruities between verbal and body communications. For example, the client may be verbally stating that they are "open" to new ideas while their arms and legs are crossed. Some of these incongruities may be usable in certain contexts or they may be ignored; however, there is no substitute for paying exquisite attention to your client.

One of the major uses of pacing is to then be able to *lead* your client into other states, feelings, or postures once you have paced them. When you have matched the walking pattern of a companion, you can then get them to increase or decrease their stride or pace by simply varying yours. When you have matched the breathing rate of your client, you can get them to breathe faster or slower by modifying your own breathing rate. This, of course, has obvious uses. You can literally lead someone out of a depression by first pacing, and then changing your bodily and verbal patterns.

Pacing and Leading Exercises
This verbal pacing exercise can be done in dyads or triads. Person A and person B stand or sit back-to-back so that they are making contact with their backs, and can sense each other's breathing as well as feel the vibrations generated in speaking. If C is available, then C will observe and provide feedback on the accuracy of the pacing. A says something—one short sentence works well here. It might be something like "My name is Harry and I am feeling a bit uncomfortable about doing this exercise." It is B's task to repeat A's statement to A's satisfaction that B has their speech patterns accurately paced. Alternate several times doing this before moving on to practicing with someone else. Both A and C can coach B in how to do better. Being back-to-back rules out visual cues and forces you to concentrate on your hearing. B can also practice matching A's breathing patterns while doing this exercise. You can also practice verbal pacing in the privacy of your home while listening to the radio or the television. Another good place to practice is in your car while listening to the radio or tapes. Once you are aware of individual speech patterns you can even mentally rehearse matching people during ordinary conversations since this mental rehearsal actually activates your vocal cords and other relevant speech structures within your body. In practice you will be pacing representation systems, as well as speech patterns at the same time!

A second verbal pacing exercise is also done in dyads or triads. *A* is the client, *B* is the therapist, and *C* is the observer. In the framework of carrying out an initial interview with a client, find out what happens when you pace their speech patterns *and* when you deliberately "violate" their speech patterns. If pacing will lead your client to be more comfortable in your presence, then deliberately not pacing will "drive" them away. *A* and *B* switch roles (or *C*, too) and repeat the exercise. After everyone has had a chance to practice all parts, then process what went on. It is important to find out how the client reacted to the things you did. Now that you have had some success at pacing, do the exercise again, but this time consciously *lead* the client by changing one aspect of their speech patterns. Observe carefully what occurs so you can do this better and better. The body posture exercise is done in a similar fashion with dyads or triads. It is the therapist's task to mirror in a subtle way some aspect of the client's body posture, to "violate" that mirroring, and to observe what happens. Once you have successfully learned to mirror body postures (and you need to do only *one* at a time), then use this postural pacing to *lead*. Get the client to shift positions or change movements. You can sometimes subtly lead a client out of an emotional state by just shifting your body posture. Try it.

As a final exercise, put the pacing of representational systems, speech patterns, and body postures together so that you actually remember and try to match in *all* channels of communication. This exercise can be done in dyads or triads. Remember to process the exercise afterwards and to ask your "client" about internal states they experienced during the exercise. People daily demonstrate pacing and leading—all you have to do is be aware.

6.6. Eye Accessing Cues

The observation of eye movements when you are working with someone can be of use. There is much controversy in the literature about the validity of eye accessing cues. My own approach is that if you are aware of a consistent pattern of eye movements in your client, and that the pattern matches the NLP assertions about this phenomenon, then you would be foolish not to use them. One assertion is that people tend to have a consistent association of an eye movement down and to their own right when accessing kinesthetic states internally. The pattern for most right-hand/left-brain individuals is shown in Figure 6.2. You are *looking at* this person. When a person looks up and to the left they are accessing stored mental images or pictures. When they look up and to the right they are constructing a mental image or picture. Looking straight left is accessing remembered auditory sounds. Looking straight right is constructing sounds. Down right is for kinesthetic states—from memory or current; and down left is for talking to yourself. Down left is internal auditory dialogue on messages. Check these out for yourself to convince yourself of their validity. Some people demonstrate a mirror image of the patterns shown in the figure. It is sometimes difficult to ascertain an individual's eye accessing patterns.

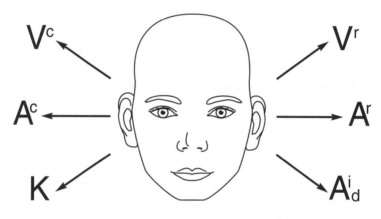

Figure 6.2
Eye Accessing Cues. Looking at the person

There is a practical aspect to knowledge of eye accessing cues: it is useful to know what your client's internal states are and what they are feeling or doing mentally while they are talking to you. Are they looking at old pictures in their heads, talking to themselves, listening to someone talking to them in the past, or accessing (kinesthetic) feelings? You can seem like a mind-reader when you ask "What are you seeing now?" You can practice eye accessing cues by observing your clients' responses, by observing performers in the movies and on television, and by observing people in casual conversations. If it makes sense to use eye accessing cues, then use them.

6.7 Anchoring

Anchoring is a word used in NLP and other disciplines to mean the *obtaining of a conditioned response by an associated stimulus. Anchoring* is any stimulus that elicits a consistent response. In one sense, you cannot *not* anchor in any interaction with another person. A typical culturally installed anchor is the hand-shaking response. Someone raises their right hand towards you and you automatically start raising your own hand.

Anchors may be set by touch, sound of voice, cue words, hand movements, odors, tastes, body postures, voice location, physical surroundings, or other stimuli. It is well known, for example, that students do better on exams given in the same lecture hall in which they received instruction. Just being in the same room aids in the recall of the lecturer's words or writings and other associated material.

In working with a client, the easiest stimulus to use is that of touch. Touch has an additional advantage in that there is a *kinesthetic over-ride* which appears to operate in that touch is more powerful for most people than other stimuli. The sense of smell is perhaps the most powerful stimulus to memory since it bypasses consciousness, but it doesn't lend itself to convenient use in a therapeutic situation! (Aromatherapists may have found a way to use the sense of smell therapeutically.) Since the physical arrangement of your office is under your control, use this to position yourself and your client in such a way that it is both convenient and natural to be able to casually reach over and touch a shoulder or a knee or an arm or a hand. However, *permission* should be obtained before touching a client. Since it is important to be able to reproduce a kinesthetic anchor *exactly*, you should pick a location that is easy to reach and easy to touch in exactly the first way you touched it. Knuckles are useful here. It is also important to reproduce exactly the amount of pressure used. Remember that the sense of touch varies in sensitivity depending on the part of the body touched. Fingertips and hands are much more sensitive than the middle of the back or the thigh. So, you would need more precision to reproduce a kinesthetic anchor on the hand than on the shoulder. Generally use a hand or an arm or a shoulder for anchors.

There are several rules for effective anchoring. They are: (1) Have your client access the desired experience which you wish to anchor as powerfully and as fully as possible. They will probably need to be verbally guided to do this. (2) "Insert" your stimulus at the moment of fullest expression or the most intense response. Timing is crucial here. Use your senses to detect the peak experience by paying attention to breathing, facial color and tone, pulses, etc. Behave congruently with the type of response you are seeking. It is usually convenient to place the anchor lightly as the client starts to access the desired state, and then to slowly increase the pressure of the anchor as the client gets deeper into the desired state. Remember that these are *gentle* pressures, and that small subtle changes are readily detected. (3) Be sure that the stimulus can be repeated *exactly*. (4) Always *test* to be sure that your anchor works. "Triggering," that is, touching the anchor, should get the response that you originally anchored. Observe!

One of the simplest use of anchors in your office is to have a "guided imagery" chair, i.e., one chair that you use for this purpose only. They will automatically know when they sit in that chair that it is time to relax. Some therapists use a particular voice tone or delivery style that transmits the same information. It could also be the way that you sit or hold your head.

The most important thing about the concept of anchoring is that it does exist and that people are capable of one-trial learning. Once you are aware of this, then you can use it in appropriate contexts.

Anchoring Exercises
Practice with anchoring is best done in dyads. One person is the operator and the other is the person having the anchor installed. As the operator, be sure to control your physical space arrangements with your client. (You don't want to stretch awkwardly to place an anchor.) For the first exercise, have your client access a pleasant or happy experience and then anchor it. Test by triggering the anchor outside of the client's awareness by first engaging them in casual conversation. As a second exercise, you will be anchoring two experiences, one of which is the opposite of the other. These could be pleasant and unpleasant, happy and sad, a good meal and a bad one, etc. The two anchors could also be used for an undesired behavior, and a desired one, or a present state

and a desired state. Once the two anchors have been installed, then trigger both at the same time and observe what happens. You can influence the outcome by using slightly more pressure on the desired/positive state than the other one.

6.8 The Utilization Approach

In many ways the *utilization approach* (Zeig, 1999) is the heart of the famous psychiatrist and hypnotherapist Milton H. Erickson's approach in working with clients. He accepted clients as they were and then moved on from there. It was said of Erickson that a client never knew what Erickson would do when the client entered Erickson's office. Erickson felt that every client is unique and deserves to be treated in an unique way. For example, if a client is a devout Catholic and you are an atheist, you can still help the client by working within their belief system since *yours is not germane*. (Remember, if *your* belief system gets in the way, then you *must* refer the client.) If you are a Republican and your client is a dyed-in-the-wool Democrat, then *use* that information. If your client believes in past lives and you don't, or vice versa, then use that information and belief system to help the client. Of course, being aware of belief systems is extremely important in doing cross-cultural work.

One of Erickson's most quoted observations involves the Greek thief Procrustes who was in the habit of kidnapping people. He kept them in an iron bed. If they were too short for the bed, he stretched them to fit the bed. If they were too tall for the bed, he cut them down to size! By too rigorously applying any given approach, you are in danger of becoming a Procrustes.

In the utilization approach, you simply accept and utilize the client's observable and non-observable behaviors and beliefs. By non-observable we mean paying attention to what the client says about themselves. Pacing these behaviors establishes rapport and leading them moves the client along. Everyone is unique.

Utilization Exercise

This can be done in dyads or triads. In a triad the third person is an observer and commentator and assistant to the operator. The framework for this exercise is to hold an intake interview with the client, paying attention to their uniqueness. Then, using that uniqueness, devise and carry through a relaxation, or a guided imagery session.

Chapter 7

Language for Guided Imagery

7.1 Introduction

Perhaps the most useful exercise my students perform in learning how to construct guided imagery sessions is the micro-analysis of the language used in published imagery scripts and audio tapes. Following the preparation in the previous chapters and the material in this one, they become quite sensitive to both the language and the method of delivery. The next chapter is devoted to analyses of published scripts. This chapter is devoted to a study of language for guided imagery and is an abbreviated version of Chapter 5, "Language Forms," in Battino and South (1999). Since there is so much in common between hypnotherapy and guided imagery, it behooves the serious student of this work to get training in hypnosis. Within the United States the three most reputable sources of training in hypnosis (in the author's judgment) are: (1) The Milton H. Erickson Foundation, Inc. (3606 North 24th Street, Phoenix, AZ 85016-6500; (602) 956-6196); (2) institutes affiliated with the Milton H. Erickson Foundation—write or phone them for a list; and (3) The American Society of Clinical Hypnosis (2200 East Devon Avenue, Suite 291, Des Plaines, IL 60018-4534; (312) 645-9810).

The most common mistake found in scripts and audiotapes for the general public is that they are *too* specific in their imagery. Going to the beach and listening to the mesmeric pounding of the waves may be *your* special place for relaxing, but it will be frightening to someone who nearly drowned or who lost a loved one to drowning or who got a very bad sunburn on their last outing or…. Being in the woods can be relaxing; or scary if you got lost in the woods as a child, are afraid of the outdoors, are allergic to bee stings, etc. Language for guided imagery tapes for a general audience needs to be open, vague and permissive. This chapter will explore systematically the structure of such language. In large part this style of language usage was popularized by Milton H. Erickson, M.D. through his use of *indirect* language for hypnosis. It has been said that Erickson was a master of the **precise** *use* *of* **vague** *language*. We especially emphasize both the word "precise" and the word "vague" in this description. By *precise* we mean conscious choice of the exact word(s) for a particular purpose. But, the words are *vague* in the sense of comparing "going to the beach" to "going *somewhere* that is *safe* for you." The word "somewhere" is open and vague and the listener creates or finds that place. I have a sense of what "safe" means to me, but *your* idea of safety is unique to you and your experience.

Another way to examine these ideas is to use the transformational grammar concepts of surface and deep structures. As a class exercise we state, "Jo(e) hurt me," and after the students have considered their reaction to this sentence for one minute, we ask them: (1) Is Jo(e) male or female? (2) Is the "hurt" physical or mental? (3) What is the relationship (husband, wife, significant other, relative) between Jo(e) and "me"? (4) Who is "me"? The sentence, "Jo(e) hurt me," is an example of a *surface structure* which contains only the *partial* meaning of the communication. The full linguistic meaning is in the *deep structure* and may be a sentence like, "My husband Joe hurt me by holding onto my left arm very tightly." This sentence is more specific and detailed and could probably be made even more complete. Yet, the *real* meaning (internal reality) for this woman is well beyond the deep structure sentence since it incorporated her: (a) physical sensations; (b) her memories of other similar incidents of hard connection; (c) her memories of related incidents; (d) the words that she uses to describe the experience to herself; and (e) her entire life's experiences and memories to that point in time.

When we attempt accurate communication using language, we can at best use deep structures. The implied "but" here is that even deep structures are only an approximation of the *real* meaning to the listener. In fact, *the meaning of any communication is the **response** that you get.* It is the nature of language that you can only hope that the response is connected to your intention in the communication. How many times have you been misunderstood or had to repeat yourself, particularly when you thought you were being very clear?

Fortunately, good guided imagery language is more often surface structure rather than deep structure. When you are designing a guided imagery for a particular person, you specifically incorporate *their* words and phrases and images into your delivery. If known, you also use words that are part of their representational system.

Another way of emphasizing the importance of vague language is to consider the differences in your experiences of *reading* a novel, *listening* to it on audiotape, or *seeing/hearing* it as a movie. How many times has a movie made from a favorite book disappointed you because they didn't get the characters or the scenes just "right," i.e., the way that *you* pictured the scene in your mind, and heard the dialogue in your mind? Good novels and short stories are successful because they provide only sufficient information for you to fill in the details.

There are three more common mistakes in general audience guided imagery audiotapes. A good tape is usually built around just one image. Poor tapes use too many ideas and images. After all, if fifteen minutes is a good length for a session, there just is not sufficient time to develop more than one image. A related idea is that most deliverers of guided imagery talk too much and too continuously. (This is also a common problem with neophyte hypnotherapists.) The listener needs time to develop his/her image and a response. In Transformational Grammar the search for response and meaning is called a *transderivational search*. Effective tapes and deliveries incorporate both short and long pauses. The last common mistake is to incorporate music into the tape—the music may be too loud and intrusive, and it may be of a style and from a period that is foreign to the client. Tastes in music differ so much that it is best to leave the music out. If music is important for your client, then they can play their own special music in the background using separate equipment. It is my practice to *not* use music.

Practitioners of neuro-linguistic programming (NLP) have contributed much to the systematic study of language. Some accessible NLP sources are Lewis and Pucelik (1982) and McLauchlin (1992). For a more linguistically oriented approach read Bandler and Grinder (1975) and Grinder and Bandler (1976).

7.2 Delivery

The effective delivery of guided imagery goes beyond the rapport building skills discussed in the last chapter, but necessarily builds on those skills. For effective communication, insofar as possible, you still need to speak your client's language the way that they do—this is pacing. It always helps to incorporate particular words or phrases that they use (but beware of exact mimicry). Your interview session notes should record idiosyncratic language usage for future utilization. When you are starting out in this field, it really helps to listen to many different people to develop a sense of *how* they deliver their material. In fact, in the initial stages you may wish to copy the delivery style of someone you particularly like. When I was learning how to do hypnosis in the Milton Erickson style, I consciously copied many of his mannerisms to later adapt them to my own style. It is also the case that students in my workshops tend to mimic my style initially—there is nothing wrong with learning in this way. (This is only a problem if you stay stuck in someone else's style.)

It certainly helps to have experience on the stage or in front of students to sharpen your speaking/acting skills—I have been fortunate to have a background as a professor of chemistry and many years in community theater. For example, actors and actresses have long known the value of the *dramatic* pause. *Timing* is central to all comedic routines: just think of the way that Cary Grant used pauses and double-takes in *Arsenic and Old Lace*. *Pauses* are a way of ... adding ... emphasis ... to words ... and phrases. Read the previous sentence aloud with and without the pauses indicated by the ellipses, and play with varying the length of each pause. We earlier mentioned the concept of a *transderivational search* wherein you search internally to find the deep structure for your own meaning or interpretation of a particular word or phrase. *Pauses allow the client time to carry out such transderivational searches.* The most common problem in delivery with neophytes in guided imagery and hypnosis is that they talk nonstop. It's almost as if they are afraid to give up control or direction or lose their train of thought. If you err at all, then do it on the side of more and longer pauses. Again, the *client's internal* work is what is important in a guided imagery—give them the time to develop their own responses.

When you develop a guided imagery script, it is important to mark by underscoring or capitalization or boldface the words and phrases you wish to emphasize in your delivery. In fact, it would be useful to have two or three levels of emphasis. In the delivery itself, particular words or phrases are *marked* by: loudness *or* softness of delivery; speed of speaking; adding a musical quality; pauses; and by intonation. How many interpretations can a good actor give to Hamlet's "To be or not to be"? This is the *art* of delivery. If your client's eyes are open and they are looking at you, then body language can be used for marking. Dragging out a word can mark it: *yessss* … The human ear is sensitive to the source of a sound, so you can use voice locus for marking. With practice, you can even "pitch" or "throw" your voice in a particular direction. Certainly, you could also shift your head position. Within limits, using slang, an accent, and ungrammatical usage can also mark words and phrases. Puns and rhymes and homonyms and well-known quotes and confusion can all be used for marking.

In the *interspersal* technique you weave especially significant words and phrases into your conversational flow as a way of marking them. In some way, these interspersed words and phrases seem to slide right by the conscious mind, but are heard by the unconscious or inner mind since they are different, out of context, or out of the ordinary. And, how *surprised* will you be, about the changes that *have already occurred?*

Analogical marking uses non-verbals to mark out particular words and phrases as separate messages. If your client has their eyes open, you can use natural movements, such as head nods or tilts or other body movements to mark. A movement like a head nod can be associated with a word like "comfort" to anchor it. If eyes are closed, then this is done using voice dynamics.

Quotes are a useful way to add emphasis as in, "My minister once said, 'God is always with you'." I particularly like to quote Jean Valjean in the musical *Les Miserables* as saying, "To love another person is to see the face of God." People tend to listen more acutely to statements in quotes.

Suggestions and *presuppositions* can be embedded within questions. (More will be written later in this chapter about the importance of presuppositions, which imply the existence of some state or feeling.) Some examples are:

> "Just how comfortable are you, now?"
> "And this, too, will pass, will it not?"
> "Are you enjoying your quiet time?"
> "What haven't you done yet that you can do?"
> "And, just being relaxed.... "

It is, or course, important to be *congruent* in your delivery. The word "fast" is spoken quickly, the word "soft" softly, the phrase "... and you can sense that ..." with conviction, and "I believe in miracles" in a way that conveys your deep inner commitment. If you do not believe what you say, will your client believe or be helped? (As a point of irreverence here, I quote Flanders and Swann from their song "The Reluctant Cannibal" who said: "Always be sincere—whether you mean it or not!" As another aside, the interesting thing about flattery is that it appears to make people feel good even when they are doubting the speaker!.... The readers of this book are a select and wonderful group....)

7.3 Words

In terms of impact some words are "more equal" than others. This section presents classes of such words. (Again, much is owed to NLP for this organization.)

a. *Nominalization*—When a verb or "action" word is converted into a noun or "static" word, this is a nominalization. Consider the difference between "I am a cancer victim," and "Cancer is victimizing me." Also, "I am depressed," or "I am in depression," versus "I wonder what is depressing me." Nominalizations seem to be cast in concrete, and when you think of yourself in nominalizations the situation appears hopeless. Bernie Siegel's statement, "Cancer is not a sentence, it is just a word," de-nominalizes "cancer" within the context of word play. Since depression is a common concomitant of life-challenging diseases, it is important to denomalize this state by saying "I wonder how you are (have been) depressing yourself." The denominalization opens the possibility of change. *Denominalization* involves converting a noun into a verb.

b. *Unspecified Verbs*—In a sense, no verb is completely specified in terms of an action. There are particular verbs that are sufficiently vague to be useful. Some of these are: know, learn, understand, feel, change, wonder, do, think, and fix. The listener fills in the specifics; some examples are:

> "And you may wonder just how much you can learn."
> "Change is easier to do than you think."
> "Just in what specific ways will that be fixed?"
> "And you can feel the change starting."
> "The body knows just how to do that."

Some of these sentences use an *unspecified referential index* in words like: that, how, learn, know, body, etc. That is, these words do not have a specific reference. A good example is the word "it" as in, "It really will help."

c. *Causal Connections*—These constructions exist in compound sentences where a connection is implied or stated between one thing and another. There are three levels of connection. The weakest is using the word "and" as in:

> "You are paying attention to your breathing, *and* becoming even more comfortable."

The next strongest linkage uses words related to time such as: while, during, as, when, and soon:

> "*As* you pay attention to your breathing, you become more comfortable."
> "*Soon* your breathing will slow down, *while* you relax even more."

The strongest level of causal connection uses real causal words: makes, causes, forces, and requires.

> "*As* your breathing slows, it *makes* you calmer."
> "*While* you pay attention to that spot on the wall, it *makes* your eyes blink more."

Start these causal connections with something that is already going on like sitting, blinking, or breathing, *and* then connect that to another condition. (This is an example of *pacing and leading*.)

d. *Mind-Reading*—This is a form of pacing and leading that involves some guesswork based on reading body language plus intent listening.

> "I wonder what you are hearing/feeling/saying to yourself now."
> "You are probably feeling a little nervous/scared/anxious/ tense right now."

e. *Lost Performative*—Evaluative statements are made in this speech pattern, but it is not known who makes the statement. The favorite generalization is "it."

> "It's not important just how fast you relax."
> "It is good to be at peace with yourself."

f. *Modal Operators of Necessity*—These words *imply* particular actions and lack of choice. Here are some of them: will/won't, can/can't, should, have to, must, no one, and necessary. One of Loretta LaRoche's favorite admonitions is, "Don't *should* on yourself!" She also refers to people who are "*must-erbators*."

> "And, you *should* do that, shouldn't you?"
> "You *must* never give in/give up hope/cry/be weak/trust people...."

These words tend to be an inheritance from our upbringing, can be part of the unfinished business or "garbage" in our lives, and can be successfully challenged—many people are just not aware of how much control the "shoulds" have over their lives.

g. *Transitional Words*—These are words that connect or link: *and, as, while*, because, become, could, but, might, makes, may, causes, wonder, if, then, what, how, beginning, will, allow, and when. The first three are italicized since they are the ones you will use most frequently. You generally start with a truism—something the person can't deny—and then bridge to an action or thought you wish to occur.

Examples are:

> "*And,* as you pay attention to your breathing, your eyes can softly close/you become more relaxed/you become calmer/ your breathing softens."
> "*As* you sense the way that your chair supports you, *and as* you are aware how your feet touch the floor, you relax even more."
> "*While* you pay attention to the sounds of the air conditioning, your breathing becomes deeper and more regular."
> "*While* one part of your mind is busy analyzing this, the other inner part of your mind is peaceful and calm."

h. *Meaningful Words*—These words mean nothing in themselves, but are powerfully *vague* in leading people into doing inner searches. Here are some meaningful words: hopes, dreams, talents, resources, sensations, memories, thoughts, beliefs, unconscious, inner mind, love, learning, loving, genuine, really, try, and yet. These wonderfully vague words can be deliberately inserted into your imagery since they allow your listeners to fill in their "real" meaning to themselves. The word "try" is a special case since it implies *not* succeeding.

> "Just *try* harder, won't you?"
> "Please *try* to be calmer."

Use "try" consciously. Some examples of using meaningful words are:

> "Try doing that, now, but don't change yet."
> "Dreams can be so helpful."
> "Your unconscious mind really knows how much you are learning."
> "Pleasant memories are a wonderful resource."
> "And how much have you learned from your hopes and dreams?"
> "Deep beliefs are so sustaining."

i. *Or and The Illusion of Choice*—The word "or" presupposes the occurrence of one or more events.

> "You can close your eyes now *or* in a few moments."
> "I don't know whether you will be more relaxed now *or* in a minute or two, as you continue to breathe calmly."
> "Your head can stay still *or* move to either side *or* back and forth."

There *appears* to be a choice, but *some action* is presupposed.

j. *Awareness Predicates*—Words like know, realize, notice, aware, find, and understand presuppose the rest of the sentence. Their use reduces to *whether* the listener is *aware* of the point you are now making. Examples:

> "And, you are *aware* now of *noticing* those changes."
> "You really *know*, you *realize*, just how relaxed you are, now."
> "Did you *understand* all of what has already happened for you?"

These awareness predicates bring the communication to the point of *whether* your client is *aware* of the message(s) in the sentence.

k. *Adverbs and Adjectives*—These can be used to presuppose a major clause within a sentence. Some choices are: deeply, readily, easily, curious, happily, and simply.

> "Have you wondered how *easily* this happened?"
> "Just *simply, easily, deeply,* relaxing …"
> "How *curious* are you about the changes that are happening so *easily*?"

l. *Commentary Adverbs and Adjectives*—These are related to (k), but presuppose everything after the first word. Some good ones are: innocently, happily, luckily, necessarily, usefully, fortunately, and curiously.

> "*Happily*, relaxing is easy."
> "*Fortunately*, your innermost thoughts are yours alone."
> "*Necessarily*, people do change and change is the order of life."
> "*Usefully*, you've already learned how to relax deeply."

m. *Now*—Although this word can be over-used, the *immediacy* of its meaning makes it very potent. You may have already noticed how frequently "now" has been used in examples. Generally, its use is more effective following or preceding a pause. "And, ... now ... just relaxing even more." A more complete example to make this point, now, is: "And, you can know *now*, how to use this word, *now*, in the middle of a sentence for emphasis, or at the end for definitive action, *now*." To paraphrase Alexander Lowen, "To know your mind, you need to mind your no,... now."

n. *That's Right*—This was a favorite phrase of Milton Erickson's and it peppered much of his trance work—that's right, isn't it? "That" is an ambiguous word with many possible referents in a given sentence—it can mean almost anything. That's right, yes it is. Be cautious in its use, yet you'll find yourself frequently using it....

7.4 Suggestions, Implications and Presuppositions
The relaxed state, like the hypnotic trance, is a highly *suggestible* state, and clients are more open to suggestions at that time. It is even presumed by some that communications to a relaxed person bypass the conscious mind and are "heard" by the inner or unconscious mind. This means that your words take on extra meaning, must be chosen carefully, and with conscious intent. Also, the unconscious mind tends to interpret words *literally* as in thinking of a "rest room" as a place to *rest*.

a. *Suggestions*—Suggestions may be delivered to a relaxed person directly or indirectly. Contrast the following two sentences:

> "Close your eyes and relax"
> "And, breathing softly and easily, calmly, becoming even more comfortable."

Ericksonian hypnotherapists tend to use indirection more than direction, finding it effective and gentle and respectful. Yet, you always need to know your client and adapt your language appropriately.

Contingent suggestions imply a causal connection. "The more you pay attention to your breathing, the more relaxed you will become." At some point the listener makes the connection between the two ideas, and then acts *as if* the second statement were true. This has the form of "when this ... then that."

Open-ended suggestions are those which emphasize choice and are deliberately vague. (Recall that a major difficulty with many guided images is that they are too specific.) Open-ended suggestions are like master keys that can open many doors.

> "And, I don't know just when or whether your eyes will comfortably close, and you'll ...
> "Within your mind, now, you can safely drift off to your special place."
> "And, you don't need to know how those cancer cells are being eliminated, just sense their departure."
> "Your immune system will pick just the best and most efficient way to destroy those weak and aberrant cells."

With respect to indirect suggestions we can quote Erickson, Rossi and Rossi (1976, p. 269):

> With indirect suggestions, however, subjects usually do not recognize the relation between the suggestion and their own response. There thus can be no questions of voluntary compliance with the therapist's suggestion. If a response does take place, then it has been mediated by involuntary processes outside of a subject's immediate range of awareness. This involuntary mediation of responses is what we use to define the genuineness of trance behavior.

b. *Implications*—Again, let us quote from Erickson, Rossi, and Rossi (1976, p. 59) before giving some examples:

> For Erickson, psychological implication is a key that automatically turns the tumblers of a patient's associative processes into predictable patterns without awareness of how it happened. The implied thought or response seems to come up automatically within patients, as if it were their own inner response rather than a suggestion initiated by the therapist. Psychological implication is thus a way of structuring and directing patients' associative processes when they cannot do it for themselves.

"If you sit down, then you can relax."

"When you take few deep breaths and let your eyes defocus, you will be even calmer."

"Before you start relaxing, you ought to be comfortable."

"I don't know just how, or how fast, your healing will occur."

The implication is generally made up of three parts: (1) a time-binding introduction of some kind; (2) the implied/assumed/intimated/hinted suggestion; and (3) some sort of *behavioral* response to signal when the implication has been accomplished.

c. *Presuppositions*—O'Hanlon (1987) has defined a presupposition as "… the use of language, actions, and situations that *necessarily* involve certain antecedents *or* consequences." O'Hanlon (1987) also states, "Presupposition is a form of language in which certain ideas or experiences are presumed without ever being directly stated." The power of presuppositions is that they cannot be ignored and—if used correctly—create expectations for change that are outside or beyond the conscious mind. (See Battino and South (1999) for an extended treatment on the use of presuppositions.) Study the following examples for what is presupposed.

"Gloria had a good day."

"I liked the way you did that."

"Doctors can be very helpful."

"If you meditate every day, you will be helped."

"When she takes a nap in the afternoon, she feels better."

"When you eat properly, too, you are more comfortable."

"Fortunately, you have a good medical team/family support/group of friends."

"Where is the heating pad?"

"That wasn't the last bottle of pills, was it?"

"Just how much change/healing/comfort/learning is possible?"

d. *Overloading*—A speech pattern using lots of "ands" linking together many items has as its goal the *overloading* of the conscious and/or unconscious mind to ease into another state.

"As you sit there *and* pay attention to your breathing *and* listen to the clock *and* feel the support of your chair *and* move a little when your need to *and* let your eyes defocus *and* observe passing thoughts, how soon will you be deeply deeply relaxed?"You just *stack* one set of realities/truisms on another until the mind just gives up and heeds the last suggestion.

e. *Nongrammatical Language*—Since the human mind automatically fills in missing elements or gaps in speech and visual images, you can use this idea to confuse, dis-orient, embed messages, etc. This work must be subtly done. Examples follow:

"Being is or was, soon, and now … change."

"Before you relax even more … during … while these thoughts … helpful … friendly … aren't they not now … but then … for you…."

"Ain't just ain't the way to get now what you want for your-self … it ain't … is."

"And, you do not know, no you do not, exact how to change/ heal/learn/get what you want, but,… when but?"

"The moving finger is right as it writes in your rite, right? as you changed/found/got/discovered, and that is no right, or it is, yes?"

"By the dawn's beginning to sense those changes have changed what is to what was, but when and how soon is the past with all of this deep as a well behind you?"

You can certainly have fun with these nongrammatical change statements. They are effective as Gilligan (1987, p. 244) states, "… non sequiturs will have maximum hypnotic effect [read: guided imagery effect] when (1) they are delivered meaningfully (2) by a speaker assumed and expected to speak rationally and relevantly (3) in a context where the listener trusts the integrity of the speaker." The "shock" value of these statements means that they have to be used sparingly.

f. *Language Involving Time*—Consider the following sentence:

"As you change, now, thinking about all of the new things you've already learned about yourself, then, and how, will you have already begun your healing process, even while you continue to progress even more, now?"

Using time-related words and grammatical tense to confuse and presuppose that what you want *has already occurred* and all you need to do is discover and ratify it, *or* continue the already ongoing processes, is the power of this style. The use of time-related language takes practice.

7.5 Negation

As you read this, close your eyes if you will, and do *not* think about a pink polka-dotted zebra.... Human brains are wired such that you *first* have to create an image of the pink polka-dotted zebra *before* you can blank out that picture and, even then, the blanking out may not be perfect. Grinder and Bandler (1981, p. 67) state, *"No single pattern that I know of gets in the way of communication more often than using negation. Negation only exists in language and does not exist in experience."* (Emphasis in original.) And, you will now learn how to use negation, will you not?

a. *Double Negatives and Tag Questions*—Double negatives generally require a pause for processing before it is understood that an affirmative is intended, and there are residuals of one of the negatives as the other is not heard. "Don't stop doing ..." "This is not never going to happen." "When you do not know what you really know, change can happen rapidly." "Do not not be careful in using a 'no' to be a 'not'." This last sentence also plays on confusion generated by the homonyms of no and know, and not and knot.

Tag questions, at the end of a sentence, reinforce what came before, *even if* the tag statement is a negation.

> "And you can, can you not?"
> "And you will, won't you?"
> "You won't do it until your inner self is ready, will you not?"
> "And, you really do not know how fast you will, do you?"
> "You probably cannot get yourself fully comfortable, can you?"
> "It is all right to relax, is it not?"
> "And how has that healing process started already, has it not?"

Practice, practice, practice, will you not?

Milton Erickson liked to establish rapport and minimize resistance in the first session by saying at an appropriate time, "Please be sure to *not* tell me anything that you do not wish to tell me." This is an elegant way to reassure a client, even though the embedded message is, "You can tell me anything—the choice is *yours*."

b. *Apposition of Opposites*—This consists of two opposing concepts or experiences that are juxtaposed within the same sentence or context. This is partly a confusion technique, yet the apposition also reinforces the tag concept or experience. Examine:

> "And you can remember to forget, can you not?"
> "I wonder if you really wish to remember to forget, or forget to remember."
> "As that toe itches a bit more, your comfort will increase."
> "As that slight tingling appears, you know that the healing continues."
> "Learning to unlearn can be very useful."
> "Thinking about that relationship, just how much warmth can you find in coldness."
> "As you sit there, comfortably immobile, your mind can safely wander to a safe haven."

The opposites are in a single phrase in an *oxymoron*.

> "How quickly can you slow down and escalate the decrease of that discomfort."
> "As you blindly look at yourself, what is it you are not seeing?"
> "Sometimes it is quicker to crawl."
> "And just how smooth can your life be on that rocky road?"

c. *Not Knowing and Not Doing*—In this language pattern, the "not" is ignored, resistance is by-passed, and the client acts as if only positive statements were made. Some of Milton Erickson's statements from Erickson, Rossi, and Rossi (1976) with page number in parentheses follow:

> "You don't have to talk or move or make any sort of effort. You don't even have to hold your eyes open." (p. 23)

"You don't have to bother to listen to me because your unconscious can do that and respond all by itself." (p. 24)

"Now the important achievement for you is to realize that everyone does not know his capacities. (Pause) And you have to discover these capacities in whatever slow way you wish." (pp. 36–37)

"You don't know when you're going to change your rate of breathing [or whatever]." (p. 154)

"You don't need to know [whatever] for when the occasion arises, your unconscious will supply that knowledge." (p. 198)

And you don't know, now, how much you have learned already about negation, have you not?

d. *Truisms and the "Yes Set"*—In using the "yes set" you make a series of statements and questions whose obvious answer is "yes," that is, they involve *truisms*. This establishes rapport, for you are affirming what the client already knows or experiences. Then, the client will *continue* in a receptive and affirmative manner to other things that you say. These are statements like, "Today is Tuesday, isn't it?" "And you are sitting on a straight back chair." "Your husband's name is Harry?" "There are a lot of books in this room, aren't there?" "It was raining this morning, wasn't it?" … "And how soon do you think you will be deeply relaxed?" "Your healing sense is strong today." The last two sentences are part of your opening suggestions. It is generally useful to begin a guided imagery session with truisms to connect the person to the present and their environment and their bodily senses.

e. *Ambiguity*—The word "ambiguity" applies to the case where there is more than one deep structure to a surface structure—there is some doubt and uncertainty. Puns may be used for their ambiguity.

Phonological Ambiguity occurs where words have the same sound sequences, but different meanings. These are homonyms like: knows/nos/nose, dear/deer, way/weigh, weight/wait, rein/reign/rain, there/their, bare/bear, road/rode, and to/too/two. The English language has many *individual* words which sound the same and have the same spelling, but have different meanings—it is the context that supplies the meaning. Some examples are: moon, hold, comber, ship, tire, cow, card, bowl, die, train, fast, and founder. Can you hold something *fast* to you while you are moving *fast*? Or, can you *train* a dog on a *train*? A sentence like, "To know how to say no may be the right rite for you when you write bearing baring your deepest thoughts." Use these ideas sparingly and consciously.

. *Syntactic Ambiguity* occurs when the syntactic function of a word cannot be uniquely determined by the listener from the context in which the word is used. Some examples from Bandler and Grinder (1975, p. 233) are:

> "... flying planes can be dangerous."
> "... investigating FBI agents can be dangerous."
> "... they are murdering peasants...."

Another form is the nominalization of a noun:

> "The touching woman...."
> "The running leader...."
> "The feeling of the chair...."

Punctuation ambiguity is a nongrammatical form where two unrelated sentences or ideas are connected by a word that can reasonably fit into both parts.

> "Now you can notice your *hand* me that paper."
> "You can take that *turn* around your life."
> "When you're at the *store* away what you have learned."
> "The clerk gave you the *change* that has already begun."

7.6 Binds
Binds and double binds have been well discussed by Erickson, Rossi, and Rossi (1976, pp. 62–76) and by Erickson and Rossi (1979, pp. 42–49). The former book gives good definitions (pp. 62–64).

A *bind* offers a free choice of two comparable alternatives—that is, whichever choice is made leads behavior in a desired direction. Therapeutic binds are tactful presentations of the possible alternate forms of constructive behavior that are available to the patient in a given situation. The patient is given free, voluntary choice between them; the patient usually feels bound, however to accept one alternative.

Double binds, by contrast, offer possibilities of behavior that are outside the patient's usual range of conscious choice and control.... The double bind arises out of the possibility of communicating on more than one level. We can (1) say something and (2) simultaneously comment on what we are saying.... What is a bind or double bind for one person may not be for another.

Although the idea of binds and double binds may appear to be simple, their construction and delivery is not. Some examples follow:

> "Would you like to deeply relax in this chair or that one?"
> "Would you like to work on your healing imagery now or in a few minutes?"
> "Would you like me to read your bedtime story to you now or after your bath?"
> "When do you think your eyes will get heavier and close?"
> "Just how soon will your special healing light begin its work?"
> "Those old sensations of pain will safely and easily change to a mild tingling in how many minutes?"
> "It doesn't really matter what your conscious mind does, because your inner mind will do just what it needs to in order to achieve that analgesia/anesthesia/relaxation/healing force/body cleansing."

A central characteristic of all binds is an *illusion of choice*. This is fostered frequently by mentioning *all* possible responses: "Your eyes may close now, or they may close in a minute or two, or they may become softly de-focussed." "Change may come about momentarily or in a few minutes, or at 10:16 pm this evening or, even, some time after that." "This discomfort may increase temporarily for a moment, or it may stay the same, or it may have already significantly decreased."

7.7 Summary

This *abbreviated* introduction to language for guided imagery may appear to be overkill, but it is the foundation for this work. This will become abundantly evident in the next chapter where we do a detailed linguistic analysis of some published guided imagery scripts. At this point, you may feel a bit overwhelmed by all of the material—do not despair—just as it took you a while to learn how to swim or ride a bike or drive a car or learn a foreign language, before you know it, you will know without even knowing how you know what you know even if at times you wanted to say "no." Practice, practice, practice! Remember that learning theory states that new knowledge begins with a state of confusion. So, if you feel confused now....

Chapter 8

Analysis of Guided Imagery Scripts

8.1 Introduction

It seems like everyone is preparing guided imagery tapes—not only can you find them in catalogues, but also in chain bookstores. Over the years I've listened to many tapes, including ones that are meant for relaxation and are primarily, if not solely, sounds like ocean waves or especially composed music. How can you evaluate these materials? There has been no *Consumers Report* style study that could provide guidance. Certainly, this is a task well beyond the scope of this book. Since it is my contention that guided imagery tapes need to be designed for each unique listener, this chapter will provide some guidance, via a two-column format, for an in-depth analysis of portions of four published guided imagery scripts. The emphasis on language usage and several generic scripts of my own throughout the book can serve as the basis for the preparation of such general-audience tapes. In fact, the four scripts studied in this chapter are all generic scripts. Again, it is emphasized that you should write out your script, record it, analyze and rewrite based on listening, and then repeat the process until you are satisfied. (I have been preparing tapes long enough so that I generally work from notes of key points, but I still write out scripts for special purposes.)

There is one special videotape for relaxation that I would like to single out. It is by Jon Kabat-Zinn and is entitled "The World of Relaxation" and runs for 57 minutes. It is designed for an in-patient hospital channel video program. The tape features Kabat-Zinn (shows only his upper body or face) talking with background music. The tape is described in chapter 13 of Kabat-Zinn (1990) and is available for purchase.[2]

Out of the myriad of music tapes available, I would like to mention the work of David Ison who has made an intense study of the impact of music on people. He has designed and sells[3] a mat with

---

[2] Stress Reduction Video, University of Massachusetts Medical Center, 55 Lake Avenue, North Worcester, MA 01655.

[3] Thera Sound, Inc., 92 Shadyside Avenue, Concord, MA 01742.

many speakers and especially composed music. He also sells a recliner chair with similar music, but for chemotherapy and dialysis units. Thera Sound Inc. sells a set of music tapes designed for particular personal improvement purposes.

Finally, I need to mention the work of Therese Schroeder-Sheker and her "Chalice of Repose Project." She is a musician who founded a program to ease dying by playing harp and other music to dying patients. Materials about the project, including audio and videotapes are available.[4]

8.2 The Wellness Community Script

The Wellness Community was started by H.H. Benjamin, Ph. D., in 1982. It is a non-profit and non-fee support network for people who have cancer. They have branches in a number of cities, but you may write to the national headquarters[5] for further information. The program is described by Benjamin (1995). Of particular interest is Appendix C (taken from Benjamin, 1995, pp. 210–212) which is a patient/oncologist statement indicating expectations for both patients and physicians to establish a healing relationship.

Appendix 4 of Benjamin's book (1995, pp. 234–240) is a script for directed visualization. I will analyze parts of this script in a two-column format. The first column contains a quote from the script and the second column contains commentary, and suggested alternate wording in *italics*. The purpose of this analysis is to teach the reader about effective language usage for guided imagery work. This particular script has undoubtedly been of help to many people—revision along the indicated ways could make it more effective for more people.

---

[4] Therese Schroeder-Sheker, c/o Sandy LeForye, 2705 Vassar Drive, Boulder, CO 80303. For information about the project contact: The Chalice of Repose Project, 554 West Broadway, Missoula, MT 59802.

[5] The Wellness Community, 2716 Ocean Park Boulevard, Suite 1040, Santa Monica, CA 90405. (310) 314-2555.

Original Script

This is going to be a time of complete relaxation ... a conscious effort to relax as completely as possible.

Get into as comfortable a position as you can, and close your eyes.

For the next couple of minutes, concentrate on just your breathing.

To the best of your ability, see your lungs ...

Commentary

Promising "complete" relaxation is probably an oversell. A "conscious effort," is much like "be spontaneous," and also implies work. "... as possible ... " creates the idea that this may not occur. *This is a time to relax, to be at ease.*

"... as you can ..." creates standards and goals, and permits the possibility that you may not be able to get into a state of maximum comfort. It is not necessary to close your eyes to relax/meditate – in fact, many people strongly resist closing their eyes. *As you adjust your position to become even more comfortable, you may wish to close your eyes now or later, or to just leave them softly unfocused.*

"... next couple of minutes ..." sets a time limit. *And, concentrate on just your breathing, now ...* This is a direct suggestion and can be followed with, *Noticing each breath – just how it feels, and any sounds – continuing to breathe softly and easily.*

Again, this creates a challenge that is not needed. The word "see" is visually oriented—either match the listener's representational system, or consciously do overlapping, or use all three systems, or use

119

generic words. *And, just sense how the air moves into and out of your nose, throat, lungs …*

... see how they feel, consciously see how they feel while they're completely expanded, and see how they feel after you exhale.

How do you "see" a "feeling?" The word "consciously" reminds the listener of volitional activity which is minimized the greater the relaxation. *Sense your breathing … becoming more relaxed with each breath.*

Be aware that there's no right way and no wrong way to do what you're doing now ... that whatever results you get are perfect results, and that if all you do is relax, that's wonderful.

Recall the material on negation in the last chapter—stating that there is "no right way and no wrong way" implies that there is a right and wrong way. It is better to avoid judgmental statements completely. This also refers to "perfect" in terms of results. "... if all you do is relax ..." sets up the possibility of failure. Simple assertions are all that are needed—*Just continuing to relax in your own way.*

This is not a time to be worrying about any of the things that are happening in your day-to-day life.

Negation, again. The listener hears, "... a time to be worrying ..." This also brings attention to day-to-day events, rather than to this quiet calming time. *Your time now, a peaceful time …*

This is a time for only you, let it all hang out.

Let what "hang out," and what does this phrase mean? The word "it" starts a transderivational search. *This is your time.* And, if you really must say something,... *leaving all that back there …*

For this very short period of time, you can completely relax. You are never out of control. You can feel completely secure.

Why emphasize "very short period of time" rather than have the relaxation experience be open-ended? "can" implies possibility *and* "can not." Is "completely" too much to ask for? Just, *relax*. Mentioning "never" with "out of control" suggests the possibility of being out of control. Why raise this idea at all? The last sentence is a good one.

You are never out of control. You can feel completely secure.

Negation again. *Feeling in control and secure ...*

[Jumping to the middle of the script.] And now perhaps, if you want to, you'll see yourself at the top of a flight of ten steps going down.

"... if you want to ..." breaks the flow and so the listener debates whether or not to follow the directions. If they do not "want to," then what? "See" forces a visualization and a dissociation. Some people are afraid of stairs. In general, avoid stairs, escalators, and elevators.

We are going to walk down these steps together, if you want to ...

From "seeing" yourself on the stairs, you are now accompanied by the speaker "if you want to."

And now, if you want to, and it's easy for you to do ... perhaps you can see yourself on a lovely, lovely, warm, comfortable beach.

Again, "if you want to" sets up internal dialogue, as does "[if] it's easy for you to do." "Perhaps" is open-ended, and "see" is visually oriented. The writer may like beaches, but how many people have had bad experiences on beaches? Too specific an image.

121

And see if you can smell what the ocean smells like. Really try to smell it. Be there.

How can you "see" an odor? But, do this "if you can." "Really *try*" has failure built in. "Be there" is pushing the listener into *your* comfortable place.

[The next part uses a "lovely golden light" as a healing metaphor.] It's an extraordinarily powerful elixir.... And you can tell the golden light to crush any cancer cell, and to diminish any tumor.

Healing light can be a useful general metaphor if used vaguely. *You now become aware of a healing light of just the right color and intensity to rid your body of un-needed and strange cells, gently locating them and eliminating them just as fast as your body can do this.* How does light "crush," and aren't "elixirs" substances you take orally? The word "eliminate" lets the listener fill in the mechanism.

And now, if you'd like, see yourself at the bottom of the same flight of stairs you just came down, and we'll walk up those stairs together.

What *if* you do not wish to "see" yourself at the bottom of the stairs? Walking up together— where was the listener during the healing light imagery? If you have trouble going up and down stairs or are bed-ridden, then what?

... feeling completely alert and at least as well as you felt when you started, and most likely much better...

Why not imply that the listener *will* feel better and *has already* profited from this experience? The session ends on an ambiguous note. *Feeling completely alert, and having already done so much for yourself, work that will continue, moment by moment, feeling and being better, minute by minute and day by day, continuing, easily and comfortably, returning to this room.... Thank you.*

8.3 Achterberg, Dossey, and Kolkmeier Scripts

The previous script has many areas for improvement and also contains some good material. Careful attention to language would improve it. The delivery should involve many judicious pauses … We continue this detailed analysis with portions of several guided imagery scripts from Achterberg, Dossey, and Kolkmeier (1994). The first is a general relaxation script (p. 60) on healthy breathing.

Before you begin your imagery journey, find a quiet comfortable place, and give yourself permission to spend fifteen or twenty minutes taking care of yourself.	This is a good opening sentence. The word "journey" could be replaced with the more neutral "session" or "time." "Give yourself permission" implies a conscious decision and is probably not needed.
Lie down, or sit with your back and neck completely supported. Allow your chair, or bed, or wherever you are to hold you.	These are well thought-out instructions, with minor quibbles about "completely" and "hold." *Find a comfortable position with your back and neck supported* …
Let tension melt away …	*And now, resting comfortably …*

The previous script for relaxation is well-done and involves paying attention to breathing and a body survey like a progressive relaxation. Again, instead of saying, "… letting go of any tightness or restriction you find …" it would be more useful to say, "and, bringing ease and comfort to places where they are needed …" We continue with some portions (pp. 75–76) of an imagery script for handwarming. (Note that handwarming via biofeedback or other modalities is frequently used for the relief of headaches by increasing blood volume in other parts of the body.)

As your mind becomes clearer and clearer [insert your name]..., feel it becoming more alert.

Do you really want the listener's mind to become "clearer" and "more alert" at the beginning of session? It is important at the opening to *focus* or *concentrate* on some ongoing phenomenon like breathing or the ticking of a clock or a spot on a wall.

Somewhere deep inside of you ... a brilliant light begins to glow. Sense this happening.

The image/metaphor of a "brilliant [internal] light" is used throughout their guided images as a way to start a session. This is an example of the speaker's preferred imagery becoming central to the process. What if the listener has a bad reaction to radiation or sunburn or bright lights? Also, the word "brilliant" is too strong—do you need some sort of eye protection? "Sense" is a very good word.

... The light grows brighter and more intense.... This is the bodymind communication center. Breathe into it ... Energize it with your breath.

Again, do you want a bright and intense light within you? (This idea scares me.) How can "light" be a "bodymind communication center"? The light might originate in such a place, but ... Besides, the phrase "bodymind communication center" is probably "New Age" jargon and would not make sense to many listeners without extensive explanations. "Breathing" into a light or a center is also standard New Age jargon, but is easier to understand although, strictly speaking, you can breathe only into your lungs. The words "energy" and "energize" are popular and sufficiently vague to sometimes be useful. Oxygen is a necessary component of the body's metabolism, so breathing and energy are connected … check these ideas with your client.

The light is powerful and penetrating, and a beam begins to grow out of it. The beam shines into the area of your hands and feet.

"Powerful" and "penetrating" are strong words for some amorphous light within you— this can be scary. Then, a "beam" appears from within what is now a glow of light and this beam from *within* you (the bodymind center) can now shine from *outside* you on your hands and feet. This is complicated imagery which defies literal interpretation. It would be simpler and better to avoid the light and beam altogether and simply suggest that the listener focus or concentrate attention on their own feet and hands, although it would be more useful to do them separately. Also, the script does some biologically accurate things with blood vessels before returning to the hands. The last sentence in the other column is premature.

[after a description of the circulatory system] In your imagination, now maybe you can see that circle of blood vessels in your palm, much like a warm,

Within your mind, now, just feel and sense and see that circle of … this is more directive than "maybe you can." The metaphor of a "warm, golden-red sunset" may be helpful, or you can say, … *and, just feeling a warmth, a gentle warmth spreading*

golden-red sunset in each hand.	*softly and easily through each finger to your fingertips.* Besides, for some people, sunsets are a time when it gets *colder*!
… Can you hear the color of the pulsing flow of warmth?	Good juxtaposition of all three representational systems with the helping question mark.
… As you look even more closely …	The visual representational system can be replaced by "examine" or "study" or "sense."
…You might let yourself imagine for a few moments what happens to the blood flow into your fingers when you are feeling anxious, afraid, or threatened. …	This section gives a too vivid description and can be heard as "you are feeling anxious …" *When you need to relax and warm your hands and feet, just …*
[The session ends with the following:] Take a few reenergizing breaths as you come back to the full awareness of the room. Know that whatever is right for you at this point in time is unfolding just as it should, and that you have done your best, regardless of the outcome.	The first sentence is well-structured. "… and that you have done your best" implies a judgement. The ending phrase "regardless of the outcome" reinforces the idea of potential failure. The second sentence would be better if it just ended after " … as it should", perhaps with a "Thank you" added.

We conclude our study of Achterberg, Dossey, and Kolkmeier's scripts with parts of a script designed for general pain relief (pp. 103–104).

[After the brilliant light opening.] The beam shines into your body now as you prepare to reduce your perception of pain or discomfort.	The connection between the beam of light and preparing to reduce perception is tenuous. "Discomfort" is better than reminding about "pain." The word "hurt" is descriptive, but not as painful as "pain." In general, once the listener knows that the script is for pain relief, then it is best to avoid reminding them about their pain(s) by repeated use of the word.
If you feel that cold will help block your pain … imagine breathing in an icy blue-green mist with each breath … Recall the color of icebergs or deep, frozen glaciers…. [many more details and images about cooling the painful part]	"If you feel that cold will help …" Unless you *know* about the listener's experiences with cold (or warmth) for diminishing pain, it is best to be general. *Just imagining, now, feeling the right amount of cold, coolness, soothing and numbing, just where you need it, as long as you need it, safely, easily, the coolness dulling and remove these sensations, yes, just where you needed it. That's better, isn't it?*

8.4 Belleruth Naparstek Scripts

Belleruth Naparstek (1994) has written a book with many guided imagery scripts. Audiotapes are also available.[6] We start our analysis with segments from a "Favorite Place Imagery" (pp. 76–79.)

To begin with, see if you can position yourself as comfortably as you	"See it" is a visual direction for a kinesthetic process. "If you can" contains an implication that you may not be able to carry out the

---

[6] Image Paths, Inc., 2635 Payne Avenue, Cleveland, OH 44114. (800) 800-8661.

can, ... Try to arrange it so that your head, neck, and spine are straight.

next direction which is, "position yourself as comfortably as you can." *To begin with, position yourself in some comfortable and easy way.* "Try to" implies a difficult task with potential failure. It is not necessary to have head, neck, and spine straight for a useful session.

And taking a deep, full, cleansing breath ... inhaling as fully as you can ... breathing deep into the belly if you can ...

And taking a deep, full, cleansing breath ... inhaling deeply ... feeling that breath fill you and relax you ... and exhaling fully... This removes the "as you can" and "if you can" and the speaker's emphasis on breathing into the belly as being important.

And again ... breathing in ... and this time, seeing if you can send the warm energy of the breath to any part of your body that's tense or sore or tight ... and releasing the tension with the exhale ... and breathing it out ...

"Seeing if you can" versus *letting the warm energy of the breath soothe and relax those parts of your body needing calm and peace and ease.* "Releasing the tension" implies the existence of tension, so part of the listener's mind is diverted to looking for tension so it can be released.

So you can feel your breath going to all the tight, tense places ...

See the recommended phrasing above.

And any unwelcome thoughts that come to mind, these too

"unwelcome" implies that thoughts will be unwelcome. *And, any stray thoughts which* can be sent out with the breath … released with the inhale … so that for just a moment, the mind is empty … for just a split second, it is free and clear space, and you are blessed with stillness …

wander through, just observe them, thank them, and return to your relaxed breathing. An "empty" and "free and clear" mind for a moment can be scary; why just for a "split second"? *As you continue to softly breathe, enjoy a special peace and quiet, a safe stillness within your mind, and your body.*

And any emotions that are rocking around in there … those, too, can be noted, and acknowledged, and sent out with the breath … so that your emotional self can be still and quiet … like a lake with no ripples … .

If you want to call attention to emotions, why describe them as "rocking around in there" which can be a disturbing thought. It is better to not call attention to emotions, but use the "stray thought" formulation above. Or, you could refer to "stray feelings." "like a lake with no ripples" is a highly specific image which requires an internal search for an image/experience of a lake, and then another effort to make it rippleless. The "unwelcome thoughts," "rocking around," and "lake with no ripples" are incorporated in many of Naparstek's scripts— they must be especially meaningful to her.

And now, imagining a place where you feel safe and peaceful and easy … a place either make-believe or real … a place from your past … or

This section is well-formulated with open-ended and permissive language. Although the following sections (not copied here) describe many possible ways to experience this safe place, there are too many

somewhere you've always wanted to go … it doesn't matter … just so it's a place that feels good and safe and peaceful to you …	possibilities offered and they are often quite specific. Just let the listener fill in the details, and allow sufficiently long pauses so that they may do this in their own time and manner.
… and very gently and with soft eyes, letting yourself come back into the room whenever you are ready … knowing in a deep place that you are better for this … and so you are …	This is a well-written ending for the session and ends almost all of her scripts.

Naparstek's book contains a number of imagery scripts for specific conditions like enhancing the immune system and improving cardiovascular functioning—these are by-and-large well done although the beginning formula can be improved (unwelcome thoughts and rocking around emotions, etc.). The many scripts in her book are well-worth studying in terms of the principles presented in this book—you may wish to re-write segments or entire scripts for practice.

8.5 Bernie Siegel Imagery Scripts

Siegel (1989) gives the scripts for four meditations (pp. 261–270) in his book, *Peace, Love & Healing.* He has produced many healing meditation tapes, and tapes to help people for specific concerns like surgery and radiation. Many people find these tapes to be quite helpful—in fact, they started me in this work. Ruth Lapp, Ph.D., and I sent a detailed analysis of one of Bernie's tapes to him for his consideration. Bernie's 60 min. audiotapes typically contain four separate meditations, so he early discovered the usefulness of a fifteen minute session. In the following, we analyze segments of his Meditation I (pp. 261–264).

Begin by taking some deep breaths. Breathe in peace. Breathe out conflicts and thoughts and fears. Just fill up a balloon with them and let them go.

There should be reasonably long pauses between these three sentences. "Breathe in peace" is a good generalized phrase—each listener will interpret it individually. Breathing out "conflicts and thoughts and fears" first requires locating and identifying them before they can be exhaled. Should "thoughts" be on the same footing as "conflicts" and "fears"? It is one thing to breathe out these abstract ideas, but filling a balloon with them requires both a conscious and a physical effort. (Besides, as a chemist I need to point out that balloons filled with air sink rather than rise!)

And when you're ready, look up and let your eyes close gently if they haven't by now.

Eye closure is not necessary for imagery work. Looking up fatigues the eyes and can be a preliminary for eye closure, but generally needs some time.

And now let a wave of peace move down through you body. You might give it a color if you like, or repeat a word like "peace" or "relax" to yourself.

A "wave of peace" is a good image. Giving it a color at this point is only useful if this image is used again—it is not. Repeating "peace" or "relax" to yourself can be helpful if this is given sufficient time to develop into a self-relaxation method.

Let go of the tension in your jaw muscles, and your neck and shoulder muscles.

To release a tension, it must first be identified—this script almost directs you to have tension in your jaw, neck, and shoulder. *And, just let your jaw and face and*

131

neck and shoulders relax, become soft and easy.

I'd like you to try to remember sitting in a school room ... the teacher at the blackboard filling the board with lessons ... when the lesson was done the teacher would erase the blackboard. Do that now. Clean your slate and erase the blackboard of your mind so that you are ready for new lessons and new experiences.

I generally avoid the phrase, "I'd like you to ..." since it sets up a request/response relationship where something is done to please the requester. "*Try* to remember" creates the possibility of failure. *And, within your mind now, you can gently and safely drift back to being in a classroom. [Pause] You may recall a blackboard covered in chalk marks and the teacher cleaning it. [Pause]* Bernie's last sentence is a good one setting up expectations via a common experience. However, this blank slate idea does not recur in this meditation.

Once you've prepared the slate for new images, words and lessons, we'll go on a journey. You know where we're headed.

"We'll" and "we're" imply going and doing things together. It is generally best to leave yourself out of the imagery. The last sentence is nicely open-ended. This segment could use significant pauses.

We're headed for the middle of nowhere, to your corner of the universe, your own special place in the middle of nowhere, with its vivid colors, textures, aromas and sounds.

For me "the middle of nowhere" which is somewhere out there in the void is a very scary place! "Middle" and "corner" are mixed images. *And now you can drift to your special place, with whatever things and sounds and colors and odors, your special safe place.* Why go to the "middle of nowhere" to find your place?

This is a particularly busy meditation which incorporates the following situations: (1) a wave of peace that may be colored; (2) a classroom and a slate and chalkboard and eraser; (3) the middle of nowhere; (4) your corner of the universe; (5) a den or nest in (4); (6) absorption of energy from earth and sky; (7) a time for self-healing; (8) a bridge from your corner of the universe over a river connecting with your path; (9) dressing for work with a weaving and garment metaphor; (10) crossing and evaluating the bridge (what kind of connection do you have with the universe?); (11) meeting and interacting with all the people in your life; (12) entering an old house with a chest and examining a message or gift in the chest; (13) finding a seed and planting it in the house's garden with a growing plant metaphor; (14) entering your own body to repair, rebuild, mend, recreate your body and then clean and clear out your mind; (15) see this new self in a mirror; and (16) return to the here and now. Please note that all of the above are crammed into a fifteen minute tape! Some of the language is excellent. But, Bernie's tapes tend to contain too many images with no time to process before the next one pops up. The classroom and chalkboard metaphor can be built into the central theme of *one* guided imagery session with sufficient pauses to allow the listener to fill in their own personal details, needs, and solutions.

8.6 Summary

The creation of an effective guided imagery script (and its delivery) involves much conscious effort, particularly to choice of language. The detailed linguistic analysis, with suggested alternative language, presented in this chapter was designed to get you started on preparing your own scripts. This chapter should have sensitized you to what to listen for in commercial tapes, and what to be aware of in your work.

Chapter 9

Some Guided Imagery Scripts

9.1 Introduction

In this chapter we will provide several *general* guided imagery scripts. These scripts are designed to be used for groups of people in circumstances where you do not have any information about the nature of imagery that would work for a particular person. It has been my practice to offer groups several general ideas and obtain a consensus for a preferred approach. Typically, I will mention: healing hands, a healing presence, healing light imagery, and angels. These general imagery scripts can be adapted for one person, if that approach appeals to them.

Some particular themes I have used for individuals are: a healing angel; a healing angel assisted by another angel who specialized in bone regeneration and reconstruction (this second angel, or several assistant angels, can be used for particular purposes like tissue regeneration, rewiring of brain connections, production of specific biochemicals for pain control (or whatever), reduction of nausea or other side-effects of treatments, appetite enhancement, sleep, etc.); a group of cowboys who ride around a cancer site blasting away at cancer cells; a personal Indian tribe of fierce warriors who are adept at tracking down, ambushing, and scalping/killing abnormal cells; a gardener who weeds out strange cells; a miniature submersible (as in Asimov's *Fantastic Voyage*) that seeks out and destroys cancer cells and clumps of cells by crushing them with mobile pincers at the end of retractable arms; and Jesus who lovingly persuades cancer cells to leave. Again, it is important to match the images with the individual.

Other imagery that has been used includes: animal predators like wolves, sharks, catfish, piranhas, cats, various dog breeds, snakes, and raptors; ray guns like *Star Trek* phasers, etc.; heat and cold; chemotherapy as a God-given golden healing fluid; healing persons such as God, Jesus, Mary, particular saints, powerful doctors, nurses, family members, wise men or women, and "power" spirits, healing substances, particular dietary regimens, supplements, juices, and detoxification regimens; prayer and prayer circles; and biologically accurately described functioning of the immune system [see pp. 317–328 in Achterberg, Dossey, and Kolkmeier (1994)]. Another image, "desired you," takes the form of an image of yourself free of cancer and in full health, and just letting your immune system and body/mind figure out its own way to attain that desired state.

There are many, many images which can be used: remember to match them to the person—we are all unique. Also remember that the word "imagery' refers to *all* senses and that the imagery can be specifically kinesthetic or auditory in nature.

9.2 Review of the Components of an Imagery Session

A guided imagery session is in three main parts; a relaxation and preparation section of about five to seven minutes, the delivery of the imagery in nine to seven minutes, and a re-orientation to the present for about one minute. This is about fifteen minutes in total. The typical session lasts from fifteen to twenty minutes, although it is sometimes useful to go to a full one-half hour which is the typical length of my preparation-for-surgery and sleep tapes. As explained earlier, I do not use music on my tapes since musical tastes are so varied. The listener is free to listen to the imagery tape on a personal cassette player, and play their own preferred music on a stereo system or boom box in the background. We have emphasized the careful choice of language, the importance of delivery, and the writing out of entire scripts or key points. In the following scripts one ellipsis … is a short pause, two are for a longer … … pause, and three … … … are for a very long pause.

9.3 Healing Presence Imagery Script

Hello. Find a way of being comfortable … just shift around some now … moving your head or arms or … so that you are even more comfortable. Feel free to move at any time … This is your time, nothing at all to bother you, nothing else to do. Your special quiet time … And, you can begin with paying attention to your breathing … noticing each breath as it comes in, slightly cooler … and each exhale … slightly warmer and moister. Just one breath at a time. Simply, easily. And you may count your breaths. One … two … three … four … five … … And back to one … two … three … simply and easily. One breath at a time. Softly. Simply relaxing into that quiet rhythm … one … two… three … …

From time to time a stray thought may wander through ... notice it ... thank it ... and go back to ... ... one ... and two ... and three ... and ... ... Another thought may come through ... notice it ... and ... yes.... Thank you ... back to... ... Easily and simply, so restful, as you continue to become even more relaxed ... more at ease ... easily... ... ...

And, within your mind, now, you can drift off to your own special, safe and secure place, I don't know where it is ... or what it is like ... or even if it is real or imaginary ... just your special ... safe ... healing ... place. A place that is just yours ... ... Enjoy being there ... noticing, looking around, sensing, hearing ... maybe there are some special odors. Your place ... resting even more fully ... ...

While you are there, you notice that someone, a special healer, a powerful and knowledgeable healer, is there with you, too. Just the two of you ... Sensing that healing presence ... perhaps there is some music or singing or words that are ever so full of meaning ... ... And I don't know who your special healer is ... this healing presence ... someone from your past, or future, a religious figure ... your healer ... here ... with you ... Just being there, and enjoying being cared for ... ... your time ... ... your place ... now ... ...

And the healer comes close enough to touch you ... gentle, warm, energetic, knowing hands ... and they lightly touch those parts of your body that are in need. And with each touch you can sense, you really feel, a special tingling or warmth, or perhaps coolness, find its way to those places where healing is needed ... eliminating unwanted cells swiftly, easily, automatically ... just as fast as your body can handle this now ... ... Maybe crushing or destroying or simply eliminating those cells and masses ... the power of the healing presence moving to wherever it is needed, knowing just where to do its work ... yes ... and yes ... and yes ... ...

And, in those other places where a repairing or rebuilding or reconstructing or rewiring kind of healing is needed, you can sense this healing presence, your healer ... repairing, rebuilding, making appropriate connections and adjustments, simply and easily ... ... Knowing just where to work, effectively and efficiently ... repairing ... like new ... maybe better ... ...

Your healer is also a teacher ... improving your immune system ... showing it new and better ways ... reminding of older ways that are still helpful ... teaching ... so that this healing work can go on and on and on ... just as long as you need it ... ... Remembering ... learning ... storing away ... your healer gently completes the work for now ... slowly withdrawing ... ... a last touch or two ... ... while you know somewhere deep inside just how this work will continue and continue and continue ... ... your time ... your healer ... ...

Thank you for letting me spend this time with you ... When you are ready, you may take a deep breath or two, blink your eyes, stretch, and return to this room ... here and now.

Yes ... Yes ... Yes ... ...

9.4 Healing Light Imagery Script

Hello. Find a way of being comfortable ... just shift around some now ... moving your head or arms or ... so that you are even more comfortable. Feel free to move at any time ... This is your time, nothing at all to bother you, nothing else to do. Your special quiet time ... And, you can begin with paying attention to your breathing ... noticing each breath as it comes in, slightly cooler ... and each exhale ... slightly warmer and moister. Just one breath at a time. Simply, easily. And you may be counting your breaths. One ... two ... three ... four ... five ... ... And back to one ... two ... three ... simply and easily. One breath at a time. Softly. Simply relaxing into that quiet rhythm ... one ... two... three ... ...

From time to time a stray thought may wander through ... notice it ... thank it ... and go back to ... ... one ... and two ... and three ... and ... ... Another thought may come through ... notice it ... and ... yes ... Thank you ... back to ... ... Easily and simply, so restful, as you continue to become even more relaxed ... more at ease ... easily ... ...

And, within your mind, now, you can drift off to your own special, safe and secure, place, I don't know where it is ... or what it is like ... or even if it is real or imaginary ... just your special ... safe ... healing ... place. A place that is just yours ... ... Enjoy being there ... noticing, looking around, sensing, hearing ... maybe there are some special odors. Your place ... resting even more fully ... ...

And, enjoy just being there, peacefully and quietly ... ... An interesting thing begins to happen ... the light is shifting and changing ... becoming more focused in some gentle way. This is a healing light, coming from above and around, somehow, especially for you ... and I don't know exactly what color or hue it is ... or how bright ... or how focused or diffuse the ray or rays ... or just how warm or cool it is ... you know ... ... and you can adjust it so that it is just right for you, now ... just the right intensity ... ... And this healing light, perhaps from above, has its own way of knowing just exactly where to focus its energies to heal and correct and adjust and rid your body of those unwanted cells and masses ... ... gently and safely moving through your skin in as many places as it is needed ... ... and only doing its healing and eliminating work on just those spots and places, oh, so very carefully and safely selective ... where it is needed ... so easily and gently and softly ... ... touching, covering, shining, and cleansing your body with rays of hope and energy and power ... your healing light ... ... and doing this just as fast as your body can get rid of the debris, the fragments, the shriveled and vanishing unwanted cells ... ... It is almost as if a Higher Power or some Cosmic or Universal Force, something outside you, is beaming on you with love and compassion and healing energy ... working ever so quickly and efficiently ... cleansing, restoring ... ... yes, restoring, for this healing light with its special colors is restoring and rebuilding ... ... and bathing your healthy cells with extra energy so that they become healthier, and the healthy cells increase naturally and simply ... you can almost feel that now, can you not? ... ... how this light is re-energizing your immune system, giving it a boost and renewed vigor, to be alertly protective ... yes, that's right, isn't it? ... ... becoming stronger, doing more, doing more so easily ... feeling the healing light all over and through you ... your healing ... ...

And, when it has done its work for now, the light gently withdraws and fades, leaving you feeling ever so rested and relaxed, yet strangely, full of energy, too ... ... When you are ready you can take a few energizing deep breaths, blink your eyes, open them, and return to this room.

Thank you for letting me spend this time with you ... Yes ... Yes ... ...

9.5 Healing Hands Imagery Script

Hello. Find a way of being comfortable ... just shift around some now ... moving your head or arms or ... so that you are even more comfortable. Feel free to move at any time ... This is your time, nothing at all to bother you, nothing else to do. Your special quiet time. ... And, you can begin with paying attention to your breathing ... noticing each breath as it comes in, slightly cooler ... and each exhale ... slightly warmer and moister. Just one breath at a time. Simply, easily. And you may be counting your breaths. One ... two ... three ... four ... five ... ... And back to one ... two ... three ... simply and easily. One breath at a time. Softly. Simply relaxing into that quiet rhythm ... one ... two... three ... ...

From time to time a stray thought may wander through ... notice it ... thank it ... and go back to ... ... one ... and two ... and three ... and ... ... Another thought may come through ... notice it ... and ... yes ... Thank you ... back to ... ... Easily and simply, so restful, as you continue to become even more relaxed ... more at ease ... easily ... ...

And, within your mind, now, you can drift off to your own special, safe and secure place, I don't know where it is ... or what it is like ... or even if it is real or imaginary ... just your special ... safe ... healing ... place. A place that is just yours ... ... Enjoy being there ... noticing, looking around, sensing, hearing ... maybe there are some special odors. Your place ... resting even more fully ... ...

Your special place, somewhere, somewhen, with interesting things ... ... enjoying a calm and relaxed time, your time ... ... and, you know, you know, just how important touch and being touched is for healing, do you not? ... connections with another, or many others, sensing their caring and love and compassion ... ... and the desire to heal, to help heal, to help your healing in any way possible ... ... and while you rest in your special place, can you not sense, now, the presence of a pair of healing hands? ... ... slowly coming closer ... and I don't know whose hands they are ... maybe someone from your past or childhood, maybe a spiritual healer, perhaps the hands of a saint or religious entity ... ... important, powerful, knowledgeable, healing hands ... ... soft and gentle ... yet stronger, much stronger, than whatever within you needs healing ... ...

And, those hands gently move over your whole body, just an inch or so away, sensing where their healing touch, their healing energy is needed ... ... Then, ever so gently, the hands touch you just in those places where their power is needed ... sending healing feelings and energy through your skin to surround and encompass and eliminate those cells and groups of cells ... to reduce them ... crumble them ... so your body can easily get rid of the debris ... ... many places ... wherever that healing touch is needed ... ... reaching into all parts of your body ... simply, naturally, powerfully ... cleansing and clearing and eliminating ... ... just as fast as your body can handle this clean-up work ... ... knowing that this cleansing, healing, process will continue ... just as long as you need it to ... to be healthy and whole again ... the magic, the power, of healing hands ... yours at this moment ... ... and later ... you can still feel that touch working ... tonight ... tomorrow ... next week ... and all the way into your future ... ... for you know you can never touch without being touched ... ... the contact brings a kind of fusion of minds and bodies and spirits ... ... sharing, working together, being the more powerful for that touch, that touching experience ... ...

And, your body will remember the touch, the touching, of your healing hands ... ... continuing the work long after they've gone to help someone else. And, you can sense that the hands do a final gentle scan of your body for now, and then leave ... ...

When you are ready, will you find yourself waking, returning to this room, full of energy, yet as refreshed as awaking from a satisfying nap? Thank you ... Yes ... Yes ... ...

9.6 Ken's Cowboys: Prostate Cancer Imagery Script
(My friend Ken has had a remarkable recovery from prostate cancer. He was in his mid-sixties when first diagnosed. He went through the traditional medical treatments of surgery, radiation, and chemotherapy. Yet, he attributes his cancer-free state as much to his special imagery sessions as to the conventional treatments. Ken loves western novels and reads one or two per week. This script is a *specific* one based on Ken's chosen imagery.)

Hello. Find a way of being comfortable just ... shift around some now ... moving your head or arms or ... so that you are even more comfortable. Feel free to move at any time ... This is your time, nothing at all to bother you, nothing else to do. Your special quiet time. ... And, you can begin with paying attention to your breathing ... noticing each breath as it comes in, slightly cooler ... and each exhale ... slightly warmer and moister. Just one breath at a time. Simply, easily. And you may be counting your breaths. One ... two ... three ... four ... five ... ... And back to one ... two ... three ... simply and easily. One breath at a time. Softly. Simply relaxing into that quiet rhythm ... one ... two ... three ... ...

From time to time a stray thought may wander through ... notice it ... thank it ... and go back to ... ... one ... and two ... and three ... and ... ... Another thought may come through ... notice it ... and ... yes ... Thank you ... back to ... ... Easily and simply, so restful, as you continue to become even more relaxed ... more at ease ... easily ... ...

And, within your mind, now, you can drift off to your own special, safe and secure place, I don't know where it is ... or what it is like ... or even if it is real or imaginary ... just your special ... safe ... healing ... place. A place that is just yours ... ... Enjoy being there, noticing, looking around, sensing, hearing ... maybe there are some special odors. Your place, resting even more fully ... ...

Resting and relaxing, with one of your good books, perhaps remembering a favorite episode where a posse finally tracks down the bad guys for a shoot-out ... ... or just slowly scanning your body, focusing on the area of your prostate, the two lobes on either side of the urethra ... sensing and seeing in full color and three dimensions, bright or dim as you wish ... ... hearing the sounds of hoofbeats, and the creak of leather, and the snorting of the horses ... ... as your favorite cowboys, somehow miniaturized, ride, round and round those prostate glands ... getting to the size where they can distinguish individual cancer cells, and groups of cancer cells ... tracking down, yelling, riding, kicking up dust, under a blazing sun, clearly illuminating those bad guys, those desperadoes ... ... and, your cowboys, each and every one a dead shot, shooting from a moving horse ... ... your cowboys pick and choose a cancer cell each, wasting no shot, and with deadly accuracy, blast away with their forty-four six-shooters, feeling the recoil, smelling the gun smoke ... ... and in a blazing stream of fire

142

they just destroy, demolish, shoot to smithereens any and every cancer cell that rears its ugly head ... ... blasting away systematically, efficiently destroying any of those remaining cancer cells ... and any new ones that dare to raise their heads ... the cowboys knowing exactly where to shoot, not being fooled by any disguises or shamming ... creating a clear and clean field ... and, after they've done their work, cleaned out the bad guys, they go off singing to a campfire and a meal and rest ... ... and a strong wind blows up, dust devils appear, and all the debris of their shooting just gets blown away, eliminated, scattered like so much chaff in the wind ... ... as your prostate gets healthier and healthier, returns to normal size and functioning ... knowing that your cowboys will return ... any time you need them they can be whistled up ... and their work continues ... yes, it does ... your cowboys ... clearing the way ... ...

When you're ready, you can return to this room, perhaps continuing to read one of your favorite westerns, or just going over one in your mind ... rested and relaxed, and ready for the next chapter of your life ... Thank you ... ...

9.7 Cindy's Story

My involvement with Cindy and her husband John started at one of the regular Charlie Brown Exceptional Patient Support Group meetings. My co-facilitator Mary told me about a woman who was in Hospice, and that she had recommended to them that they get in touch with me and work with me. I visited Cindy and John the next morning. This was now five years after her initial diagnosis with breast cancer. She had been through several rounds of chemotherapy and radiation, following the initial surgery. Cindy and John had explored many alternative avenues. They were both deeply religious. Unfortunately, their minister was uncomfortable around people who had cancer, so they no longer invited him to visit. But, there was a great deal of church and community and family support. I found out later that Cindy's cancer was so advanced that no one expected her to live beyond seven to ten days. I met her on about her fifth day in Hospice. The cancer had metastasized to her bones and she was on a special air bed since the slightest movement would bring pain. The sound of the air system for this bed was omnipresent. Cindy was medicated for comfort and was alert and aware. Even in these extreme circumstances,

Cindy maintained such a cheerful and hopeful and considerate outlook, that Hospice staff would just drop in to see her from time to time as a pick-me-up for themselves. John effectively lived at Hospice using the convertible chair/bed in the room.

I explained to Cindy and John the kind of free personal work I did with people. (This book details the kind of multi-modal work that I do.) I was initially surprised when they asked if working with me meant that they had to give up the other things they were doing. (There are helping professionals who ask for exclusivity for their approach.) I assured them that it was my hope that they continued to do whatever made sense to them, and that what I did was independent of other treatments and regimens. In that very first session I mentioned the research that indicated that doing any kind of weight-bearing exercise anywhere in the body told the body to increase bone density everywhere. The body apparently reacts globally to strengthen bones. Cindy could not move her legs, so John took on the job of moving her legs for her several times a day so that there was some slight stress on the bones there. Cindy started doing exercises to strengthen her arm muscles and the bones in them. She began with lifting a paperback book.

Following the initial session, I visited twice weekly. My visits (John always left us alone after some initial talking) started with some friendly chat and some questions as to how she was doing, so I could structure what I said next and the guided imagery session to match her needs on that day. Cindy had two problems: the first was the cancer itself, and the second was the destruction of bone tissue that the metastases had caused. Our early imagery work involved getting rid of the cancer. After discussing what images might work for her, Cindy told me of a personal angel named Gwen. So, Gwen became the focus of all of the imagery work for eliminating cancer from Cindy's body. The script at the end of this section incorporates the way I used Gwen for healing purposes. As Cindy's health improved (recall the 7–10 day prognosis!), she got more and more concerned about her bones. So, together we discovered that Gwen had a helper angel named Rosie who was a specialist in bone reconstruction and strengthening. All of the subsequent imagery work used both angels. This is reflected in the script.

After seventy-one days of being in Hospice Cindy walked out under her own steam with a walker! Cindy continued to improve and within about a month was walking with a cane, and then in about two months without a cane. She went back to work half-time and then full-time. She was doing quite well and pretty much back to a normal life except that there was some irremediable bone damage, and her right leg ended up about two inches shorter than the left one. A special shoe took care of this. Her orthopedic surgeon could not believe the rapidity of her recovery until he examined the first set of x-rays taken after she left Hospice. The bone structure actually returned.

I was out of the country for about seven months on leave and saw Cindy upon my return. To my sadness, the cancer had returned again. This time there was nothing that we could do together, or the many other things and people she and John were working with, that helped. I saw her in Hospice the day before she died, and she was eager to have another session then, which we did. There is just no way of knowing how much the imagery work contributed to her miraculous recovery and "graduation" from Hospice, just as there is no good way of knowing what brought the recurrence on in such a way that nothing helped. She was comfortable until the end, and maintained a cheery attitude and smile that I can still see. Do miracles happen? Yes. Are they reproducible? No,… and sometimes. For me it was a privilege to have spent time with Cindy and John and to have participated in their lives and her death. John recently gave me permission to not only write Cindy's story for inclusion in this book, but to also use their real names as a memorial to Cindy. The script for a guided imagery session using Cindy's angels follows. The relaxation portion is short since Cindy knew my voice and almost immediately went into a trance. (Note that pauses are not indicated.)

Cindy's Angels: Breast Cancer and Bone Reconstruction Script
Hi. And, again, we can start with you just paying attention to your breathing. Feeling the air coming in and going out. Just one breath at a time. Easily and simply. Imagining that each breath in is a kind of healing breath, and each breath out a cleansing and clearing breath. Relaxing even more. Feeling the support of your chair, breathing easily. Your time now, nothing to bother you, just a peaceful, quiet, resting, healing time. And, if a stray thought

wanders through, just acknowledge it, thank it for being there, and go back to your soft and easy breathing. Good. Just one breath at a time.

And, within your mind now, you can just drift off to your special safe and secure and healing place. Enjoy being there. Such peace, resting easily, comfortably. And, what is that you hear? The soft beat of wings, and you can feel the air moving, can you not? Musical laughter and joy. And you can sense that Gwen has come to visit with you again, bringing her healing love, smiling. Her angel wings touch you, and somehow, somehow, Gwen knows just where in your body her healing energy is needed. You can sense her presence in those places where the power of her love gently persuades the cancer cells that it is time to go. And, if there is a particularly resistant cell or group of cells, she just swaddles them in a cocoon of love, and gently escorts them from your body. And she does this just as fast as your body can handle the removal of those cells. Gwen has this special knowledge, she knows just where to go, where to work, where to use her gentle persuasion, easing out those aberrant cells, gently, yet swiftly, not missing any. There are some that try to trick Gwen, but she is never fooled. Gently, softly, easily, removing them. Working even faster and faster, just as fast as your body can tolerate. One cell here, and another there, and a whole bunch of them over there. Eliminating them with the power of her love, her healing force. Sweeping them away on waves of prayer and joy. Yes. Yes.

And, while Gwen continues to do her work, clearing and cleansing, you can hear another angel coming near. It is Rosie, her special helper, who knows how to rebuild and correct, and reconstruct bones. Rosie is like one of those medieval stone masons who dedicated their lives to build cathedrals. Rosie has special knowledge and powers. You can feel, can you not, Rosie's presence? And, she begins to work where she left off, rebuilding, reconstructing, gently and easily, swiftly, the bones in your hips and pelvic area. Chipping away and clearing out the debris. Removing any cancer cells that might be there and discarding them. And then, just one cell at a time, like building a brick wall, building up your bone tissue. Rosie knows the exact pattern, the original way your bones were put together. So she builds up one cell at a time. You can just feel where she is working, the bone growing, strengthening, forming into just the right pattern. Just as fast as your body can handle these changes. Strengthening, reinforcing, reconstructing. One bone cell connected to another, building up bone mass, becoming even stronger and more dense. In just the right places, in just the right patterns. Rosie concentrates on one area at a time. But, she knows all of the places that need rebuilding, reconstructing, strengthening; and moves from one place to another, working swiftly and accurately. Your bones rebuilding, stronger and stronger as Rosie does her healing and rebuilding work.

Both Gwen and Rosie, working separately, and yet working together. Coordinating their healing work. Your two angels. Listen to their music, their singing, their laughter as they work. So joyously, happily, easily. Gwen and Rosie. And, you know that they are also teaching your own body, your own immune system, your bone rebuilding system, so that this work can continue and continue on its own. Gwen and Rosie have others to help. And, when they have finished their work with you and in you, just for now, they gently take their leave, fluttering, feel the gentle wind from their wings, their voices fading. Their work will continue, moment by moment, minute by minute, hour by hour, day by day, until your body is clear and functioning normally. Whenever you wish to have them help again, you can listen to the tape, or just close your eyes, take a few breaths, and feel them being with you, continuing their work, eliminating, persuading, rebuilding, strengthening. Yes and yes and yes.

Cindy, thank you for letting me spend this time with you. Peace and love and healing ...

9.8 Summary

In this chapter we have provided for study three general scripts and two specific scripts. How would you adapt one of these scripts for a particular client? As you read through a script, are you automatically marking out words and phrases for emphasis? Adding your own pauses? Critiquing the choice of words and phraseology? These scripts can be improved—how would you do that, specifically? For practice, you might make a tape of a particular script and then listen carefully to *your* delivery. You might want to deliberately play with reading a script in different styles. We trust that these scripts are true to the principles outlined earlier.

Chapter 10

Preparation for Surgery

10.1 Introduction

Among the many physically invasive techniques that western medicine uses, surgery is one that many people fear. Their fears may be unfounded for a particular surgery that has a very high success rate and with very few post-surgical complications. For example, the repair of an inguinal hernia, an appendectomy, or the reduction of a bone fracture are done routinely and with rare complications. The term "physically invasive" also sounds rather threatening. In the old days before effective anesthesia and antisepsis, major and minor surgeries had low success rates. In a modern hospital setting there is *generally* little to fear in surgical procedures, even for those long and complex operations like organ transplants and the surgical removal of brain tumors.

However, fears about surgery are realistic since there are documented instances of serious and tragic mistakes and accidents. General anesthesia is effective, but it comes with a price of complications and a relatively long period to remove all of the after-effects from the body. A rule of thumb is that it takes about two months for all of the effects of general anesthesia to wear off. Where there is a choice it makes sense to use local anesthetics or spinals. *Iatrogenic* (the word means "doctor-caused") problems are those caused by medical doctors who make mistakes. These are rare, but do occur. *Nosocomial* problems are those that are caused by mistakes made in hospitals. These are not as rare as iatrogenic problems. For example, the incidence of patients getting infections of various kinds, both fungal and bacterial, in hospital settings is increasing. We earlier cited the incidence of hospital-caused difficulties due to mistakes in prescription drugs (adverse drug reactions, or ADR) that actually appear to be one of the leading causes of death in the U.S. (Lazarou et al., 1998)

This means that many people approach surgery with anxiety and fear. In this chapter are presented the techniques that I use to help reduce anxiety and to prepare people for surgery. The preparation usually takes two sessions.

10.2 Details on the Preparatory Sessions

During the first session we explore previous experiences with surgeries to find out how they reacted in the past, and what it is that they specifically react to. Is it the hospital, the surgeon, the anesthetist, the anesthetic and recovering from its effects, loss of control, the operation itself, the recovery period, pain, old fears and memories—particularly ones from childhood, potential loss of a body part, memories of bad experiences that happened to loved ones and friends, dying on the table, dying, becoming a vegetable, losing the ability to do certain things, the sense of the procedure being a gamble, insurance, paying for the procedure, being away from work or home, the effect of the procedure on their employment status, and the reactions of significant others like spouses or children or close friends? This information about what it is that they anticipate about the procedure is obtained in an open-ended way, doing the minimum of leading or suggesting since you do not want to put ideas in their heads. (Do not repeat the list above.) This information is essential to be able to design a unique tape and set of instructions. The initial stance of the interviewer is that of concerned listening, since a major goal of the first session is establishing rapport and obtaining the confidence of the client. Since the main intervention is that of a posthypnotic suggestion, the client's experience with hypnosis is explored and its nature explained. It may be important to deal with myths and misconceptions about hypnosis at this time. It may also be necessary to use the last part of the first session simply to have the client experience some hypnotic phenomena, and also to experience the relaxed state that is part of the hypnotic experience. If this is the case, then three sessions will be needed for a thorough preparation for surgery. The last part of the session is devoted to a preliminary hypnotic experience incorporating the five parts of the hypnotic preparation for surgery.

There are certainly other ways to prepare someone for surgery. Since I am a practicing hypnotherapist, my approach is based on using hypnosis. If you are not adept at hypnosis and hypnotherapy, then you should not attempt to do the work as outlined in this chapter. On the other hand, if you are experienced at constructing guided imagery sessions for clients, you should be able to adapt the essence of the approach in this chapter to your own work. Training in hypnosis is important for this work.

The reader is probably concerned at this point about the length of the first session. Since I do not work to the clock, my sessions are always open-ended and the first session might last as long as three hours. If you are constrained to work within the framework of a fifty or sixty minute session, then you may need to use up to six or more sessions for the preparatory work described here.

One of the things that is always discussed in the first session is the fact that people can hear what is said in the operating room, even under the plane of full surgical anesthesia. The evidence for this and its nature is discussed separately in Section 10.3.

As indicated above, the hypnotic session is composed of five parts. Before beginning the session, you need to find out from the client where she would like to go within her mind for the duration of the entire surgical experience. Later in this chapter there is a complete transcript of the tape that I used to prepare a friend named Esther for surgery. Esther's safe haven is her garden. The *safe haven* is a real or imaginary place that the client is guided to go to at the end of the relaxation portion of a guided imagery session. It is their unique place where they feel safe, secure, and protected. Deliberatively permissive language is used for this purpose. Amongst other things, the posthypnotic suggestions involve a dissociation in space and time. It is therefore important to know just where (and perhaps even when) their safe haven is and some details about the place. Of course, the haven can be real or imaginary. The five parts of the hypnotic session are:

1. Induction and relaxation
2. Pre-operation experience
3. During the operation
4. Post-operation recovery period
5. Returning home and to normal functioning

At the end of the trance session, the client is asked if there is anything she would like to change in the content and/or the delivery since I will be preparing an audiotape based on this preliminary hypnotic session for her to listen to once or twice each day in preparation for the surgery. The essence of this preparation method is a *posthypnotic suggestion* that activates just prior to the beginning of the surgery experience for the client. This could be the night before going to the hospital, upon arriving at the hospital, during the pre-operation preparatory time in the hospital, or upon entering the operating theater. The client is given a choice as to the most appropriate time for them to begin their trance experience. Erickson cites an instance (Erickson and Rossi, 1981. pp. 22–23) of a posthypnotic suggestion he gave that was activated some fifteen years after the suggestion! This indicates that a posthypnotic suggestion that is activated in a few weeks or less would not lose its strength. The clients who use this preparatory work are highly motivated towards its success. This makes it relatively easy to work with them. Each of the parts of the hypnotic session are commented upon below.

1. *Induction and relaxation*—The simpler the induction the better, since the client will, in effect, be going into a self-hypnotic trance for this work. I generally use focusing on the breath with counting of breaths as an induction. In the second session, I will typically have the client start the hypnosis part of the session on her own to give her practice and confidence in her ability to do this. The relaxation portion of the induction uses words and delivery to enhance relaxation. This portion of the work lasts no longer than five minutes, but with sufficient pauses.

2. *Pre-operation experience*—The pre-operation time is not confined to the immediate hours before the surgery—it may extend to the beginning of the work with the client. Ideally, at the end of the first session the client will feel confident and not apprehensive about the upcoming surgery. They are actively doing something for themselves, they have had their questions answered, and have experienced one relaxing hypnotic session. The pre-operation time effectively includes all of the time between the decision to go ahead with the surgery and the actual operation. In practice this time period is usually confined to departure for the hospital and entering the operating room. The client is told that she can go into her trance at any time that she feels it is appropriate—this may be the night before, while she is being prepped, or when she actually enters the operating room. The choice is hers to make. Esther, for example, was actually listening to the audio tape in her hospital room and while she was being wheeled to the operating room.

The suggestions that are made concern relaxation, going to the safe haven, sufficient details about the safe haven to establish its "reality," comments relating to time distortion in the sense that her time spent in the safe haven is long and the external pre-op time is short, that she is able to respond appropriately to reasonable requests and queries from the hospital staff and family, and comments establishing a dissociation of where she is in the safe haven from what is happening to her body. For example, she can observe from time to time, from the perspective of the safe haven, her body "over there" being competently cared for while she is in complete comfort "over here." This dissociation is established during the pre-op time and maintained throughout the operation and recovery times.

3. *During the operation*—During the operation two things are provided for comfort. The first is continuing time in the safe haven with a sense of dissociation and time distortion (long internal time and short external time). The second is the series of statements made to the client by the surgeon, the anesthetist, or some designated person in the operating room. The person giving the statements is identified beforehand and the client knows who this person is and can recognize their voice. These statements are given in detail in Section 10.4 in the letter to the surgeon. Basically, these are statements of reassurance about how well the procedure is going and for her rapid and easy recovery. The audiotape and the hypnotic sessions incorporate the healing statements in this segment. It is the combination of *all* of these elements that makes for successful outcomes.

4. *Post-operation recovery period*—This period generally comprises three parts: the recovery room, the hospital room, and home recuperation. The elements of being in the safe haven, dissociation, and time distortion are continued. Additional suggestions are given for a rapid and complete recovery, and for minimum discomfort. She will be "surprised" at how comfortable she is afterwards and how little medication she needs. She is urged to ask for whatever comfort medication she needs, no matter how little. She will be "surprised," and so will everyone else, at how rapidly she recovers, how quickly she can be up and about, and how easy all of this was. She may continue in her trance if she wishes, but with

the ability to converse normally with those about her, and to behave and react appropriately.

5. *Returning home and to normal functioning*—It is her choice (given as part of the posthypnotic suggestions) as to when she will return to full consciousness and awareness and leave her internal safe haven to resume normal activities. This can occur during the recovery period in the hospital or upon returning home. She can be "surprised" at how fast everything went and how easy it all appeared to be. The whole experience was something like a dream—one in which she thoroughly enjoyed her visit to her safe haven while competent others took care of her bodily needs. She is told that if she ever needs to do this again, that she already knows how to take care of herself in this way, and that simply listening to the tape will sharpen her skills in this particular self-care procedure.

Obviously, the audiotape and the hypnotic sessions need to be longer than the standard fifteen or so minutes used for a guided imagery session. Typically, the surgery preparation tape runs for thirty minutes, and is repeated on the second side of the tape. Repetition helps, and the client is urged to listen to the tape at least once each day, with two times being optimum.

10.3 Hearing Under Anesthesia

Does a person hear what is said in an operating room when in the surgical plane of anesthesia, i.e., deep anesthesia? If the answer is yes, then what is said in the operating room can have beneficial or harmful effects. Imagine if you heard the following in the totally helpless state of deep anesthesia, "can't stop this bleeding," or "oops!," or "can you find that ...?", or "not much hope," or "this is worse than I thought," or "watch it, one slip and he's a vegetable!," or....

By functioning under the assumption that patients can hear under deep anesthesia, and certainly during procedures using local anesthetics like a tooth extraction, I have prepared myself and others for surgery. As an example, in the past few years I have had two oral surgeries. The surgeon in each case was sent a letter well in advance of the operation explaining the rationale for making certain healing statements during surgery. (See Section 10.4 for the letter and typical statements.) For these particular surgeries I added statements about: no swelling, no bleeding, and minimal discomfort after surgery for my surgeon to say. On both occasions all three statements were realized. In using these statements there are no side effects for the patient and recovery can be more rapid and comfortable.

There is an extensive literature on hearing under anesthesia and in comas. If you are interested in reading more about this, see Pearson (1961), Cheek (1959, 1960a, 1960b, 1961, 1964, 1965, 1966, 1981), Rossi and Cheek (1998, pp. 113–130), Dubin and Shapiro (1974), Liu, Standen and Aitkenhead (1992), Clawson and Swade (1975), and Bank (1985). For some reason, surgeons in the United Kingdom do more healing talk to their patients during surgery than in the United States.

10.4 Letter to the Surgeon and Healing Statements

To aid you in doing this kind of work, this section includes a copy of the letter I gave Esther M. to give to her surgeon at whatever time Esther felt was most appropriate. This could have been well in advance of the surgery, it could have been mailed, or it could have been just prior to the surgery. Circumstances differ, although I think it is important that the surgeon have some warning about your expectations in sufficient time to respond. Discuss the timing with your client. The letter from me is on my formal letterhead and contains information to provide a rationale for the statements, as well as my credentials. This is not to be treated as some "kooky" request, but a serious one that is based on research and efficacy. The letter establishes that the client has been doing preparatory work of a particular kind, and the client's expectations. The statements are included as a separate page in the large font indicated. The statements are also provided to the surgeon mounted on a 5 x 8" index card. On occasion, we have laminated these statements so that they can be made sterile. The letter and statements follow. Please feel free to adapt them for your clients. Also, please adapt the list of statements to match the particular surgery and your client's needs.

Battino Counseling Services
440 Fairfield Pike   *(937) 775-2477 (work)*
Yellow Springs, Ohio 45387   *(937) 767-1854 (home)*
June 25, 1998   *FAX: (937) 775-2717*
email: rubin.battino@wright.edu

Dr. Mary Smith
Cincinnati, Ohio

Dear Dr. Smith:

I am writing this letter on behalf of my friend Esther M. She has consulted with me concerning her breast cancer and the kinds of things I can do to help her at this time. I have been working for seven years now as a leader or co-leader of support groups based on Bernie Siegel's principles for people who have life-challenging diseases and those who support them. I do individual work with some of our members which involves teaching them guided imagery for healing, relaxation methods, ways for resolving unfinished business in their lives, and preparing them for surgery and other medical interventions. As to my credentials, I am a licensed professional clinical counselor (LPCC) in Ohio and a National Board Certified Counselor. I recently co-authored a book on hypnosis and hypnotherapy and have taught courses for many years for Wright State University's Department of Human Resources (counseling) as an Adjunct Professor.

There is a great deal of evidence that patients, even under the surgical plane of anesthesia, can hear what is said in the operating room. It is believed that if the surgeon (or a designated person in the operating room) makes encouraging and healing comments directly to the patient during the surgery, that this has a beneficial effect on outcomes and recovery. This has been both my personal experience and the experience of the people I have prepared for surgery. To this end you will find enclosed a brief set of directions and some simple statements that we hope you will be willing to say to Esther at appropriate times during the surgery. These statements need to be made only a few times, and should always be prefaced by using Esther's name so that she knows the message is directed to her; and ended with a "Thank you," so that she knows the message is over. By the time of the surgery I will have spent some time with Esther preparing her for the surgery and the recovery period. She will have an audiotape to listen to in advance of the surgery. I would certainly be willing to talk with you or your staff about my preparation methods.

Sincerely yours,

Rubin Battino, M.S.,
Mental Health Counseling
Licensed Professional Clinical Counselor (Ohio)
National Board Certified Counselor

copy to: E. M.

*****

Dear Dr. Smith:
I would be pleased if you would make the following statements (and/or other relevant statements) to me at appropriate times during my surgery. So that I know you are talking to me, please preface each statement with my name, and end each statement with, "Thank you."

1. **Esther—please slow down (or stop) the bleeding where I am working. Thank you.**
2. **Esther—please relax your muscles in this area. Thank you.**
3. **Esther—this is going very well. Thank you.**
4. **Esther—you will heal surprisingly quickly. Thank you.**
5. **Esther—you will be surprisingly comfortable and at ease after this. Thank you.**
6. **Esther—your recovery will be very rapid. Thank you.**

10.5 Esther's Surgery Preparation Tape

The surgery tape I prepared for Esther after our first session together follows. The tape runs for about thirty minutes. It is for your guidance in preparing such tapes and may be adapted for your own work. Not all of the pauses and their duration are indicated in the script. Recall that I had already established that Esther's safe haven was her garden. You will need similar information for each client. (A copy of a tape containing this material plus two other guided imagery sessions may be purchased along with this book.)

Esther's Surgery Preparation Tape Script

Esther, this is the special tape I told you I would make for you so that you will be able to go through your surgery in complete comfort, and to be able to recover as fast as possible.

We'll start again with just paying attention to breathing, being sure that you're in some comfortable position ... that your head and neck are free and easy ... jaw loose, knowing that at any time you can move a little bit to adjust how you're sitting or lying so that you're even more comfortable. For this is your time now. Nothing to concern you, nothing to bother you, just your special, quiet time.

And perhaps now counting your breaths ... one, two, three, four, five, and back to one, two, three, in any pattern and in any way that's comfortable to you. Just slowly and easily enjoying this time ... a quiet time ... your time.

And you know that you can change the words I use and how I say them so that they are just right for you at this time. Continuing to count. Perhaps some stray thoughts wander through your mind. You notice them and thank them for being there, and then go back to one, and two ... and that's right, just continuing to breathe easily, softly and gently. And your inner mind will let you know just when it is the right time for you to drift away, inside your mind to your own special, quiet place, your own small garden. And that time may be the evening before the surgery, or that morning, or when you enter the hospital. You'll know just when to start your counting of breaths, drift away to your own special garden. And yet, at the same time, you'll know that you'll be able to respond appropriately to those people who have questions, assist them in any way, so that this all goes comfortably, quickly. And they would be surprised if they knew that you were already in your garden. One part of your mind perhaps dealing with all those mechanical details, competently, while you are immersed completely in your garden.

And I don't know what the first thing will be that catches your attention there ... it may be bird song ... one, two, three ... many birds, just listen to their trilling. It may be a sudden rush of wind rustling the leaves in the upper branches in the trees ... perhaps swaying the bush ... flowers moving gently ... feeling the wind's softness brush against you, just the right amount of coolness. Or maybe the color of a flower or a group of flowers ... just observing them very carefully, whether they're still, or move a little bit in the breeze, just how tall they are, the variations, the shades and hue of color. The delicacy of each petal, stamen and pistil and leaf. How artistically each flower is formed. Continue to enjoy being in your garden, and knowing that at this time you are being prepared for the surgery, but that that seems to be happening somewhere over there. You are so engrossed in the smallest details of your garden. ... The time goes so quickly, almost as if the minute hand on the clock were moving as fast as the second hand; and yet, strangely, your time in your garden seems to go on and on and on, peace and quiet ... sensing the beauty there. .

And then your other mind knows that you're in the operating room now ... while you continue to be in your garden, observing, enjoying. Perhaps you respond to the comment of the surgeon or the anesthetist, I don't know who. And then all is really quiet in your body. Being strongly alive and yet willing to assist them in any way so that this experience goes successfully and rapidly. And I don't know when you first become aware of the sounds of water trickling, running. And over there, you can see it now, the little miniature fountain's bright streams of water sparkling in the sun, splashing, splashing noises, seeing the little droplets form, the reflections in the water ... almost mesmerizing; watching, listening to that wonderful sound. Remember being near some clear stream where the cold water rushes over small and large stones, the rippling light of whiteness of the waterfalls. So quiet ... so pleasant.

And Esther, you should know that the procedure is going very rapidly, very well. Thank you. And Esther, you should know that you'll be recovering from this rapidly, easily, simply faster than you could have ever believed. Thank you. And what is it that you now see over there? Two butterflies. What wonderful colors in their wings. Dancing around each other, fluttering, flitting in the air. Lighting on a leaf that's folding up a little bit ... and then darting off to another place, floating, shimmering in the sun.

Esther, you know that you'll be very comfortable after this is all over, being able to request whatever medications you need and yet surprisingly needing very few, being very comfortable within yourself, knowing that the healing has already started. Your body regenerating, reconstructing, pulling together, doing what it knows how to do, automatically, without any awareness on your part. So rapid, so simple. Thank you.

And Esther, now the procedure is over and you sense somehow that it has been successful. You have been in the care of very competent, concerned, caring professionals all this time. Knowing that they are using their skills at peak efficiency to help you, and that's comforting, isn't it? And you continue to enjoy being in your garden. Perhaps, now you look up, within your mind in your garden, at some glorious white, fluffy clouds moving majestically along, high in the sky, floating, soft and cushiony, observing the billowing pillow-like shapes and forms changing, perhaps seeing interesting forms and faces and shapes in those clouds. Enjoying the peace, the quiet of this moment. Your time. A safe and quiet time. And, from the clouds, your gaze moves to the tops of some trees, watching the way the leaves move in the wind, the breeze. Hearing the wind as it rustles through, feeling its caress, its coolness on your skin and your hair, your time. And yet this time is moving slowly, slowly in your enjoyment while the external time goes very, very fast.

And before you know it, that other part of your mind is aware that you're in the recovery room and you respond, of course, appropriately to any comment, any questions, aware of who is there and being with them. And yet, at the same time continuing to enjoy your special garden. And your eyes now fall on the grass, perhaps seeing many, many blades at one time. And then focusing on the magic, the individuality of one blade, noticing how it fits among the many, and yet how it has individual beauty, being part of and yet a part of an incredible greenness. And you may notice in the grass other plants growing there. Perhaps, at this point, you hear the buzzing of a bee nearby, and watch its erratic path from flower to flower, stopping here, stopping there, gathering pollen, buzzing along, following its own path, its own destiny, many byways, many things, gathered and collected. And over there is another flower, a solitary one, glorying in its stature, its color, its robust delicateness, showing its face to the world at this moment, now.

And soon you know, with that other part of your mind, that you're in that regular room at the hospital, feeling very comfortable, asking for whatever you need, as you need it, sensing within you how rapidly the healing is going on. Perhaps little sensations of warmth or coolness, tinglings. I don't know exactly how your body will be speaking to you, in some way, letting you know just how fast this is going on, how much you have already been helped by this procedure, looking forward to going home to familiar surroundings, so that you can be both within your mind as you are now, and yet in reality, physically in your own special garden.

And all of this is going on within an awareness of comfort, calm, ease, peace, simply, rapidly. And at some point you become aware that time is now again at its regular pace, state. And you wonder, with some surprise, that this is already all over, done, and you're home again. Almost like awakening from a dream, yet a dream where you've been so peaceful, so calm, where within your mind you may have relived many other enjoyable, quiet, calm, peaceful moments. Your time. This moment, now, quietly, peacefully.

And you know that your mind is somewhat like a tape recorder; and you will remember whatever it is that I've said that's helpful that you need to recall, so that you can play it over and over as you need to in preparation, in wonderment, looking back at how simple and fast this has all been. And when you know in some way inside that it is now okay to be fully conscious and aware of whatever place, and whatever way you are, with this all over at this time, will you find yourself taking a deep breath or two, blinking your eyes, perhaps stretching a little bit, feeling very rested, and yet somehow full of energy? Just come back to this room, here and now. Esther, thank you. Thank you for letting me spend this time with you. Yes, yes, yes ...

Part Two

Psychotherapy Based Approaches

Chapter 11

Introduction to Psychotherapy Based Approaches

The kind of individual work I do with people who have life-challenging diseases uses guided imagery as one part of a more comprehensive approach. Part Two of this book deals with psychotherapy based ways of helping people with diseases. In fact, most of this work is directed at *healing the illness*, that is, helping the person to be more comfortable with themselves and with the physical manifestations of the disease. Dealing with unfinished business, helping someone to discover meaning in their life, or helping them realize earlier hopes and dreams are ways of handling the illness. Although this work appears to be the same as traditional psychotherapy, there are significant differences. When I do this work I avoid the words "therapy" and "psychotherapy." The client does not approach me for help with mental or psychological concerns, but rather for ways of dealing with their physical disease that might have an effect on the course of the disease. Lawrence LeShan's decades of work (1974, 1977, 1982, 1989) with terminal cancer patients is a good reference point for this perspective. Helping clients clean out the garbage in their lives invariably leads to some degree of healing, and there are sufficient instances of improvements in physical health that the element of hope is always present. (I am always careful to explain these distinctions.) LeShan's successes have been anecdotal and by self-report. To my knowledge, he has yet to do a systematic, scientifically controlled outcome study of what he does. Yet, the indicators for significantly helping people are there.

In Section 2.7 David Spiegel's controlled study of the effect of a weekly (for one year) psychotherapy support group for women with 4th stage breast cancer describes the hallmark work in this field. To Spiegel's surprise, the women in the support group lived about twice as long on the average from the start of the study as the women in the control group. This work has been replicated and shows that psychotherapy can have profound effects on the body, including impacting supposedly untreatable cancer.

On the average needs to be emphasized because there are no guar-antees that *everyone* in a psychotherapy support group will live significantly longer. On the other hand, standard medical treat-ments like chemotherapy and radiation *all* come with their own percentage success rates for different cancers at different stages of development. You buy insurance and wear a seat belt and don't smoke and eat a sensible diet because you are playing the odds and enhancing your own chances for well-being. After all, most heavy smokers *do not* get lung cancer, and there are non-smokers who do get lung cancer, but a wise person knows that not smok-ing (or to a lesser extent stopping smoking) decreases the likeli-hood of getting this particularly virulent form of cancer. So, you play the odds and do sensible things, even though what is sensi-ble has some of the characteristics of a moving target as new stud-ies are published.

Spiegel's work shows that psychotherapy support groups and, by implication, psychotherapy, can have a significant effect on the progress of a disease. Will all psychotherapy and support groups be equally effective? No, since individual outcomes depend on the skill of the therapist and the client's involvement. Also, there are many kinds of support groups (see the next chapter). You need to shop for a therapist or a support group at least as carefully as you do for a major purchase. Only, in this case, your life may be at stake.

There is much evidence (see chapter 2, for example) that the mind (thinking) can have significant effects on body functions. Milton H. Erickson authored a number of papers where he described psy-chophysiological changes. In Vol. II of his collected papers (Erickson and Rossi, 1980) see Section I on visual processes (pp. 1–78), Section II on auditory processes (pp. 79–142), and Section III on psychophysiological processes (pp. 143–220). One can consider all placebo effects to be psychophysiological—so the thesis of this book that psychological work (which includes guided imagery—Part One—and placebo effects) can bring about physical changes is well-grounded. For example, how many instances of pain con-trol via hypnosis are needed to establish its efficacy for this pur-pose? Hypnosis does not work equally well for all people, but neither does chemotherapy or blood-pressure reducing drugs. Is the one more scientific than the other?

If the placebo effect essentially depends on belief, then the belief systems of the patient are also important. It is well-known, for instance, that one of the characteristics of survivors—whether it be a concentration camp or a disease—is that they have a strong religious faith, or a strong belief in some dogma. Working with beliefs can be life enhancing. Viktor Frankl characterized this by emphasizing man's search for meaning. If your life is meaningless, if you have no goals, then you might as well give up and die. Sometimes people have given little thought to what is important in their lives. Helping discover such events or activities can help focus their energies forward, and bring meaning to their lives. This is central to Frankl's system of *logotherapy*. Frankl also emphasized that people always have choices in *how* they respond to a particular challenge in their lives. Are they stuck with "why me?" and "why now?" and "why this?" *or* do they explore how they can use this challenge to increase meaning in their lives, and how they can respond to become more just, more compassionate, more loving?

A related aspect has to do with unfulfilled and unrealized hopes and dreams. LeShan emphasized the importance of finding and being able "to sing your own unique song." Joseph Campbell described this as "finding your bliss." All-too-often our hopes and dreams get put aside by what we consider to be practical reality—things that *must* or *should* or *have to* be done. Generally, these "musts" are not of our own choosing, and you can slide through life without ever even attempting to test the reality of those dreams, to experiment. One part of the work I do is to explore unfulfilled dreams and hopes, probing to discover their importance and helping towards attainment, if at all possible.

Sometimes, along with an understanding and acceptance of mind/body interactions comes a kind of guilt, dubbed New Age Guilt, that has its origins in the belief that,... somehow I've brought on this particular cancer by my lifestyle and actions.... If proper thoughts can improve my health, then I must have had improper thoughts or had done bad things which brought on the cancer. Some healing professionals even invoke a kind of "pop psychology" genesis of types of cancer by finding those who "can't stomach things" getting stomach cancer, those who "don't give a shit" or are "tight-assed" or who "hold everything in" getting colorectal cancers, those who are anorgasmic getting prostate or ovarian cancer, those who have evil thoughts getting brain tumors, and the like. **There is no evidence for these assertions.** Just as fecal matter can happen, cancers can happen. We can occasionally point to environmental factors like DDT and halogenated hydrocarbons, smoking, asbestos, and vinyl chloride as being known carcinogens, *but* not everyone exposed to these factors gets the related cancer or *any* cancer. This means that there are known factors that can contribute to a person getting cancer, but that individual responses are just that—individual and highly variable. If mental attitude can lead to healing and remission, is it possible that mental attitude can bring on cancer? Yes, it is possible. Lerner, in his careful study (1996), indicates that it is probably significant at about the 15% level. Stress certainly diminishes the immune system's ability to protect the body. Is it a factor in cancer? The answer is Yes. Does high stress invariably produce cancer? No. We are all unique individual beings. All that we can do, as I have stated above, is to live our lives as best we know how, doing sensible things in nutrition, exercise, relationships, activities, and stress reduction or, better, enjoyment and relaxation enhancement.

It may be easy simply to dismiss the concept of "New Age Guilt" in all of its (sometimes subtle) manifestations. A word of caution is needed as in some circles this idea is endemic and, even unspoken. There is sometimes the implication (which is always heard and understood) that you brought the cancer on yourself. So, be wary, be careful, and challenge this harmful idea wherever it appears. Cancer happens in some people. Viktor Frankl advised that no matter what hand life deals us, we *always* have the choice of how to respond. That choice is what makes us human.

Chapter 12

Support Groups

12.1 Introduction

When someone rings me up for information about the Charlie Brown Exceptional Patient Support Group that I work with in Dayton, Ohio, I am always careful to point out that it is only one of many support groups in the Dayton area. I urge them to go to several groups before deciding about which group to join. Everyone's needs are different. The group must *feel right* to you on some personal level before making any commitments about attendance. Most hospitals offer support groups and/or services to people who have cancer or other serious diseases. These hospital-based groups may be solely for the patient, solely for those who support the patient, or for both. These groups are generally free.

There are many support groups organized around a particular disease like emphysema, cancer, colorectal cancer, asthma, etc. These groups are generally associated with a national organization, e.g., The American Cancer Society. Usually there are no fees. Typically, the specialized support group meetings are heavily oriented towards information about the disease and coping with it. Support groups may be classified by the amount of time spent on information and lectures versus the amount of time spent on emotional or psychological support. This is why it is so important to check out support groups, and being open to going to groups with different styles as your own needs change. Above all, it is important to recognize that seeking help and support is an indicator of *strength* on your part, and is one area under your control. Although the members of a particular group may be quite ill indeed, the atmosphere is generally that of hope and courage—they are brave people who have gone through or are going through whatever is your specific disease. You learn from each other's experience. These are generally not "downer" groups, and there is a surprising amount of humor present—this "in" group can share jokes or so-called "black" humor which they would find to be uncomfortable in the presence of healthy people. This is an important point since a person with a disease frequently feels isolated and different and even stigmatized with respect to "healthy" people. There is a sense of unreality, of separateness, of estrangement—on some core level they do not recognize themselves; the disease has transformed them into a different and strange person. It is not so long ago that these people were ostracized, isolated, and driven out of their community. Recall the history of the way that those with leprosy and tuberculosis were treated. Echoes of these old behaviors and fears still reverberate.

There are a number of psychotherapists and social workers and other helping professionals who offer fee-for-service assistance for people who have life-challenging diseases, and those who support them. Sometimes, this is straight psychotherapy for the individual or their family. Sometimes, they offer programs for grieving, and sometimes there are privately run support groups. These groups may reflect the particular orientation of the provider in terms of nutrition, body work, and alternatives to conventional medicine. Always remember that you are in control and that the choice to use or stay with a particular practitioner is yours. Michael Lerner's book (1996) is the essential guide to evaluating complementary practices for cancer.

In this chapter several specific support groups or styles will be described.

12.2 David Spiegel's Breast Cancer Support Groups

Spiegel et al.'s support group (1989) for women with metastatic breast cancer is a classic psychotherapy based group. (Spiegel et al.'s research is described in section 2.7.) Such a group is run by a trained psychiatrist, psychologist, counselor or social worker with typically two leaders working with a group of ten to twelve participants. Meetings are weekly or biweekly and run for a fixed time period of ten or twelve sessions or from three to twelve months. Participants make a commitment to attend all of the sessions. Once a group has started, new members are rarely admitted since the group quickly establishes an identity and a strong group loyalty. In a disease-based group (versus a psychotherapy-based group) the members are encouraged to be in contact with each other outside of the meetings.

The Spiegel groups meet for ninety minutes. Although other groups may meet for longer times, up to three hours per session, it is rare that a group would meet for less than ninety minutes. One reality constraint is that ninety minutes may be as long as a person with an active disease can comfortably attend a meeting. In the Spiegel groups, an extra measure of rapport was attained by having one of the leaders be a person who had breast cancer in remission.

The following quote from the 1989 paper (repeated in part from Section 2.7) describes the nature of Spiegel et al.'s group interventions.

> The groups were structured to encourage discussion of how to cope with cancer, but at no time were patients led to believe that participation would affect the course of the disease. Group therapy patients were encouraged to come regularly and express their feelings about the illness and its effects on their lives. Physical problems including side-effects of chemotherapy or radiotherapy were discussed and a self-hypnosis strategy, was taught for pain control. (Spiegel, 1985) Social isolation was countered by developing strong relations among members. Members encouraged one another to be more assertive with doctors. Patients focused on how to extract meaning from tragedy by using their experience to help other patients and their families. One major function of the leaders was to keep the group directed toward facing the grieving losses.

This is a succinct statement of the way these groups functioned. As pointed out in Section 2.7, the results were remarkable—which establishes the effectiveness of psychotherapy-based support groups for working with cancer patients. The Spiegel support groups were run by trained psychotherapists. Although it is not necessary, the inclusion of group leaders who were models of healing in that they were in remission from the same disease, must have been an important contributory factor.

12.3 Exceptional Cancer Patient (ECaP) Groups
ECaP was started by Bernie Siegel about twenty years ago. His initial motivation was to establish a group where his cancer patients could talk to each other between office visits. He had found that his concern and empathy and hope sustained his patients during

their office visits, and reasoned that regular support group meetings would be of help. The style of the groups evolved. Bernie (he prefers to be called by his first name) reports that it took him six months to learn how to shut up in the groups and *listen* to the members talk. He found that the most important aspect of the support group was the sharing amongst group members.

Several years ago I went to ECaP headquarters (then in New Haven) for training for ECaP group leadership. I discovered while I was there that their way of organizing and running groups was significantly different from the way the Charlie Brown Group in Dayton (see next section) was run. First, they used paid professionals to run the groups. There was a two hour intake interview (fee = $100.00). The groups were limited to twelve people and one professional leader. Attendees agreed to a fixed number of sessions (usually twelve) and paid a fee for this bloc of meetings. (There was a sliding fee schedule and no one was turned away because of fees. Note that these groups were led by paid professionals.) There was a significant psychotherapy orientation to the sessions. Music was often used. Since Bernie feels that drawings are helpful, art therapy was part of the intake interview and the sessions. The groups were for only people who had a life-challenging disease, as there were separate groups for people supporting those with an active disease. There were also separate groups for people who had AIDS. Hugging was always important. As far as I know, there are no systematic outcome studies. After some financial difficulties, ECaP's activities were considerably reduced, and they moved their headquarters.

ECaP puts out an excellent catalog of materials featuring Bernie's tapes (both audio and video) and books, as well as a fairly comprehensive offering of other major contributors to the field of alternative or complementary medicine. ECaP also puts out a yearly directory of support groups across the U.S.A. This guide lists individual practitioners as well as groups, with information about the services offered. Their address is: Exceptional Cancer Patients, 522 Jackson Park Drive, Meadville, PA 16355. (814) 337–8192.

12.4 The Charlie Brown Exceptional Patient Support Group (Dayton)

I will state at the outset that I am biased to the way this support group is structured and run, and its operating principles. I am one of the three leaders (the other two are Clarissa (Chris) Crooks and Mary Dyer, both of whom were among the founders of the group) of this group which began in 1990. We meet at Hospice of Dayton which provides us with a free meeting room and coffee on the first and third Thursday of each month year round. The meetings start at 7:00 p.m. and run to 8:30 p.m. on a fixed format.

The group was started by Charlie Flynn after he "graduated" from Hospice. Charlie was Chris's patient. After he read Bernie Siegel's first book while a patient with a short life expectancy in Hospice, Charlie decided he liked Bernie's philosophy, and that he wasn't going to die of cancer. His cancer went into remission and Charlie walked out. With the help of his surgeon, Dr. George Brown, and Chris and Mary and psychologist Pat Merriman, the Charlie Brown Group was launched in October of 1990. Charlie died three years later on Christmas Eve of a heart attack, but his group continues.

The leaders have always served on a volunteer basis, as have the other facilitators like our treasurer, secretary, and board. The operational expenses are about $200.00 per year for supplies for parties, cards and postage, and donations to Hospice in the memory of any member who dies. There are no fees, but there is a donation basket for the suggested common amount of $1.00 each. The group maintains a free lending library of books, audiotapes and videotapes. Members can keep these items as long as they wish. The library is stocked by donation. There are cookies and coffee and tea available at all meetings.

Members find out about the group by word-of-mouth, by referrals from ECaP or physicians, and by occasional announcements. There is no screening of any kind—anyone who walks through the door is automatically a member. They attend meetings as often as they wish. No distinction is made about why they are there since anyone who has or has had a life-challenging disease, and anyone who supports such a person is welcome. Frequently, just the support person attends. Whole extended families have come to meetings. Visitors are welcome. We are simply there year-round to provide a healing and supportive environment.

There are a few rules, perhaps the most important one is confidentiality—we expect that anything said in the room stays there. Each person gets a chance to talk, and they can talk for as long as they wish. Interruptions or comments are not permitted—each person talks until they are done. It is our expectation that everyone else gives the speaker their undivided, respectful, and caring attention. Even if there is time after everyone has spoken, we do not permit commenting (asking questions or offering advice, for example) during this time. After the meeting is over, people do talk to each other and share in a private manner. The leaders also do not comment, interrupt, or offer suggestions. We are trained to work with people like those in our group, but we do not perceive this as our role within the group setting. We start and end the meeting, do the healing meditation at the end, and chair the non-sharing portions of the meeting. On rare occasions we may privately talk with a member who is just too verbose and wanders in their sharing time.

The order of a typical meeting starts with hugs on entering—we even have an official "chief hugger." Coffee and cookies are available throughout the meeting. Everyone wears a name tag with their first name in large letters. These tags, as does our library and literature, stay in a cabinet in the room between meetings. We always sit in a circle so everyone can see all of the people at the meeting. One of the leaders of the group calls the meeting to order and relates the history and purpose of group if there is a new member present. The operating rules are also repeated. New members get a list of our operating rules, a flyer, a hug card, and an address list. If there are any business or announcements, they are handled rapidly. Next, we ask for updates on members who are not present. At that time we decide who gets a hope/healing/we're-thinking-of-you card. These are circulated along with an attendance sheet. Everyone is expected to write a few encouraging words or greetings, whether or not they know the addressee. We are then ready for sharing time. One of the leaders decides the direction (clockwise or counter-clockwise) of the order of speaking so that any new members get to speak later in the meeting. If there is time after all have spoken, then anyone can enlarge or add to their own *personal* statement.

The meeting ends with dimming the lights and moving the chairs so everyone can hold hands in a large circle. One of the leaders then does a healing meditation that lasts for 5–10 minutes. This healing meditation usually weaves into its content some theme or themes of the day or the meeting itself. The leaders are skilled at doing these meditations *ex tempore*. The meditation always ends with the *Serenity Prayer* (some people start with God and some do not; some end with "Amen"):

(God) grant me the serenity to accept the things I cannot change, the courage to change the things I can, and the wisdom to know the difference. (Amen)

The lights are raised, hugs are available for those who want them, and people chat with each other for a few minutes.

We have found the group to be an instrument of healing, and our members are quite loyal. Needless to say, the style of the Charlie Brown Group is my preferred way to organize and run a support group. I often "adopt" two or three members of the group at any given time, and keep in regular contact with them. If they are interested, I do the individual multi-modal work described in this book with them on a non-paid basis.

12.5 Residential and other Support Groups

There are a number of residential support groups for people who have life-challenging diseases that admit patients for typically one week. Fink's book (1997) *Third Opinion* is, as its subtitle states: "An international directory to alternative therapy centers for the treatment and prevention of cancer and other degenerative diseases." In addition to these residential centers, Fink also gives information about alternative treatment programs worldwide. A brief description is given for each entry, along with contact information and estimated costs. Lerner (1996) has an extensive appendix with the names and contact information for alternative therapy programs.

Perhaps the two best-known residential programs are Commonweal (Lerner is its director and Rachel Naomi Remen, M.D., is its medical director. Their address is: P.O. Box 316, Bolinas, CA 94924. (415) 868-0970) and the Simonton Cancer Center (O. Carl Simonton, M.D., is the director. Simonton Cancer Center, PO

Box 890, Pacific Palisades, CA 90272. (800) 459–3424). There are other centers and programs, but they all need to be thoroughly checked and, if possible, you need to visit to find out if that is the right program for you.

The Wellness Community (2716 Ocean Park Blvd., Suite 1040, Santa Monica, CA 90405. (310) 314-2555) is a national, free, support group with chapters in many locations. The American Cancer Society sponsors support groups in many cities, and is a good source for information (1599 Clifton Road, N.E., Atlanta, GA 30329. (800) 227-2345). The National Cancer Institute of NIH has an informational hot line (800-4-CANCER) and a Web site (www.nci.nih.gov). Also, see Appendix F for some relevant Web sites and phone numbers.

Chapter 13

Working Through Unfinished Business

13.1 Introduction

In addition to all of the objects and things we accumulate in our lives that fill closets and drawers and boxes, we also accumulate many items of unfinished business. By this I mean all of the things we've wanted to do or planned to do which somehow never got done; this includes all of the things we've wanted to say to others and never got around to saying. So, there are many things in our lives that are in an incomplete or unfulfilled state. There was that "thank you" note that you never got around to writing or posting. There was that empty place in your life when you never got to tell a parent that you loved him or her. Another empty place arose from never telling off a particular person. There were un-read books and experiences never attempted. Some of these things are "garbage" we've carried for years, but never got around to throwing in the trash. Of course, many bits of unfinished business turn out to be unimportant or trivial on further examination, and they can be dispensed with quickly. Other items are of such deep personal importance that they take on major significance for a person with a life-challenging disease who faces a fore-shortened life.

This chapter is concerned with uncovering and eliciting items of unfinished business, and the many ways of facilitating satisfactory resolutions. Why is this important? Why do some religions make a special point of death-bed confessions? Gestalt psychologists have demonstrated repeatedly the propensity of the human mind to fill in gaps and complete pictures where pieces are deliberately omitted. It is almost as if human beings have a wired-in need for closure, for completion. Religions and societies have provided formalized ways of attaining this closure. But people who are nearing the end of their days sometimes miss out on seeking this closure, of completing significant bits of unfinished business.

People with life-challenging diseases need to have some way to do this work, and a variety of approaches are given in this chapter. Some of these methods require considerable skill and experience on the part of the facilitator, i.e., they should not be attempted by an amateur. In that sense, **this chapter is designed for mainly experienced practitioners in the helping professions**.

Lawrence LeShan (1977, 1989) has spent a considerable part of his professional life as a psychologist working with terminal or last-stage cancer patients. He has written eloquently about the importance of helping individuals work through unfinished business. This work is a form of psychotherapy that is highly specialized and is aimed towards the particular goal of helping terminal cancer patients be more comfortable with themselves and their memories. They are not "sick" or "neurotic" or "mental cases," but *normal* people who are doing end-stage house cleaning, if you will. LeShan always spends time eliciting hopes and dreams, and the daydreams that motivate and inspire us. Sometimes these are youthful fantasies—being lost in them was particularly fulfilling and satisfying at one time. Sometimes, they were more mature ambitions, the goals and hopes we had set for our professional lives or years of maturity. Sometimes reality, or our *interpretation* of reality, makes it appear that these goals and hopes are unrealistic or unattainable, and we set them aside. I believe that we are incomplete when at the minimum we do not give voice to our hopes and dreams. This is especially important for people who are nearing death. LeShan found that facilitating access to the various levels of unfinished business and their closure had a profound effect on the comfort of the people with whom he worked. He cited examples of remission and increased longevity among his patients, although these are not explicit goals of his work, which was designed for healing.

13.2 Secret Therapy—Content vs Process

The heritage of Freud's methods in psychoanalysis, as continued in psychodynamic-oriented therapies, is an emphasis on *content*. In these approaches the therapist takes a detailed history, may use various diagnostic tests, and delves deeply into the origins of the presenting problem. The therapists feel that they need to know the problem's etiology, details about the client's current emotional state, and much information about relevant relationships, both current and past. So, a significant amount of therapeutic time is spent on content, the nature and history of the problem. Much emphasis is placed on what *caused* the problem in the first place— there is less interest in how the problem is maintained.

Psychoanalytic theory maintains that once the client knows and understands these causal factors, that the problem will disappear. This theory is maintained even though most people who smoke, are over-weight, anxious or depressed can provide detailed reasons for their behavior. It appears that within the framework of content-oriented therapies that knowledge about causes is not always effective.

Milton Erickson's goal for his clients was to help them *change* in some way that they desired. People go to their therapists because they are *stuck*. Typically, a given stimulus in their life results in *one* response (dashed line). If the stimulus is modified by the brain, then it evokes *one* interpretation which has only *one* response. In terms of this model, the function of the therapist is to assist the client to have more than one interpretation and/or more than one response to a given stimulus. The cure for being stuck is discovering many choices in your life. Generally, this is a change from automatic or non-volitional responses to volitional ones.

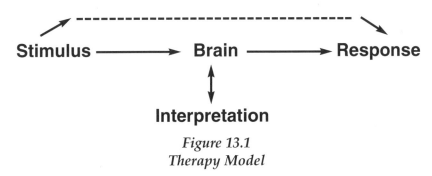

Figure 13.1
Therapy Model

The discovery of choices can be made via *secret therapy* in which clients are guided to find their own solutions within their own minds. By contrast with content-oriented therapy, this secret therapy is *process* oriented. This chapter contains a variety of process-oriented secret therapies. These therapies are, by and large, more effective and significantly shorter than content therapies. They are also more respectful of the client who does not have to disclose intimate details of their life. Of course, some information is needed, but this is kept to a minimum. Clients can tell you more, if they wish, but this is not expected. People with life-challenging diseases need to have their privacy protected, so secret therapies are the preferred modality.

13.3 The Gestalt Therapy Two-Chair Approach

The Gestalt Therapy Two-Chair Approach was developed by one of the founders of this form of psychotherapy, namely Frederick S. Perls. Some basic references are: Perls, Hefferline and Goodman (1951), Perls (1969a, 1969b, 1973), and Polster and Polster (1974), and Polster (1987). Perls was superb at doing therapy in groups, and his two-chair approach evolved out of group work. However, it is equally effective in one-on-one therapy, and this is the way that I use it.

As its name implies, two chairs are used. When the client is sitting in the first chair they are themself in the present moment. As the dialogue develops they may "regress" to an earlier age which is appropriate to the dialogue. In the second chair they place the person with whom they have some unresolved conflict or unfinished business. This person may be a parent, a spouse, a relative, or some significant figure from their past. It is not unusual for the persona in the second chair to be another aspect of themselves, such as the way they are when they behave aggressively, submissively, angrily, out-of-control, childishly, scared, anxious, or depressed. The second chair can hold more than one person, but with a spokesperson. The second chair person may be living or dead. In the latter case this approach is an opportunity to resolve old business or gaps in the client's life, like never having told a parent that they love them.

First, a word about the physical arrangements. The chairs should not be the ones normally used for a regular session. Since it should be easy to get in and out of the chairs, straight-back chairs work best. The chairs are placed a few feet apart, and facing each other. The spacing and orientation may be changed as needed. If the client is in a wheelchair, then they wheel themselves between two designated locations. If the client is confined to bed, they can speak to the other person who is imagined to be in a space near them, and then close their eyes or hold something symbolic to indicate switching positions (chairs).

The two-chair work is begun by explaining the process, and eliciting the identity of the occupant of the second chair. Start with the client in the present. They can make statements to or ask questions of whoever is in chair two. The art of this work, which develops with practice, is knowing when to ask the client to switch chairs. Generally, the process works even if you are not "perfect" in your timing. You keep them switching until the conflict is resolved or all has been said that can be said at this moment. Some useful comments by the therapist are: "Okay, switch." "And what/how do you (does he/she) respond to that?" "What do you think of that?" "Okay, ask again." "Tell him/her what you really think now." "What did/do you resent about him/her?" [Elicit a number of resentments. This should be followed by:] "What did/do you appreciate about him/her? [Elicit a number of appreciations.] By paying close attention to body language and voice quality in each chair, you get clues as to how to guide the process—follow the client's lead. Of course, you need to maintain rapport and respond congruently.

One of the characteristics of two-chair work is that the client typically slips into trance states. The "as if" reliving that occurs means that people appear to get into earlier states, personas, and the other person's patterns of behavior. There may be regressions in either chair, changes of voice and posture. The useful response after this work is over is a sense of completion and resolution, almost the hearing of a sigh of relief at finally having taken care of an old problem. Follow the client's lead in terms of the extent of processing what has occurred.

13.4 Changing Personal History

I recall vividly one training session in Gestalt Therapy. One man in the group started talking about a situation where he had strong emotions two days *before* our meeting. The trainer pointed out that when someone discusses an emotion that is more than about thirty minutes old, that what they are reporting is the *memory* of that emotion rather than the emotion itself. This observation raises the question of the accuracy of memories—did the things we remember actually occur, and if they did, in the way we remember them? We experience something in the present—then it gets stored in our memory. Upon recall, how much does our present emotional state distort or change the memory, and how much do all the experiences between the original event and the present time modify the memory? Accurate memory recall is an important part of evaluating witness testimony in trials—even if the witness is telling the truth as they know it, the judicial system always seeks some corroborative evidence. The essence of the tactic of "changing personal history" as practiced by people trained in NLP (Neuro-Linguistic Programming) is that since memories are so malleable, why not *change* them in ways that are helpful or useful to the person in their present life? This means that one thing you can do for people who have life-challenging diseases to help them be more comfortable with their lives is to guide them via the process described below to modify their memories so that they have happier memories. Is this ethical? If the client chooses to do the procedure once the nature of memory has been explained, then it is their choice and operates within the framework of how we understand memory function.

The following seven-step process should be used by only therapists who are adept at NLP and how to set and use anchors.

Step 1. Identify the nature of the present concern, i.e., what are they finding difficult that relates to origins in the past.

Step 2. There is generally a kinesthetic component that can be identified that is related to the concern. Anchor this kinesthetic part so that the concern can be accessed by triggering the anchor.

Step 3. Holding the anchor in Step 2, have the client do a transderivational (or internal) search to recall the first time they had the kinesthetic reaction or response to the behavior or mental state they wish to change.

Step 4. Access or develop a present-day resource, or way of coping, or confidence in a present-day competence, that can be used to help in the past. Anchor this present resource or resources.

Step 5. Trigger the present-day resource(s) and the kinesthetic component related to past origins. Hold both until you get positive indications that the process is working, i.e., that the resources are being used to modify and/or correct the origins of the behavior.

Step 6. As a satisfaction check ask, "How do you know that you feel good?" or "How do you know that this residue from the past no longer bothers you?" or "How do you know that you are now experiencing your past in a positive way?"

Step 7. Future Pace. Imagine the original concern, but without the anchors. Notice what has already changed, and how this will change your future experiences. If necessary, establish an anchor that will activate the present-day resources in situations in the future where they might be needed.

The "changing personal history" approach is readily adaptable to many circumstances. It should be used only where you have knowledge that it will be useful.

13.5 Reframing and Seven-Step Reframing

Taking a picture to a frame shop and having it reframed *alters the way you look* at the picture, but does not change the content of the picture. In psychotherapy the concept of *reframing* refers to the way you help your client change their interpretation (see Therapy Model in Section 13.2) of a given stimulus so it no longer appears to be the same. Psychologically, reframing is similar to discovering how to solve a particular riddle or puzzle; you are rarely fooled again in the same way. Reframes tend to be permanent changes in perception. For example, a typical first session reframe for a client is stating at some time during the session, "You know, you've shown a lot of courage in taking care of yourself by coming to this office." In fact, you might recall the famous statement of, "It is not the things themselves which trouble us, but the opinions that we have about these things."

Straight *verbal reframing* involves a statement like the one above that changes the client's perspective with respect to a particular behavior or thought. NLP practitioners define a *complex equivalence* as two statements which are equivalent in the person's model of the world. A causal connection is often implied—two examples are:

"She's always yelling at me ... she hates me"
"He acts differently ... he's crazy."

You do a *content* or *meaning reframe* with a complex equivalence by asking, "what else could this behavior mean?" Instead of only one possible response (the statement after the ellipsis), you explore other meanings and responses with the client, i.e., choice vs certainty.

Since all behavior occurs within a given context, then you may consider reframing to also be a re-contextualization. The context has been an anchor for a particular set of responses. Every behavior is useful somewhere—identifying where is called *context reframing*. You can ask yourself and/or explore with your client the question, "In what context would this particular behavior be of value?"

In addition to verbal reframing, the NLP people have developed a seven-step reframing process whose function is to provide choices for a given stimulus. [see Bandler and Grinder (1982)] The steps follow, but again we note that facilitating a change process like this requires skill and practice.

Step 1. Identify the pattern to be changed. Ask the client to pick a symbol for this pattern so it can be easily referred to. Using a symbol like a letter or a number or a color keeps the therapy secret and avoids the reinforcement of repetition. Let's just call the behavior or pattern X.

Step 2. Establish communication with the part responsible for X. We are assuming here that the client has some internal "part" or way of thinking or reacting that controls X. You can also suggest that this communication is most easily done with the eyes closed. When you ask the following question inside, please be aware of any physical change or response in your body. The question is, "Will the part of me that runs X communicate with me in consciousness?" There may be a direct internal response as "yes" or "no" or there may be a physical response of some kind. If the last, ask the client to intensify that physical response a little bit if the response means "yes" and to diminish it if it means "no." This procedure gives the person an internal response to ratify yes/no answers.

Step 3. An essential part of this total process is to distinguish between the behavior of pattern X and the *intention* of the part that is responsible for X. Next, guide the client to ask the following question internally, "Would you be willing to let me know in consciousness what you are trying to do for me by pattern X?" (a) If they get a "yes" response, have them ask the part to go ahead and communicate its intention, knowing that this intention may be surprising to consciousness. (b) If they get a "no" response, have them reassure the part that they appreciate what it has done for them in the past and that its intention is helpful. The part may wish to communicate the reason(s) for X at some future and more appropriate time.

Step 4. Create new alternative behavior to satisfy the intention. Suggest that they have a *creative part*, a way of feeling or acting or being, like when they are solving puzzles or problems or creating new things. Then, at the *unconscious level* have the part that runs pattern X communicate its intention to the creative part, which generates many alternative and realistically appropriate ways to satisfy the intention at the present time. The part running X picks three of these alternative ways. You can ask the person to raise a finger every time an alternative is selected. [Note that the purpose of Step 4 is to provide choice.] "Let me know when you have done that."

Step 5. Give the part running X responsibility actually to choose one of these new alternative and more appropriate behaviors: have the client ask that part internally, "Are you willing to take responsibility for utilizing one or more of these new ways of taking care of yourself in appropriate contexts?" The almost invariable response is "yes" since this part has already accepted the alternative behaviors and knows that they are congruent with its intention.

Step 6. The next step is an "ecological check." Have the client ask internally, "Is there any part of me that objects to the three new alternatives?" If the answer is "yes," recycle to Step 4 above to find alternatives that are acceptable to the objecting part(s). The objecting part(s) consult with the creative part to generate acceptable behaviors. The keys to successful seven-step reframing are the separation of intent from behavior, and using the person's own internal resources to generate choices. Occasionally, you may need to suggest that the creative part can call on (imagined) outside assistance in the form of a creative "helper." If the answer to the ecological check question is "no," then go to Step 7.

Step 7. Future pace or establish that the new responses will be used. Think of a circumstance that will occur in the near future where you would normally X. What is the first thing you would see, feel, or hear that would let you know that you would soon be X-ing? Know that when you experience that signal, that you now have other, more appropriate, choices available. The future pacing response may need to be rehearsed so that the new choices become automatic.

13.6 Time-Line Therapy®

Time-Line Therapy® was developed and promulgated by James and Woodsmall (1988) and James (1989). Their book provides details of the method, case studies, and background material. It is an elegant and rapid way to change personal history and as such may be considered to be a kind of reframing. Just a brief outline of the method is given here—consult the book if it makes sense to you.

Everyone has a way of representing for themselves the progression from past to present to future events in their lives. People who read from left to right have a tendency to think of the past as being off to their left, the present in front of them or where they are, and the future off to the right. Another common representation is to have the past behind you, the present where you are, and the future in front of you. The way that you think about the sequencing of events is your timeline. To aid the facilitator in guiding someone through the process, it is helpful to find out how that person thinks about time.

Before starting the time travel two anchors are installed (touching two places on a shoulder or a hand). The first anchor is to the present. The second anchor is to present-day skills, knowledge, strengths and resources. The person is asked to think about some event or series of events earlier in their life which began the behavior or attitudes they wish to change. Maintaining the two anchors the client is then asked to somehow move or drift safely back along their timeline to *before* this critical event(s) occurred. It is best to have the client imagine that they move back into their past by being above or to the side of their timeline to give them the perspective and protection of being dissociated from the timeline itself. That is, they are *observing* rather than experiencing as they move back in time. Once they have found the event and are at a time prior to its starting, they can then (within their mind, of course, since this is a version of secret therapy) step onto their timeline, being in contact at all times with the present and their present-day resources. At this point you might say something such as:

> Having with you what you know now about yourself and your capabilities, knowledge and experience you didn't have then, notice how you can change those events and interactions to obtain the outcomes you want for yourself now. Your present self would not have responded in these ways or let you be stuck with these no-longer-needed consequences. Stay with that time and events until you are completely satisfied about the outcomes. Now, facing forward to the present, move as fast as you need to through all relevant intervening experiences, noting how they have already changed for the better for you, all the way up to the present. These changes in perceptions and feelings have also changed the way you view your future. So, move forward into your future to some significant time noticing how your life will have changed already. When you have absorbed, and are comfortable with these changes from your past into your future, you may return to the present, perhaps being surprised at how much better and more comfortable you feel. Thank you.

Of course, this script can be modified to suit your particular client. The delivery will involve significant pauses. You can directly ask for feedback and indications of progress as the person uses their timeline to help themselves. The timeline process may be repeated for other concerns. There is a variant of this work that has the client walk beside and along their timeline with the facilitator holding anchors as they are guided through the process, but with the extra power of their own kinesthetic movement.

13.7 Beliefs

Personal belief systems contain the essence of how we motivate ourselves. We absorbed these beliefs into our behaviors and they've become an almost unconscious basis for our actions. For example, believing that cancer is incurable and always involves excruciating pain and physical debilitation will control how you respond to a diagnosis of cancer. On the other hand, a deeply held belief that faith and prayer can overcome any adversity has other outcomes in terms of actions. To a large extent you are what you believe, and your perceptions are controlled by these same beliefs. Some beliefs may be directly challenged by credible authority figures in a person's life. Other beliefs may need to be made conscious before helping the person to change them for their own benefit. The ethical problem here is that some way must be found to change personal beliefs with informed consent—otherwise it would be inappropriate interference. This is a touchy and difficult area.

If you are interested in pursuing working with belief systems, read Andreas and Andreas (1989), Andreas and Andreas (1994), Bandler (1985), Andreas and Andreas (1987), and Dilts, Halbom and Smith (1990).

13.8 Submodalities and the Swish Technique

The "Swish" Technique, which is named for a change occurring as fast as you say "whsst," is based on a kind of guided visualization using submodalities. See Bandler (1985) for a brief description and Andreas and Andreas (1987) for more details.

A *modality* is a primary sense like vision or hearing or taste or touch. A *submodality* is a smaller element within each modality. Submodalities are literally the ways that our brains sort and code our experience. Within the visual modality, like making a picture in your mind, the submodalities would include: color, distance, size, depth, clarity, contrast, scope, intensity of hue, moving or static, speed of movement, aspect ratio or proportion, orientation, whether bounded or framed, tilt, and foreground/background relationship. These are ways in which you can alter an image. Although kinesthetic and auditory modalities may be used, the visual one is preferred since it is relatively easy within the mind to work with two or three visual submodalities at the same time—it is difficult to do this for kinesthetic and auditory. Musicians might find it easy to work with sounds.

The client should first be tested with respect to several visual submodalities. Ask them to visualize a picture of themselves in some *mildly* unpleasant situation. Call this the "original" picture. Have them alter this picture within their mind by: (1) making it larger and smaller; (2) moving it closer to themselves or farther away; (3) making it brighter and dimmer. Return to the original condition after each change. Then ask them about the effects of these changes. A typical response is that making the picture smaller, more distant, and dimmer reduces the mildly unpleasant feeling. It is best to work with 2–3 submodalities changing at one time as in Step 3 in the process described below.

The distinction between associated and dissociated states is important in this work. When you are *associated* with the image, you are re-living the experience in some way, e.g seeing it from your own eyes. The *dissociated* state means that you are looking *at* the image from any point of view other than your own eyes. Associated is *being in* and dissociated is *looking at*. The ideal way to recall pleasant memories is associated, and unpleasant or painful memories dissociated. Dissociation can be used for pain control, i.e., if you *watch* yourself, your body over there, having pain, you're not in your body feeling it.

The Swish Technique adapted specifically for healing purposes has four steps. (Practice this under supervision first, please.)

Step 1. *Identify Cue Picture*—This is picture #1. It is of you in your present condition with whatever ailment or emotional state you wish to change. See yourself in some full representation of that state. See this cue picture associated, i.e., be in it seeing yourself with your own eyes as perhaps in a mirror. Then, blank this image out like turning off a TV set. If it is difficult to do this associated, then it is okay to just create a #1 picture of yourself.

Step 2. *Create Outcome Picture*—This is picture #2. Create a second image of how you would look when the disease has gone into remission, disappeared, and/or you are healed. Keep adjusting this picture until you have one that is really attractive to you, one that realistically meets your needs. Seeing this outcome or "desired you" image as dissociated creates a direction for hope and change.

Step 3. *Swish*—Start with seeing picture #1 big and bright, for example. Then put a small dark image of picture #2 in the lower right-hand corner (or wherever makes sense to you). This small dark image will grow larger and brighter as picture #1 gets dimmer and smaller until picture #2 completely replaces picture #1 which has faded and dis-appeared. Blank out the images. Then "swish" this again five more times, getting faster and faster, being sure to blank out the images at the end of each run. You can even repeat the whole process five more times, until the last one just goes "phsst."

Step 4. *Test*—Now *try* to see that first picture. What happens?

The Swish Technique is a kind of behavior modification approach where the brain is programmed to replace one image or depiction of yourself with another. The repetition and speed are important so that you achieve an almost automatic replacement of how you perceive yourself. Brains can learn very rapidly.

13.9 "As If" and the Miracle Question

The power of the "As If" frame is that if you act *as if* you feel a particular way that both your emotional and physical responses appear to be the same as whatever you consider to be the "real" reactions. Tests have been carried out with skilled actors and actresses who were told to portray given emotions during a particular scene. Their physiological markers (like pulse rate, blood pressure, oxygen consumption, and stomach acid secretion) changed in the directions characteristic for relaxed, depressed, anxious, or grief-stricken people. "Pop" psychology statements like: "Smile—you'll feel better," "Laugh and the world laughs with you. Cry and you cry alone," "You need to be/act brave now," "Don't give up," and "Cheer up," appear to have a basis in fact.

A related caution is to be careful about asking people for details about traumatic experiences like: surgical operations, heart attacks, accidents, how they felt when they were first diagnosed about cancer, and a loved one's death or trauma. In recalling the experience, what is brought to life is not only the thought memories but also the physiological memories. On a trivial level, recalling a really good dinner activates the salivary glands. Singing to yourself can be detected in the vocal cords. Athletes can improve their performance by thinking through their event. Guided imagery utilitizes the same phenomenon.

The *miracle question*, which is one of the main devices used in solution-focused or solution-oriented therapy, is an effective method to activate and reinforce the *as if* model. The four books by Steve de Shazer (1985, 1988, 1991, and 1994) and the one by Miller and Berg (1995) are good resources for learning about this work. These therapists have found that if you are solution-oriented (What has worked for you this past week? Tell me what was different about the times: you were feeling good about yourself, you were not depressed, you weren't drinking or taking drugs, you were working well, you and your spouse really were communicating) rather than problem-focused (What went wrong? How depressed were you? How much did you drink? What went wrong between you and ...?), and listen attentively at the first session, that most clients will wind down their story in five to ten minutes. (If you are problem-focused, you can probably keep them describing their woes for hours.) When the client reaches this pause, it is time for the miracle question.

The *miracle question* approach was designed for people with personal behavioral problems that can be severe: de Shazer's Brief Family Therapy Center operates in inner-city Milwaukee. For someone with a life-challenging disease you would elicit information about how they have been coping and the minimal necessary information about the disease itself. The miracle question is the same for both groups. "Suppose, that after you fell asleep tonight, that some time during the night a miracle occurred. This miracle was that whatever you were concerned about before you went to sleep was completely and realistically resolved by the time you wake up tomorrow morning. This is a miracle and such things can happen. So, tell me, tomorrow morning when you wake up, what would be the first thing you would notice that would let you know that this miracle has already occurred?" The therapist assumes that change of some kind has happened. In the case of a cancer, for example, this would not be a complete remission or cure in such a short time, but indications that the remission/cure had started and was well on its way. The art of the therapist at this point is to elicit as much detail about the post-miracle changes in the person as is possible. Not only are questions asked about the client's own perceptions, but they are asked about how these changes will be noticed and obvious to everyone in their post-miracle lives. What would your husband/wife/children notice that is different? Could they see this in the way you walk/sit/move? in your face? in the things you say and the way you say them? The elicitation of post-miracle detail is an elaboration of *as if* behavior. The greater the detail in observable behaviors, the greater the likelihood of change. Please note the careful use of the word "realistically" in the miracle question formulation. Breasts do not regenerate after a mastectomy, but cancer cells can be eliminated from the body. The miracle question can be of significant utility at the right time.

13.10 Rossi's Moving Hands Model for Mind/Body Healing

E.L. Rossi has developed a simple, but sophisticated, four-step model for doing therapy. The details of the process are given in the second part of his book, *The Symptom Path to Enlightenment* (1996). The first part of this book attempts to provide via chaos theory a theoretical basis for the effectiveness of hypnotherapy. It is an altogether intriguing book. Briefly, this four-step model is:

Step 1.   Establish a kinesthetic signal that the person is ready to work on a particular concern.

Step 2.   Suggest that they can quickly do a thorough review of all *relevant* memories related to this concern.

Step 3.   Suggest that they can now quickly find realistic ways of resolving that concern.

Step 4.   Ask for a kinesthetic response to ratify that they will use these new ways in appropriate contexts.

The process uses kinesthetic responses for all four steps as a reinforcement for that step. When you think about it, these four steps incorporate the minimum number of actions required for effective change. The language that Rossi uses is carefully chosen to elicit appropriate responses at each step, and should be carefully studied. This is another example of *secret therapy*. We have adapted his model as follows for mind/body healing. [Comments for the therapist are in square brackets.]

Step 1. Readiness Signal for Inner Work.
Place your hands up with the palms facing each other about six to eight inches apart [model this], and tune into them with great sensitivity. We know the human body has a magnetic field. We don't know if you can sense this magnetic field, or if this is an exercise in the use of imagination. Let yourself begin to experience a magnetic field developing between your hands right now. Magnetic fields can attract or repel. If your inner mind is ready to work on and resolve a particular health problem right here and now, will you find your hands somehow, moving slowly towards each other all by themselves? Take your time and notice what happens.

If there is something more important that you need to focus on first, will you find your hands, somehow, moving apart?

Step 2. Accessing Relevant Aspects
[After the hands have moved close enough to touch, *or* have moved a significant distance apart, continue with the following.] Now that you know, inside, by your hand movements that you are ready to work, and your arms and hands can continue to be comfortable in those positions, will one of those hands now begin to move down slowly all by itself to signal that your inner mind and body can now review all relevant aspects of that health concern that you don't know how to deal with yet? Only one hand and arm will move down very slowly as your inner mind and body review all of the relevant aspects. And, will your hand now come to rest [in your lap, on your leg] when that review is completed?

Step 3. Incubating Current and Future Healing
Will the other hand and arm now go down slowly all by itself as your inner mind and body explore all the present and future healing possibilities? Some of these possibilities may be surprising. [Pause] How do you see yourself? How do you feel? What will you be doing when this health concern is satisfactorily resolved?

When your hand comes to rest, let your inner mind and body review how you are going to get from your present health concern to the future when you are healed. What will you have done?

Step 4. Ratifying Mind/Body Healing

When your inner mind and body know that they can continue the healing process entirely on their own throughout the day or night, and when your conscious mind knows that it can cooperate with this healing, will you find your head nodding "yes" all by itself?

And, when your conscious mind knows it can cooperate by helping you recognize when you need to take "time out" for healing, will you then become normally alert, opening your eyes, stretching, feeling so refreshed? Thank you.

In guiding someone through this process, you need to read their body language and pace them accordingly. Of course, effective guidance utilizes many pauses of different lengths. It is okay to say at some point, "And, you know just how *fast* the mind can work, do you not?"

The "moving hands" method can also be used to deal with unfinished business and internal conflicts and to find new responses. The following has been adapted from Rossi and Cheek (1988), p. 39:

Step 1. Readiness signal for inner work:

(a) Place your hands about six to eight inches apart, and with great sensitivity, tune into the real or imagined magnetic field developing between them [therapist demonstrates]. If your creative (healing) unconscious is ready to begin therapeutic work, you will experience those hands moving together all by themselves to signal "yes." [Pause. If hands do not move together, continue with the following.]

(b) But, if there is another issue that you need to explore first, you will feel those hands being pushed apart to signal "no." In that case, a question will come up in your mind that we can deal with.

Step 2. Accessing and Resolving Problems:

(a) As your unconscious mind explores the sources and important memories about [whatever problem], one of those arms will begin drifting down very slowly. [Pause. When one does begin drifting down, continue.] That arm can continue drifting down very slowly so that it will finally come to rest in your lap only when you have completed a satisfactory inner review of that problem. [Pause after arm has come down to rest in lap.]

(b) And now your other arm will begin drifting down all by itself as it explores all the therapeutic possibilities for resolving the problem in an ideal manner that is most suitable for you at this time.

(c) When your unconscious has resolved that problem in a satisfactory manner, that arm will come to rest in your lap.

Step 3. Ratifying problem-solving:

(a) Does your unconscious want to let your head nod "yes" all by itself to ratify the value of the therapeutic progress?

(b) When your unconscious and conscious minds know that they can continue to deal with that problem in a satisfactory way, you will find yourself stretching and coming completely awake as you open your eyes.

13.11 Rossi's Use of Ultradian Rhythms for Healing

Earlier we discussed the existence of ultradian rhythms (Rossi and Nimmons (1991) which are the 90–120 minute cycles that continue throughout the day and night. Milton Erickson made use of the troughs, or naturally occurring relaxed states, for hypnotic inductions. These rhythms can be shifted, as when you start a person on a relaxation period or a guided imagery session. Rossi has developed a method which is useful for mind/body healing or pain control. (For a superb demonstration of this method with a woman who had rheumatoid arthritis in her hands, see or hear the tape made of a Rossi demonstration at an Erickson Congress, Rossi (1992).)

First, obtain background about the concern, including medications, length of time, whether under a physician's care, etc. Then ask them to scale their present level of discomfort on a scale of 1 to 100. Ask them to *increase* the pain and tension and discomfort. [This is a surprising request. But, the subtle message is that if they can increase a level of discomfort, which they hitherto had considered to be involuntary and beyond their control, then this experience must be voluntarily controllable in some fashion.] "Really enjoy that nice tension. ... Can you change it to a different kind or quality? ... Now, move it to another part of your body, and make it even worse. ... Don't lose that pain/discomfort yet. ... How does it feel, what are the sensations, in the different areas? ... Hang onto it as much as you can. [Remember to use lots of ratifying and exaggeration. Pay attention to body language, particularly changes of expression.] Let's see if your body is really becoming pain/discomfort free, or if that little sucker wants to stick up its head and play. [Look for sensory transformations, particularly while the symptom is strong. Remember that your unspoken expectation is that there will be change.] As you explore, funny, creative, or unusual things may happen—perhaps spontaneous movements or sensations may occur. [This is seeding an expectation for change.] ... How will this work of pain/discomfort control continue ... perhaps, all by itself? ... If the unconscious, your inner mind/body, can continue this healing and changing work all on its own, will your eyes flutter/ a finger move/a hand rise or fall? [When this ideomotor signal occurs, wait until they have consolidated the work. Give them lots of time. Respond to minimal cues of activity with a single word—yes, aha, okay, good—or a simple phrase—more of that, and continuing, very fine, keep that going, stay with that a bit longer—to ratify the changes and to maintain contact and rapport with them.] And, now, on that scale of 1 to 100, where is that discomfort? ... Good. [Ratify *any* change, no matter how small, which will typically be to a lower number.] When you know, when your inner mind/body really knows how this work of healing and change will continue, you can return here fully. Thank you. [The client may wish to process what has occurred for them—facilitate this. Also, check for any unfinished business or loose ends at the completion of this work, "Anything else come up that I can help you with at this time?" or "Anything else going on?"]

This process for healing or pain/discomfort control requires that you pay extraordinary attention to the client so that you can guide them with minimal statements. Give them lots of time for this inner work. From time to time it is useful to say something like, "If there is something I need to know to help you, you can tell me in a word or two or a short sentence. Thank you." This process does not involve a formal trance induction. However, when a person does the intense inner work involved, they naturally go into a trance state and usually close their eyes unsolicited at the beginning. You should not attempt to do this work unless you have had sufficient training in hypnotherapeutic work.

13.12 Ideomotor Finger Signaling

Automatic or non-volitional movements are called *ideomotor* or *ideodynamic*. They have been used for some time (Rossi and Cheek, 1988; Cheek, 1994) to elicit responses from the inner or unconscious mind. The parlor games of the Ouija board and automatic writing involve ideomotor movements, i.e., micromuscular movements that are apparently not under conscious control. The Chevreul pendulum, a light weight hanging from a thread or fine chain, has been used to indicate responses to questions. These questions are designed to obtain three responses: "yes," "no," and "I'm not ready to answer now." [The third response used to be "maybe," until it was recognized just how lazy the inner mind is, i.e., this was the most frequent answer!] In the context of the present book, ideomotor signals are used for two purposes: (1) a rapid way to resolve unfinished business; and (2) a way, taught to clients, to query their own mind/body about what is going on in their body. Both of these uses will be illustrated.

I prefer to use ideomotor finger signaling rather than the Chevreul pendulum. Finger responses are easier to read and more rapid than the pendulum. Ask the client to use three fingers on one hand. Then, ask their inner mind to select the "yes" finger, and ratify this by a number of questions whose obvious answer is "yes." Then do the same for a "no" finger. Finally, ask them to indicate the "I'm not ready to answer now finger." Ask a variety of questions to check these responses. Remember that voluntary finger movements will be smooth and usually large. By contrast, involuntary movements (presumably controlled by the inner or unconscious mind) are jerky, hesitant, and small. Most clients will close their eyes and go into a light trance for this process without formal eye-closure or trance-inducing instructions.

The process for dealing with unfinished business is like the game of *twenty questions*. It also follows Rossi's four-step model. First, elicit willingness to work. Second, have the client search and go back to the time when the unfinished business was relevant. Third, state that, "Would it be okay with your present knowledge of yourself and those events, to complete that business in a satisfactory manner?" If "yes," go on; if "no," ask if there is something else needed to resolve the issue, and then proceed to do that. Finally, you might say, "Now that that has been resolved satisfactorily, would it be okay to return to the present?" A session like this takes 15–20 min with skillful questioning. See the references cited above and Battino and South (1999) for further study.

Clients are taught how to relax and meditate. In these semi-conscious states they can ask their own fingers yes/no questions about what is going on in their bodies. This is a *programmed* meditation since the person has mentally prepared a particular enquiry of their own body. People who have cancer or are in remission get very concerned about any new pains or discomforts or sensations. Is this pain in the back a "normal" back stress pain, or does it signal a spread of the cancer? We assume that there is a body/mind intelligence which can be accessed via ideomotor finger signaling. "Should I see the doctor about this?" is a common question. This kind of body-questioning can also be done by the therapist. The procedure takes practice to make it easy to use.

13.13 Metaphors for Healing
Everyone likes a good story, particularly one with a happy ending. The literature on serious diseases is full of stories of remarkable or miraculous recoveries. There are: Norman Cousins' recovery from ankylosing spondilitis (1979, 1981); Anthony Sattilaro's recovery from cancer (1982); Wendy Williams' true stories of exceptional cancer patients who fought back with hope (1990); Rachel Naomi Remen's lifelong struggle with Crohn's disease (1996); and all of the stories in Bernie Siegél's books (1986, 1989, 1993, 1998), to mention a few. In fact, one of the things that makes Bernie Siegel's presentations so powerful is that all of the stories he tells are about people facing adversity with courage and hope, and who

frequently "beat the odds." These personal stories provide encouragement, hope, and models for action. Many of these stories are highly specific about what it was that led the person to health, be it laughter, special diets, non-conventional treatments, changes in lifestyle, or combinations of the above. The common denominator may not be explicit, but it is: if *one* person can reverse the progress of a serious disease and be cured (despite conventional prognoses), then we *all* have the *potential* and the capability of achieving similar success. These success stories reinforce efforts to fight the disease, to have hope, and to believe in a healthy future. The knowledge that many succumb despite valiant efforts appears to be minimized, for we are individual, and have a sense of our own uniqueness—in that sense, we are all exceptional. Cindy's story (Section 9.6) is a case in point: she walked out of a Hospice facility after seventy-one days, went back to her life and full-time employment, only to succumb quickly to a reoccurrence one and one-half years later. But, she did walk out of Hospice, and she enjoyed life for much longer than anyone predicted. There are many heroines and heroes on which to model action, and abiding hope. Stories are powerful and should be part of your repertoire.

There is a large literature on metaphor, which is defined as, "A figure of speech in which a word or phrase literally denoting one kind of object or idea is used in place of another by way of suggesting a likeness or analogy between them." Gordon's book (1978) systematically discusses the structure and use of metaphor for psychotherapeutic work. Lankton and Lankton (1983, pp. 245–311) give a thorough and systematic approach to the use of metaphor in psychotherapy and hypnotherapy. Barker (1985) has written a solid book on the use of metaphor in psychotherapy with many examples for different clients. There are three chapters in Battino and South (1999, pp. 297–356) on basic metaphor, advanced metaphor, and the arts as hypnotherapeutic metaphors.

When you are working with someone, stories that are real, i.e., based on people you know, are probably the most powerful. You can also relate stories of people you have read about, or heard others tell about. Books like Barker's (1985) contain many metaphors that can be *adapted* to a particular person and situation. The metaphor should be isomorphic or parallel to the person's experiences, which is a kind of pacing. Metaphors can be integrated within a particular guided imagery session, in addition to using the specific image for that person. People are more receptive to metaphors when they are in a relaxed or trance state. In fact, the telling of a story generally results in a light trance where attention is fixated. As in effective guided imagery work, the metaphor needs to be matched to the person. Guided imagery work is really a special adaptation of metaphoric work, where the particular image represents powerful healing forces.

13.14 Summary

This chapter has covered a variety of methods of dealing with unfinished business. This is a significant part of the healing process because energy tied up in these old patterns is not available for healing in the present. A caution repeated at several places in this chapter is that it takes a skilled psychotherapist or helping-practitioner to use most of the approaches herein. Training is, of course, available. It is also useful for the facilitator to have worked through their own unfinished business!

Chapter 14

Bonding Approaches for Healing

14.1 Introduction

The term "bonding" has been used in the context of male and female bonding and parent/child bonding. This means that there is some special connection or "bond" between one male and another, or one female and another. These bonds come about from growing up in a family and the tight connections that develop between family members due to the many shared experiences. In particular, these experiences usually involve some kinesthetic component: nursing between mother and baby; children sitting on laps for reading; walking, holding hands with children; hugging, carrying, and holding; and intimate activities. There is an especially powerful aspect to these physical connections. Bonding with a client makes use of a physical anchor—hand-holding. For bonding with a client it is, of course, necessary to have first established a sense of rapport and trust with them. So, these bonding approaches are generally not done in the first or second session.

In this chapter we will present the background for two kinds of bonding approaches, and also scripts for two sessions. The first kind of bonding is with the therapist who serves as a conduit for transferring healing resources from themself, and also from whatever sources within the client's world for which the therapist can serve as a passive conduit. The second kind of bonding involves a "fusion" with a projected healthy version of the client from their future or past. A variation is to imagine that a special healer connects with the client through the kinesthetic anchor with the therapist. The purpose of the physical anchor is to solidify and reinforce the experience. Both approaches are explained separately and in detail.

14.2 Bonding for Healing

Although the term "bonding" has been generally used in the context of male and female bonding, I use it for an approach in which I "bond" with the client, and serve as the conduit for giving them whatever healing or change resources they need via the bonding anchor—this anchor is generally holding one or both hands. (In the framework of this book, bonding is limited to healing. It can also be used for psychotherapy.) First, it is necessary to attain the trust of the client. Next, it is important to project in some congruent manner your deeply held belief that the connection through contact with you has the power to enhance and educate their own immune and healing systems. (For psychotherapy, the conviction is that they will be able to learn viable solutions through the contact, and that they will also be able to access their own innate resources.) The people I work with know my deep conviction that *there is always hope*, and that *I believe in miracles*. They also know of my belief that *significant change can occur rapidly*. Sit comfortably, and close enough to your client to hold one or both of their hands, but where your hand and the contact is passive. Always ask for permission for this physical contact.

As an example of how this works, the following transcript is provided. It is delivered using hypnotic language and voice control, but without a formal induction. This particular transcript was developed for a client with cancer. Prior to the delivery there will have been some preparatory informational work concerning psychoneuroimmunology, the nature of the immune system, and the effect of cancer on it. Generally, there is also some discussion about the nature and power of mind/body interactions. Be sure to put in many pauses, allowing the listener to fill in details, and to do whatever internal work they need to do.

Healing through Bonding Script

You should know that through contact with my hand you are in touch with the present, and also with all of your strengths and experience and knowledge. By the amount of pressure you put on my hand, you can control just how much strength and healing power you need from and through me at any moment. Please know that you can take as much as you need through me, for I am only a conduit, a channel for what you need, now. My body and my immune system are in very good working order, and they can serve as patterns for enhancing and strengthening your own immune system.

Just continue to relax, breathing easily and calmly. That's right, softly, and easily, and gently. Paying attention to your breathing as you relax even more, feeling the support of that chair and your feet on the floor, and the comfort of contact with my hand. Just breathing in, and out. Feeling the air move in, expanding your chest, belly rising. And, then, softly out, those muscles relaxing, becoming calmer, being aware of holding my hand, holding on, holding onto, having your own firm grasp, being connected, too, in touch, being. Good. Thank you. And, through that hand you can begin to sense the healing power and healing knowledge that is moving into your body, can you not? Just simply and naturally, flowing, moving, becoming, being. Hand to hand, hand in hand, mind to mind, spirit to spirit, the knowledge, the ability, moving atom to atom, molecule to molecule, nerve cell to nerve cell, teaching, learning, becoming even stronger. There may be a warmth, a tingling, a coolness, as this knowledge and ability moves into your body, wherever it is needed. That's right. Good.

You know—I don't know exactly where those cancer cells are, and we don't need to know consciously—yet your body knows in some deep way. In some deep internal way, where the healing work is to be done, and that's okay, isn't it? So just feel that healing power, that healing strength, that healing knowledge, move into you, through this contact, moving through your body, moving precisely and exactly to just those places where it is needed at this time. And, that healing power, that healing knowledge, just somehow, eliminates, eradicates, removes, destroys, obliterates, gets rid of the cells that shouldn't be there. One at a time, here and there. Then, faster, working on groups of those cells at a time, faster and faster, just as fast as your body can accommodate the elimination, the eradication, of those cells, the cleaning up of the debris. You may even feel a special warmth or tingling or even a mild itching in the parts of your body where this work is going on. Continuing to rest and relax. Breathing calmly and slowly, easily. That's right. Just as fast as your body can do that healing, right now. A deep inner sense of where the healing is needed, where it is going on, where it will continue. Yes. Yes.

And, at the same time, you know that your own immune system is getting stronger. Through the contact, your immune system is strengthening and learning just what to do and how to do it, more effectively, more efficiently, more powerfully, cell by cell, part of cell by part of cell, molecule by molecule, the learning continuing until your own immune system does this work by itself, stronger and stronger, faster and faster, healing, healthy, normally, naturally, easily, automatically. That's right, isn't it? Simply and easily. Just one cell at a time, as fast as possible.

At the same time, your body is rebuilding, reconstructing, fixing, correcting, regenerating, rejuvenating. Becoming healthier and healthier, stronger, naturally, easily. And this rebuilding, strengthening, will continue and continue.

And, you know that this ability, this knowledge, this strength, is now part of you, deeply imprinted in every molecule, every part of every cell, every cell, every nerve and nerve ending, and every tissue, just part of your central core, your way of living, your way of being. All yours, now, and whenever you need it, going on and on automatically. At any time during the day you can take a few minutes, pay attention to your breathing, and let this healing power move through you, doing its work, and strengthening your own internal healing powers, so they can continue on their own. Becoming part of you, being, already, already there. Slowly, and simply, and easily, and naturally. Yes. Yes. Yes. ... And, when you are ready, you can return to this room, here and now, feeling ever so relaxed and refreshed and, somehow, full of energy. Thank you.

14.3 Healing through Fusion

The fusion approach is somewhat similar to the bonding approach. The main difference is that the client obtains healing knowledge and ability from a *projected healing image of themselves*. The preparatory information again includes a discussion of psychoneuroimmunology, the nature of the immune system, and the power of mind/body interactions. It is explained that, *for whatever reason*, their immune system was caught unprepared and was overwhelmed by the cancer cells. Since aberrant or cancerous cells are being produced (from whatever causes) in us all of the time, our immune systems have been developed to rid the body of these irregular cells whose only function seems to be rapid reproduction. At some time in the past their body was perfectly capable of destroying those cancerous cells, and did so regularly and automatically. They can also imagine that at some time in the future that their immune system has cleansed their body of cancer, and is strong enough to continue to do so. The client is given the choice of being helped by their past perfectly functioning body, or the cured healthy one from the future, although there is more certainty in using the past healthy body.

It is useful to begin by establishing two anchors: one for contact with the present and the support of the therapist (holding a hand works well for this); and one for contact with their present day resources, knowledge, and strengths (this second anchor can be touching a knuckle once these resources have been accessed). The following transcript was also developed for a client with cancer, but may be adapted to other diseases or emotional difficulties. Be sure that your delivery uses many pauses as they will need time to develop and assimilate the images.

Healing through Fusion Script
You should know my contact with you, this light touch, keeps you in touch with the present and with whatever support I can give you. Even though these are difficult times for you, we did talk earlier about some recent times when you really felt good about yourself, aware of a strong sense of control and understanding, even a sense of peace. Think about those times now, really get into that sense of "right now I'm feeling okay." That's right. [Set the second anchor when you can tell that they have accessed this resource state.]

Continue to breathe easily and simply and normally. Just one breath at a time, feeling each breath come in, fill your lungs, and gently move out. A clearing and cleansing breath, softly, easily, becoming even more comfortable, enjoying this peaceful time.

You can imagine, now, that somewhere in front of you is that younger you, the you whose immune system is functioning normally, and automatically, and at peak efficiency. [Usually, they will have closed their eyes by this time, but this is not necessary.] As you look at your younger self, you can tell, you really know just by the way she is standing there, the way she moves and smiles, her stance, her attitude, that she is well and healthy, and that her immune system is strong and powerful.

As you continue to observe your younger healthy self, you notice that she is aware of you, here, now. She smiles, and slowly walks towards you. Then she reaches out and touches you, hand to hand, making firm contact. And you can feel her presence, can you not? Her strength, and her health, and her vitality ... really your vitality. And, now, an interesting thing begins to happen. Through your contact with her, hand to hand, touching, she starts to transmit from her body to yours the strength, and the knowledge, and the capability, and the effectiveness of her immune system. It is becoming, becomes your immune system. Educating, enhancing, strengthening yours. Atom by atom, molecule by molecule, part of cell by part of cell, cell by cell, tissue by tissue, organ by organ, bone by bone, fluid by fluid, nerve by nerve. And you may even feel, now, a warmth, a tingling, some mild electrical currents, as this knowledge, this strength, from you to you, moves and suffuses through your body, permanently fusing, becoming one with your essence, and all your body parts and functions. Just feel these changes, now, as they become an integral, an integrated, a permanent part of you. So they can work and work and continue to work for you, within you, now, this evening, tonight, tomorrow, the next day and the next days, for as long as you need this extra help ... ...

And, now, within your mind, you can imagine and feel this younger you hugging you, merging with you, her knowledge and strength and abilities are yours. Just fusing with you, being you, together, stronger, healthier, whole. Feeling her strength within you. You are you, yourself, again, again. What have you gained, again? And, you thank her for this gift, from her to you, from you to you.

You know the mind is remarkable, your mind/body is remarkable, full of wonders, and any time you need this extra boost from yourself, you can just find a quiet place, pay attention to your breathing, and go right to this time, her presence, and her gift, feeling it, feeling it filling you again, fusing, merging, together. Yes. Yes. Yes. ...

Thank you for letting me share this time with you. And, when you are ready, you can return to this room, here and now, feeling ever so refreshed and energized. Yes. Thank you.

14.4 Summary

These approaches presuppose that the person already has within themself all of the knowledge and resources and neuro-biological-physiological capabilities they need to bring about meaningful physical changes in their body, such as reducing and even eliminating tumors and cancerous cells and tissues. This presupposition builds upon the fact that these changes are the actual functions of a normal and healthy and efficient immune system which had kept their body free of cancer until the time when these aberrant cells somehow overwhelmed the body's own natural and normal defense systems. It is important to stress the fact that their body already possesses the necessary mechanisms to rid the body of cancer, but that these mechanisms need to be energized and reinforced. The bonding and fusion approaches are designed for this purpose. It is also always important to emphasize that these imagery-based approaches are meant to complement standard medicine and *not* to replace it. Clients should be encouraged to use every means at their disposal to help themselves and to avoid doing just one thing to the exclusion of all others (unfortunately, some practitioners of alternative/complementary and traditional treatments urge exclusivity).

Although we have presented the bonding and fusion approaches separately, it is possible to combine them and do them together as a single seamless process. When I do them together, I start with the bonding approach and hold one of the client's hands. At the conclusion of the bonding part, I just move into suggesting that the client see/visualize/sense their younger and healthier and robust self in front of them, and then go through the fusion process. The projected self will (within the client's mind) move closer to them and then hold their other hand. I continue (passively) holding one hand throughout the entire process. To reinforce closure and mark the end of the process, I usually give their hand a gentle squeeze before disengaging. I like to give people the choice of doing either process separately or combined after briefly describing them.

Part Three

Related Alternative Approaches

Chapter 15

Journaling/Structured Writing/
Videotapes/Art Therapy/Ceremonies

15.1 Introduction

Guided imagery and psychotherapy-based approaches are just two of many and varied procedures that are helpful to people who have life-challenging diseases. There are a number of adjunctive things that people can do to help them during the particularly stressful times of diagnosis, treatments, hospitalizations, and in-between periods. Bernie Siegel's third book (1993) is entitled *How To Live Between Office Visits*. What do you do with all that in-between time? Are there things that ease the day, or add meaning to your life? In this chapter a number of useful activities are discussed. The next chapter is devoted to the presentation of a large number and variety of coping skills.

15.2 Journaling

Many people have kept a daily diary at some point in their lives. I did this for several years as a teenager. This practice was more prevalent years ago than at the present time. Sometimes journals are kept for specific purposes such as: (1) recording details of a vacation trip; (2) listing amounts and types of all food ingested; (3) listing all physical activity; (4) noting the time, intensity, location, and quality of pain; and (5) noting all medications. But, mostly journals are kept as a personal log of feelings, ideas, observations, and activities.

A diagnosis of cancer, or some other life-challenging disease, immediately raises thoughts of mortality and the meaning of one's life. "What is it all about?" "Why me?" "Why now?" "Why this particular disease?" Lots and lots of questions bedevil the person. It almost seems like an unfair double tragedy to be forced prematurely into considering these questions at a time of great emotional and physical distress. The big "Why" questions need time and undistracted thinking to work through. In the immediacy of a diagnosis and treatment, there is no leisure for serious thought.

This is where the practice of regularly writing in a journal can be helpful. A person with a life-challenging disease is considered by many to be "abnormal" in the sense of not being in a normal healthy state. Many friends and relatives find it awkward to communicate with them. Some people just won't or can't listen. There are others who do—you can usually rely on ministers and psychotherapists. But, you can write anything as often as you wish in your private journal. No one judges what is written—the deepest innermost thoughts are safe. Most people find journaling to be cathartic. If it is difficult to write, an alternative is to audiotape a journal. Many people include drawings in their journals. A single tape may be re-used as needed or erased for security.

Consider journaling in a locked diary as a way to record and communicate.

15.3 Structured Writing—A Workbook for People who have Cancer

Structured writing is different from keeping a journal or a diary. The person involved is asked to answer in writing specific questions that are designed to help them solve a particular problem or deal with a specific condition. There is an extensive literature in this area, and we cite only four general references (Esterling, L'Abate, Murray, & Pennebaker, 1999; L'Abate 1992; L'Abate 1997; Pennebaker 1997) for those who are interested in studying the field in more detail. L'Abate, for example, has a Web site (www.mentalhealthhelp.com) with some ninety different workbooks for use by professionals that were developed for helping mental health clients deal with specific difficulties by writing about them in a prescribed manner. There is much evidence in the literature that writing about traumatic events helps the writer resolve them and/or minimize the impact on their lives. This kind of writing has also been called "distance writing." Distance writing can be open-ended, focused, guided, and programmed. Other dimensions for writing involve: goals (prescriptive or cathartic), content (traumatic to trivial), level of abstraction (concrete to abstract), and specificity (specific to general). (See the references cited above for more details.)

To give the reader some sense about how this may work for someone who has a life-challenging disease, this section presents a "workbook" for anyone who has been diagnosed with cancer. No systematic evaluation has yet been done of this workbook, but it has been developed with feedback and commentary by a number of people who have different kinds of cancer. Although the following workbook was initially developed with people who have cancer, it can probably be used without change, or only minor changes in wording, for a number of other serious diseases like AIDS, diabetes, and many of the chronic neurological diseases. First, there are commentary and instructions for the person who administers the workbook. Then, there is the workbook itself with instructions for the person using it. The workbook should be administered by someone in one of the helping professions. The workbook may be freely copied and used by any helping professional, but I would appreciate receiving feedback on its utility and improvement.

Instructions for the Helping Professional who Administers the Workbook for People who have Cancer

This workbook for people who have any kind of cancer was developed with the inspiration and guidance of Luciano L'Abate. Several references about workbooks designed to help people with mental health concerns and about the general subject are at the end of these instructions. You should have established rapport and a good working relationship with the person before suggesting that they take the workbook home with them to answer the questions. It should be emphasized that what is written in the workbook is *private*, and that the choice for sharing any portion of what is written with others is solely that of the writer. *If* the person chooses to share what they have written with you, then this will be quite useful to both of you in your work together. But, the choice is theirs.

References

Esterling, B.A., L'Abate, L., Murray, E.J., & Pennebaker, J.W. (1999). Empirical Foundations for Writing in Prevention and Psychotherapy: Mental and Physical Health Outcomes. *Clinical Psychology Review, 19, pp. 79–96.*

L'Abate, L. (1992). *Programmed Writing: A Self-administered Approach for Interventions with Individuals, Couples, and Families.* Pacific Grove, CA: Brooks/Cole.

L'Abate, L. (1997). Distance Writing and Computer-assisted Training. In S.R. Sauber (Ed), *Managed Mental Health Care: Major Diagnostic and Treatment Approaches*. (pp. 133–163). Bristol, PA: Brunner/Mazel.

Pennebaker, J.W. (1997). *Opening Up: The Healing Power of Confiding in Others*. New York: Guildford.

Workbook for People who have Cancer

The questions in this workbook have been designed to help you cope with a diagnosis of cancer, and with its treatment. Please find a quiet time and place to do this writing over a period of successive days. What you write is personal and should be kept private. It is your decision about sharing any part of this, or all of it, with someone you trust. If you need more than the allotted space, please continue your responses on the back of the paper or on separate sheets. There are no "correct" responses—whatever you write is the right thing for you. Take whatever time you need to respond. You should know that a number of research studies have shown that the very act of writing responses to the kinds of questions in this workbook have been helpful in resolving painful concerns.

1. Use the following space to respond to these three related questions. You may not be able to answer them with any certainty—in that case, you may have a guess or a theory about how to answer the questions.

a. Why is this happening to me (as opposed to someone else)?

b. Why is this happening to me at this particular time of my life?

c. Why do I have this particular kind of cancer?

2. Do you know, or do you have a theory, or can you guess as to why at this particular time you are doing better, or worse, or staying the same?

3. What ways of taking care of yourself are you waiting to explore? (These can be things like: second or third opinions, more research on available medical treatments, alternative or complementary treatments, support groups, support networks, or personal things like counseling/psychotherapy.)

4. What is stopping you from exploring the options in (3) now? What resources do you need to be able to do whatever is necessary to help yourself in (3)?

5. This question has to do with being able to communicate openly about your condition and your feelings about this condition with the people in your life who care. Think carefully about who you can talk to about the following items, listing *specific* people in each row (for example, you may write in the name of a particular cousin in the row for relatives). For your guidance there are a number of general categories of people listed in the first column. In each box put a "+" if you would feel comfortable talking with them about that item, a "−" if this would be a mistake and they would be unresponsive, and a "?" if you are unsure of their responsiveness. Feel free to write additional comments in each box. Where there is more than one person in a category, such as friends, please list them separately.

People	Physical Feelings	Emotional Feelings	Fears	Treatments	Information	Fun and Relaxation
Spouse						
Children						
Parents						
Relatives						
Friends						
Doctors						
Counselor						
God						
Minister						
People at Work						
Support Group						

6. Take some time to write about your fears for yourself, your family, and your future.

7. Take some time to write about your hopes and dreams, and what it is you would like to do with the remainder of your life.

What are the things that you always wanted to do? Which of them can you do now? As your health improves, what are the things that you would be sure to do?

8. Write about your feelings about surgery, radiation, and chemotherapy.

9. Some surgery (like mastectomies and prostatectomies) involves the loss of body parts, particularly those that are related to body- and self-image. Please use this space to write about your feelings concerning such surgery, if you have undergone any.

10. Write about your feelings about being in a hospital.

11. Write about your feelings about dealing with medical personnel.

12. Write about what frustrates you about having cancer.

13. It is not unusual for people who have been diagnosed with cancer to have the seemingly paradoxical reaction of considering the cancer to be a "blessing" in some way. What things have you learned about yourself and about the people around you that are beneficial to you?

14. How has having the cancer changed your spiritual life?

15. Knowing what you know now about your life, if you could, how would you have lived differently? That is, what would you change about your past life?

16. Knowing what you know now about your life, what things will you do differently starting right now?

17. Sometimes opportunities for saying things to people just bypass us. Are there significant people in your past that you never had a chance to tell what was really on your mind? Write what you would have told them if you had the chance. (These people may be living or dead.)

18. This is related to (17). Write out what things for your spouse and children (or specific others) you want to: (a) have them know; (b) leave them (personal items or thoughts); and (c) say to them. You may wish to share these writings with them now, later, leave for them, or continue to keep private.

19. Although this is a trying time, it is always wise to take care of certain "mechanical" things like wills, living wills, durable power of attorney for health, financial matters, and funeral arrangements as soon as possible. Most people make these arrangements when they are well and not faced with difficult times. Once taken care of, you no longer need to be concerned about them. If you have not already done so, make appointments to take care of these items. This space would also be a good place to write about your feelings about these items. (*Note*: This item may be difficult to handle at this time, and you may wish to put it off for a while and/or discuss it with someone you trust. The author of this workbook and his wife are both in good health and attended to these items many years ago, just so there would be no surprises or difficulties for their children. They also regularly review these items. But, please respond only to this item when you feel comfortable about doing so.)

20. Write about anything else that concerns you at this time. This is *your private* journal and you can write whatever you wish.

15.4 Structured Writing—A Workbook for Grieving

Pennebaker has two sections in his book that relate to research on the grieving process (1997, pp. 20–25, 73–88). His work is related to the use of structured writing to speed up the grieving process. One of life's major traumas is the death of a spouse. Pennebaker and his co-workers found that the more that people talked about the death of their spouse, the fewer health problems they reported having. When asked, survivors who were the healthiest emphasized the value of talking and acknowledging the pain. Two findings surprised the researchers: "First, those who didn't talk about the death often obsessed or ruminated about it. That is, people who talked about their spouse's deaths tended not to think about the death as much as those who inhibited talking. Second, ruminating about the death was correlated with poor physical health." They also found that the more people prayed about their deceased spouses, the healthier they were. Prayer seems to be a form of disclosure or confiding.

There appear to be stages in the grieving process, but they are not all agreed upon. One such three-part staging involves denial, working through, and completion. Wortman and Silver (1989) have written about the myths of coping with loss. They concluded that there are four primary coping styles that follow irrevocable loss. Almost half of the people do not experience intense anxiety, depression, or grief after the loss. They seem to roll with the punches and are psychologically well-adjusted. However, 18% are classified as chronic grievers whose distress and depression may be evident years after the loss. About 30% evolve in their feelings through stages: immediately after the trauma they are distressed and depressed, but after various lengths of time they eventually return to normal levels of well-being. Only 2% appeared well-adjusted immediately after the trauma, but were distressed one year later. Pennebaker concludes that it may be possible to speed up the coping process for about 50% of grievers. He writes:

> Although writing about ongoing crises is clearly helpful for many, the effect is neither instantaneous nor permanent.... If you are currently facing a major crisis in your life, do not expect writing to make your life wonderful.... The intense pain associated with traumas often goes away in stages. Usually, the most intense intrusive thoughts surrounding major traumas diminish significantly by about a year and a half.

Finally, Pennebaker adds the "usual admonitions":

> The ways you write or talk about upsetting experiences are important. In your writing, explore your deepest thoughts and feelings in a self-reflective way. Set aside a specific time and location to write continuously. If you talk to someone else, it helps if the person is objective and not personally involved. Don't be surprised if you feel somewhat sad or depressed immediately after writing. The work of self-reflection can sometimes be painful even if the benefits are clear.

Writing for grieving is in two parts. The first involves setting aside time to write continuously about your deepest thoughts and feelings for twenty to thirty minutes for several days. Then, return to this style of writing periodically, perhaps once a month, as you feel the need to put your thoughts down. The second part involves the structured writing in the following workbook. (There are some similar elements to the one in the last section.) If you write for yourself, that is, you do not intend on showing what you have written to anyone else, then the writing is more effective since you can be more honest and open. It may be weeks or months before you feel comfortable in doing personal writing or answering the questions in the workbook. Write in your own way and at your own pace and in your own time.

Workbook for Grieving
The questions in this workbook have been designed to help you cope with a traumatic loss. Please find a quiet time and place to do this writing over a period of successive days. What you write is personal and should be kept private. It is your decision about sharing any part of this, or all of it, with someone you trust. If you need more than the allotted space, please continue your responses on the back of the paper or on separate sheets. There are no "correct" responses—whatever you write is the right thing for you. Take whatever time you need to respond. You should know that a number of research studies have shown that the very act of writing responses to the kinds of questions in this workbook have been beneficial for both physical and mental health.

1. Write in detail about the good times you had with the person whose loss you are grieving.

2. Write about losses that you shared and experienced together.

3. What special personal characteristics will see you through this time?

4. What are your special strengths?

5. What ways of taking care of yourself are you willing to explore at this time? How will you overcome things that are in the way of taking care of yourself?

6. What is different about the times when you are able to function normally? How can you extend those times?

7. Who can you communicate with openly about your loss and your feelings? Think carefully about who you can talk to about the items in the table, listing *specific* people in each row (for example, in the row marked relatives you might list a particular cousin). (You can add more rows if needed.) Mark boxes with a "+" if you feel comfortable talking with them about that item, a "−" if this is a mistake and they would be unresponsive or unhelpful, and a "?" if you are unsure about their responsiveness. You may write additional comments in each box.

People	Physical Feelings	Emotional Feelings	Fears	Memories	Loneliness	Hopes and Dreams
Spouse						
Children						
Parents						
Relatives						
Friends						
Doctors						
Counselor						
God						
Minister						
People at Work						
Support Group						

8. Write about fears for yourself, for your family, for your future.

9. Write about your hopes and dreams, and what it is you would like to do with the rest of your life. What are the things that you always wanted to do? When will you do them?

10. Write about how this loss has changed your life. How do you plan to adapt to or overcome these changes and go on with your life?

11. How has this loss affected your spiritual life?

12. How has this loss affected your social life? Relationships with your family? Friends? Acquaintances? Fellow workers?

13. Sometimes opportunities to say things to people bypass us. Are there significant people in your past that you never had a chance to tell what was really on your mind? Write what you would have told them if you had the chance. The people you write to in this workbook may be gone or still alive.

14. Use the following space to write about anything else that concerns you at this time. This is *your private* journal and you can write whatever you wish.

15.5 Structured Writing—A Workbook for Care-Givers

Care-givers are the unsung heroes and heroines of taking care of loved ones who have life-challenging diseases. Bernie Siegel has commented about families visiting his office—he observed that the person who appeared to be under the least stress was the person with the active ailment. She knew what was wrong within her body, and had already come to terms with it in some way. It was her family who were worried and tense and anxious, not knowing what to expect or how to cope. Who cares for the care-givers; who helps the helpers? Taking care of someone you love through the months and years of cancer or the years of Alzheimer's disease is exceedingly stressful. Yet, somehow, people call on hidden reserves of energy and strength and compassion to survive these ordeals. There are many support groups for people with named diseases, but many fewer for care-givers.

This workbook has been designed specifically for care-givers, to lead them through a series of writings that provide an outlet for all of those unexpressed inner feelings and questions and tensions. Again, keeping the writing private makes it easier to "write from the heart." Caregivers, like survivors, need to let go of the regrets of the past and the fear of the future and learn to live in the present—one day at a time. Some themes which arise may become the basis for discussions with a trusted person. There are obvious similarities between this workbook and the two previous ones in this chapter.

Workbook for Care-Givers

The questions in this workbook have been designed to help you as a care-giver cope with the stress of being a care-giver. Please find a quiet time and place to do this writing over a period of successive days. What you write is personal and should be kept private. It is your decision about sharing any part of this, or all of it, with someone you trust. If you need more than the allotted space, please continue your responses on the back of the paper or on separate sheets. There are no "correct" responses—whatever you write is the right thing for you. Take whatever time you need to respond. You should know that a number of research studies have shown that the very act of writing responses to the kinds of questions in this workbook have been beneficial for both physical and mental health. This process is most helpful when you "write from the heart."

1. The following three questions are related. You may not be able to answer them with certainty—in that case, you may have a guess or a theory about how to answer these questions.
a. Why is this happening to the person I love (as opposed to someone else)?
b. Why is this happening to him/her at this particular time?
c. Why does he/she have this particular disease (as opposed to a different one)?

2. Do you know, or do you have a theory, or can you guess why he/she is doing better, or worse, or staying the same at this time?

3. Write in detail about the good times you had with the person for whom you are caring.

4. Write about special memories or experiences the two of you have shared.

5. Write about losses that you shared and experienced together.

6. What special personal characteristics will see you through this time?

7. What are your special strengths?

8. What additional ways of taking care of yourself are you willing to explore at this time? How will you overcome things that are in the way of taking care of yourself?

9. What are ways you can share the work of caring? Who can help? Can you set up a network of helpers or have someone do this for you?

10. It is not unusual to feel anger and frustration, sometimes about the person for whom you are caring. There can even be occasional thoughts about wishing it were all over already. If you are experiencing any of these things, here is a private place to write.

11. Write about fears for yourself, for your family, for your future.

12. Write about how these circumstances have changed your life. How do you plan to adapt to or overcome these changes and go on with your life?

13. How have these circumstances affected your spiritual life?

14. How has your involvement with care-giving affected your relationship with the person you are caring for? Relationships with your family? Friends? Acquaintances? Social life? Work life?

15. Are there things you would like to tell the person you are caring for at this time? When will you make an opportunity to do that? On the other hand, there may be things that you would prefer to write than speak—do that here.

16. Sometimes opportunities to say things to people bypass us. Are there other significant people in your past that you never had a chance to tell what was really on your mind? Write what you would have told them if you had the chance. The people you write to in this workbook may be gone or still alive.

17. Who can you communicate with openly about being a caregiver, about your feelings? Think carefully about who you can talk to about the items in the following table, listing *specific* people in each row (for example, in the row marked relatives you might list a particular cousin). (You can add more rows if needed.) Mark

boxes with a "+" if you feel comfortable talking with them about that item, a "−" if this is a mistake and they would be unresponsive or unhelpful, and a "?" if you are unsure about their responsiveness. You may write additional comments in each box.

People	Physical Feelings	Emotional Feelings	Fears	Memories	Loneliness	Hopes and Dreams
Spouse						
Children						
Parents						
Relatives						
Friends						
Doctors						
Counselor						
God						
Minister						
People at Work						
Support Group						

18. Although this is a trying time, it is always wise to take care of certain "mechanical" things like wills, living wills, durable power of attorney for health, financial matters, and funeral arrangements as soon as possible. Most people make these arrangements when they are well and not faced with difficult times. Once taken care of, you no longer need to be concerned about them. If you have not already done so, make appointments to take care of these items. This space would also be a good place to write about your feelings about these items. (*Note*: This item may be difficult to handle at this time, and you may wish to put it off for a while and/or discuss it with someone you trust. The author of this workbook and his wife are both in good health and attended to these items many years ago, just so there would be no surprises or difficulties for their children. They also regularly review these items. But, please respond to this item only when you feel comfortable about doing so.)

19. You may think that it is premature to write about your hopes and dreams, and what it is you would like to do with the rest of your life. Yet, this may be an appropriate time. If it is, what are the things that you always wanted to do? When will you do them?

20. Use the following space to write about anything else that concerns you at this time. This is *your private* journal and you can write whatever you wish.

15.6 Videotaping and Autobiographies

Rainwater (1979) has written of her experience with geriatric clients with respect to the importance of telling their life stories. In the telling (and re-telling) of the stories of one's life, there is a self-validation that appears that is most comforting and re-assuring for older people. This is particularly true for people of any age who face fore-shortened lives due to disease or accident. The very act of telling or writing about one's life, history, activities, achievements (and even failures) brings that life into perspective, roots it in history, and values it. This becomes an "as if" experience where the speaker/writer becomes *entranced* in their own stories, reliving and re-experiencing their lives as they evolve through memory, and the effort to relate and explain to others. In Rossi's observations about state-dependent learning and behavior, the recall of an earlier event is a re-living of it with *all* of the sensory based aspects coming to life again. The recall is in all dimensions and is phenomenal. It is this systematic review and recall whose main product is a finding of meaning and validation. It is almost a discovering of, "Oh, I didn't realize how much I had done, all the places I've been, all the lives I've touched and whose lives have touched mine, the significance of some of these little things, those magic moments I had forgotten, the specialness of ordinary living." You might recall that most poignant cemetery scene in Thornton Wilder's *Our Town* in which Emily discovers the importance, the magic, of everyday life growing up in Grover's Corner. We all need this appreciation of the mundane, if you will, to find out what is really important in life, what has been really important in our past, and what can be important in our current day-to-day lives if we only look.

The recording of your life via the writing of an autobiography is one way to attain this perspective and validation. Two of my friends have done this: one had colorectal cancer (he died in 1997), and the other has many life problems associated with adult onset diabetes and renal failure requiring thrice weekly dialysis. For my former friend the autobiography was for family and friends; the surviving friend's biography was for friends and some professional colleagues. I personally edited both autobiographies to help make them more readable, but this is not necessary. It is the *act* of writing that was important for them—polishing the words was unimportant. If you guide someone to write an autobiography, be sure to raise the question of who will be their intended audience. It is certainly okay if there is no intended audience, and directions are left to destroy the manuscript upon their death.

If the person is not a writer, at least not a sufficient writer to feel capable of writing an autobiography, then you can audiotape or videotape them telling their life story. Also, they may be in such discomfort that writing is difficult, but talking is not. I have taped a number of friends and family members. Some have knowingly been in the last weeks or months of their lives; others were in good health, but "just" old. The tapes are understood to be a heritage for friends and family and do not imply imminent death.

In my experience a two-hour videotape is about the right length of time. (Be flexible, and adjust this to the person being taped.) Sometimes, this is done in one session, and sometimes two. A typical reaction of the interviewee is that they can only think of a few things to say, maybe for ten or fifteen minutes. Yet, once they get started, they forget the camera and the time. If they do not wish to be seen on camera, suggest that you will not at any time focus on their face, but just focus on hands or objects in the room. They may want to include special furniture or knick-knacks or photographs.

I serve as the interviewer. Typically, I lead the person through their life, starting with when and where they were born. I elicit information about their parents: where and when born, where they grew up, how and when they met, where they lived, and occupations. What are some of their earliest memories? Any siblings? What was it like as a child, pre-teen, teen, young adult? What was their social life? How did they meet and fall in love with their spouse? (If I am interviewing a husband and wife, then I separately elicit this information to the point where they marry.) What was their early married life like? Bringing up children? Occupations and avocations? Travels? Grown children and grandparenting? Any special advice for children and grandchildren? (Please share what you've learned with us.) The ending is, "Anything else you'd like to say?" Then, thank them for the privilege of sharing their life with you.

Mechanical aspects need attention. If at all possible, everyone should be "miked." Lighting is not too important because modern videocameras have extraordinary light sensitivity. They all have zoom and autofocus features. To make the tape less static, vary the frame from long shots to close-ups. If it is appropriate, use the fade-in and fade-out feature. When using the zoom feature, be sure to change the frame *slowly*. Also, any panning should be done slowly. Record the data and time vocally as well as with those built-in features in the camera. As the interviewer, do not stay glued behind the camera, but change the zoom, move to the side, and move behind the camera only to make adjustments at intervals. If you have a second person run the camera, that makes the interviewing easier. I do no editing of the tapes. I do keep the original and make as many copies for family and friends as the interviewee requests. I do not charge for the tapes or this service.

There are many Hospice units that provide a loaner videocamera for the use of family members. And, of course, if you do not own a videocamera, one can be borrowed from a friend or rented.

As a related aside, therapists are encouraged to study the work of Michael White and David Epston (1990) in the field called "Narrative Therapy." They know the controlling influence of a person's understanding of their own life story, and have developed ways to use such narratives to help people change. William O'Hanlon feels that narrative therapy is a conceptual revolution in the field. Their work is well worth studying. Also see Freedman and Combs (1996).

15.7 Art Therapy

Art therapy is a projective approach that can facilitate change and a person's understanding of inner states via the symbols in their drawings. Bernie Siegel invariably features patients' drawings in his lectures and books. He (and others in the field) do much interpretation of the content of a drawing. I am more cautious; I have doubts about the universality of certain symbols and their meanings, and I always let the person who made the drawing interpret his/her own work. Neutral questions are preferred, "That part of the drawing is interesting. Does it have any special meaning for you?" Avoid leading questions such as, "There are seven limbs on this tree. Is there something especially significant about the number seven? Seven days? Seven weeks or months? Seven years?"

If people are willing, I generally ask for four drawings. They are: (1) a picture of you as you are now, in your present state; (2) a drawing of your treatment(s) and/or what you are doing for yourself; (3) a drawing of you after this is over and you are in good health; (4) how you got from (1)-present condition to (3)-full health. Please note that drawing (4) may be very different from the treatments in (2). People are asked to title and date the drawings. They may also add narratives to the back of the drawing, and give voice to elements of the drawing by balloons (as in comic strips). Drawings may be repeated at regular intervals.

15.8 Cancer as a Gift

Cancer as a gift—what a strange, seemingly paradoxical idea! Yet, just about everyone I know who has/had cancer has made this statement, or something similar in our support group or to me, personally. Others have reported hearing the same thing. How can this be?

The initial diagnosis of cancer is almost always an emotional and physical shock. Occasionally, it is a relief to have symptoms of discomfort and malaise, which may have been troubling you for a considerable time, finally diagnosed and given a name. In this latter instance, there is relief due to the disappearance of uncertainty and the unspoken implication that the physical condition is "all in your mind." Yet, that initial shock for most people leads to profound soul-searching. Why me? Why now? Why this? What do I do with the remainder of my life? How much longer do I have to live? Will I suffer? Am I capable of bearing such suffering? Who am I? What am I? Was this predestined? What can I do now?

All of a sudden life becomes predictably finite. Cancer kills. Cancer kills horribly. Can you really believe that cancer is just a word and not a sentence? Invariably, the diagnosis leads to changes in lifestyle. The treatments necessitate much of this. The questionings and re-evaluations lead to more profound changes. With a finite life expectancy, what is really important? Is it that promotion? A new car or house or...? A trip? A raise in pay? That status your ambition drove you towards? What you were going to do after retirement?

The gift of cancer seems to be the recognition of the preciousness of this moment, this breath, this touch or smile or hug, this bite of food, being able to swallow or go to the toilet by yourself, a blade of grass, a cumulus cloud, a raindrop, a glass of cold water on a hot day, a mug of hot cocoa on a cold day, some special music, quiet, serious talking, loving and being loved, a minute of no pain and of no nausea—each moment becomes precious. Suddenly, you recognize how much of your life was hum-drum, routine, automatic, habitual, controlled. Now, you have permission by virtue of the cancer to break out of that mold, that prison of musts and shoulds and can'ts. Suddenly, somehow, you become more alive, really live in the moment, tasting and touching and smelling and hearing and looking and being. It is almost like waking up from the dream of unknowingly passing through life, to being aware of each and every thing inside and outside of yourself. You are finally alive, being born to heightened awareness. That is the gift, and people respond to this new awareness with a certain kind of awe. They know that they are different from other people because of the cancer; they also perceive all of those other cancer-free people as somehow flawed, as living inside an insensate shell. Paradoxical? Perhaps. Are they denying the disease? No. They are instead becoming truly realistic in valuing and recognizing reality moment by moment. People who have had "near-death" experiences react the same way.

I, personally, do not have a life-challenging disease. It has taken my friends who do several years to teach me about their gift, and for me to live my life in ways that approximate their great lifestyle changes. You really do not need to have cancer to have "permission" to do the things you've always wanted to do. Learn about this gift. Someone has said that the *present* is called that because it really is a present, a gift. And, it is a gift that is so obvious that most of us never notice it. The stars at night. Lightning. A sunflower. A hug....

Sharp and Terbay, who both work at Hospice of Dayton, have compiled a book (1997) entitled *Gifts* which is full of stories about people and their gifts. Rachel Naomi Remen's compilation of poetry (1994) is about gifts. Her book *Kitchen Table Wisdom* (1996) is about the gift of her life.

What does a person who has been admitted to a Hospice program, with a best-guess life expectancy of less than six months, do when their cancer disappears and they "graduate" from Hospice? (This is a rare occurrence, but it does happen.) My friend Claudia graduated from Hospice over three years ago. She and her family were realistic—they had even together planned her funeral service. Coming back to life had its difficulties for Claudia and her husband and family and friends. There was an addiction to morphine to beat, and this took her two months. She and her husband continue to live one day at a time. Claudia does a lot of volunteer work at Hospice and local hospitals. She is sharing her gift. *You* don't need to be a Hospice graduate to share your gift of life.

15.9 Rituals and Ceremonies

Carl Hammerschlag, M. D., tells a remarkable story about his journey from his medical training as a know-it-all New Yorker to working in the Indian (Native American) Service in Arizona to becoming a healer. His story is recounted in two books (1988, 1993) and inspiring audiotapes available through Hammerschlag Ltd. (3104 East Camelback Road, Suite 614, Phoenix, AZ 85016). His personal story goes from traditional western medicine to healing, from doctor to healer. The subject of this section, however, is based on his book with Silverman (1997) on the use of rituals and ceremonies for healing. Readers may also wish to read the works of Steve Gilligan (1987), an Ericksonian hypnotherapist who incorporates ceremonies and the spiritual in his work.

First, Silverman and Hammerschlag make a distinction between rituals and ceremonies. *Rituals* are more like habits in the sense that they are repetitive and become incorporated into daily living. Morning rituals may be the order in which you toilet, shower, dress, shave or put on makeup, have coffee, fold towels, and put on underwear left-foot or right-foot first. These are routine actions which may or may not have had their origins as part of special religious or spiritual practice.

Ceremonies, on the other hand, have a connection to the spiritual or sacred or religious, and are special events. Brushing your teeth in a particular way is a ritual, getting married is a ceremony. Succinctly, rituals are routine and ceremonies are special. Ceremonies typically incorporate the following elements:

(1) leader to facilitate
(2) specific goal
(3) significant or sacred object
(4) group of selected people
(5) particular site
(6) mutual respect/reverence
(7) special timing
(8) specific order of service or components

For example, a western culture wedding ceremony includes a minister or rabbi, the wedding contract, wedding rings, relatives and friends of the bride and bridegroom, a church or synagogue or hall, an awe and respect of the event itself, a specific date and times for the ceremony and celebration, and an order of service prescribed by the religion, or by the bride and bridegroom.

In the rest of this section we will give details about: (1) Hammerschlag and Silverman healing circle; (2) Rachel Naomi Remen's preparation for a medical intervention circle; and (3) ceremonies designed for a specific purpose. Before doing this, however, the elements of The Navajo Talking Circle, which is common to many ceremonies, will be described.

Navajo Talking Circle. The *Navajo Talking Circle* incorporates the elements cited above. There is a person who is the focus of the circle and their healing may be the objective of the meeting. This person supplies a sacred object which is passed around the circle. You may talk only when you are holding the object. When you finish, you pass the object on. The rules are: (1) whatever is said and shared in the circle is confidential and not repeated outside; (2) each person talks about their own *personal* experience, from their own heart, for as long as they wish; (3) when they finish, the next person has the attention of the group; (4) there is *no* cross-chatter, interruption, or commenting on what others have said; and (5) everyone listens attentively and respectfully to whoever is speaking. For non-Native American groups a sacred object which is passed around is optional. In the *Navajo Talking Circle* each person speaks only once. In other groups, time permitting, a person may speak again, but only from their own personal perspective—no comments on others or by others—but, perhaps adding something they forgot to say the first time.

Hammerschlag and Silverman have facilitated many healing circles. Their book (1997) gives examples. They traditionally use a sacred object that is passed around and incorporate the elements mentioned above, as well as the rules for speaking in a *Navajo Talking Circle*. The leader is organizer and facilitator. At the beginning the leader explains the purpose of the meeting and the rules. At the end they close the meeting, perhaps with some summary comments. The significance of the sacred object may be explained. Participants are specifically invited. They sit in a circle on chairs or the floor. Lighting is controlled and may include candles or a fire. A sense of the sacred is evident. Hammerschlag says, "When you speak from the heart, you always speak the truth."

Rachel Naomi Remen (1996) gives details about a healing circle that is specifically designed to prepare a person for a medical intervention like surgery or a series of chemotherapy or radiation treatments. The group is typically comprised of a few family members and friends, and is convened for this sole purpose. They meet a few days or a week or so before the intervention. The central person brings along a small stone which is symbolically important to them. The stone is generally flat and no larger than an inch or so. The central person does not speak, but silently hands the stone to a person seated adjacent to them. *Navajo Talking Circle* rules apply. The person holding the stone tells about some traumatic or difficult event in their life. They then describe what personal characteristic(s) or action(s) helped them through that time. These characteristics are things like: courage, prayer, belief in a divine being, persistence, faith, determination, and love. This speech is concluded with, "I put *strength* into this stone so you may have it with you," and pass the stone on. Each person ends their tale with a similar statement, endowing the stone with their way of coping and surviving. At the end, the stone which is imbued with all of these personal gifts, is given to the central person. They tape the stone to a wrist or palm or foot, and inform the medical staff about its sacred significance. This special healing/preparation ceremony has been used by Remen for over twenty years. In her experience it is quite helpful—she has also received positive feedback from surgeons in her area.

I have used ceremonies in large groups and for specific individual purposes. Grief and grieving was the subject of one group (about seventy-five people) meeting. After some introductory and explanatory remarks about grief and grieving, three group members (who had agreed to do this beforehand) spoke 3–5 minutes each about their own personal losses and their way of grieving. The *Navajo Talking Circle* rules were explained—everyone had a hand-out with the rules and some references. The larger group was then broken up into smaller groups of four to six (maximum!) members who rearranged chairs to sit in a circle. Each small group member spoke in turn about their own personal experiences of grief and the ways they coped. About 35 minutes was allotted to this sharing. I served as time keeper and gave a two-minute warning. If a group finished early, then members could speak again, but only "I" talk—no comments or cross-chatter. At the end, each small group was asked to hold hands in their small circle and I did a grief-oriented healing meditation for 5–7 minutes for the whole group.

Another group experience, identical in format to that described in the previous paragraph, was held on the subject of hopes, dreams, and unfinished business. Instead of having three members publicly share their personal experiences, I instead read Minnie's story from Lawrence LeShan's book (pp. 48–54, 1989). This is an exceptionally powerful story about a woman with cancer who enlivens the last period of her life with studying her lifelong secret passion for ballet. After reading Minnie's story, small groups are formed, and people share their hopes, dreams, and unfinished business. The whole group ends with a guided meditation.

Gilligan (1987) has written and talked about the use of ceremonies (he uses the word "ritual") for helping his psychotherapy patients through crucial points in their lives. For example, a person might bury something that was symbolic of a broken marriage to put an end to the hold of that marriage on their life. A symbolic object may be destroyed. Old feelings and attitudes might be written out and then burned in a ceremony of exorcism. The therapist might suggest that a ceremony could be useful at this time of the client's life, and gives examples of things done by previous clients. It is up to the client to decide upon an appropriate ceremony—with some guidance. It is only the clients who know what objects or acts are symbolically significant to them. In this way, clients can literally "bury" feelings that are no longer useful. Such ceremonies can be quite cathartic and are powerful change agents.

Gilligan gives more detail on the use of rituals for psychotherapy and related healing in a chapter in his later book (1997, pp. 177–195). Since his approach is an integral part of his "self-relations psychotherapy," to make full sense of what he does you should be familiar with his work. He defines a ritual as, " ... an intense, experiential-archetypal structure that recreates or transforms identity." There is a four-step model: (1) suggesting a ritual as a possible solution; (2) planning the ritual; (3) enacting the ritual; and (4) post-ritual activities. The entire process takes four to six weeks with weekly sessions. Gilligan tells about the way he uses rituals therapeutically with a detailed case example.

With people who have life-challenging diseases, ceremonies can be constructed for completing unfinished business, ending old and un-needed feelings, or for marking the end of chemotherapy or radiation treatments. Generally, ceremonies are developed in conjunction with family members, and carried out by the family. I serve simply as a guide or resource, since this is their lives. The power of ceremonies is related to the specificity of the symbols and symbolic actions. Ceremonies are invariably realistic. (See Section 4.6 for related material on the power of prayer.)

Some traditions invoke angels, spirit guides and helpers, and power animals. The astute therapist always works within the client's belief systems and does things, respectfully, within those belief systems. There are many different kinds of ceremonies.

Chapter 16

Coping

16.1 Introduction

When a person is diagnosed with a life-challenging disease such as cancer they enter a whole new world from their normal everyday existence. There are new priorities and demands which seemingly cannot be postponed or scheduled for their convenience. Appointments for visiting doctors, getting treatments and being tested have to be made and kept. All other day-to-day tasks must be re-scheduled around the appointments. If a surgery or surgeries are involved, then there are hospital stays and recuperation periods. There are changed and changing relationships with family and friends. There are the hard realities of finance and insurance and employment. There may be things like changing body identity to adjust to in the case of mastectomies or colostomies or amputations, or just a decreased capacity to do everyday things like walking, going up and down stairs, playing sports, taking a shower, or going to the toilet. And, most important are the emotional ups and downs, the fears, the anxieties, the hopelessness and helplessness, the depression, the threat of death, the endless "why?" questions, and the sense of unreality that seems to preclude everything else. You have just been forced to step through the looking glass into a dream world that operates with its own strange rules. How do you cope? How do your family and friends cope? **[Please note that this chapter is both for the professional helper and the person who has a serious disease.]**

This chapter is a collection in a somewhat random order of all of the things I have learned about coping from friends and from my own investigations. It is written in such a way that it is for both patients and professionals. Patients will find many practical ways to cope. Professionals will be reminded of the many ways of coping that they can teach their clients.

LeShan's 1989 book contains an excellent chapter on dealing with hospitals and the medical establishment. Bernie Siegel's books (1986, 1989, 1993, 1998) and his recorded lectures are full of stories and advice. The American Cancer Society and the National Cancer

Institute of NIH have many free pamphlets. Support groups and societies for particular kinds of cancer and other diseases are good sources of information. There is a great deal of information on the Web. There is so much information available that it can be overwhelming. This chapter is a practical summary of the kinds of things I tell my friends and clients. Be daring. Carl Hammerschlag (1988, 1993) emphasizes that life involves change, and that if you are not changing in some way, you are probably dead. Dokay (1993) has written a comprehensive and resource-full book whose title is descriptive: *Living with Life-threatening Illness. A Guide for Patients, their Families & Caregivers.* Dokay's Chapter 1 on responses to life-threatening illness covers the subject in a helpful manner, and Chapter 2 on understanding the illness experience provides much useful guidance. (See Appendix H for some helpful Web sites and telephone numbers.)

16.2 Communicating with Medical Personnel

A standard part of the curriculum for medical doctors and nurses is how to communicate with patients. This training frequently includes practice sessions under supervision. It is also fair to say that doctors and nurses enter their professions due to ideals about helping people who are physically sick in some way. They typically begin with compassion and concern. Yet, the training of physicians when they are hospital residents involves such incredible physical and mental strains, that the system almost forces a mechanical, "scientific" and "objective" approach on them. We know of resident programs (not uncommon) where the doctor may be "on call" every other night. Being on call means being on duty, or available for duty, for a continuous thirty-six hour period. The life of a resident involves being tired and sleep-deprived almost all of the time. And, this post M.D. training can go on for up to ten years depending on the specialty. With managed care, the demands on nurses have also multiplied. The system is inadvertently (some may say intentionally) designed to strip away feeling and reduce medical personnel to technicians. The wonder, the *real* wonder of all of this, is that *most* medical personnel remain compassionate, cheerful, and involved in the welfare of their patients. The sad part is that some of these initially idealistic people do get coarsened and remote and mechanical. We have even heard of an oncologist who claims that none of his patients die. Upon further inquiry, we found that he transferred (i.e., dropped) patients when he felt he could no longer help them! On the other hand, to be fair, we also have heard doctors and nurses complain about patients who abuse them. This is not physical abuse, but rudeness, disrespect and disregard. Remember that any interaction between you and a doctor or nurse is a two-way street. You may not be able to control their behavior, but you should always be able to control your behavior and reactions. This section is about things *you* can do, that are under your control, in these interactions.

Perhaps the first thing to keep in mind is that as the consumer or purchaser of medical services, that *they work for you*. In that sense, you are their boss. One way to think about this is the distinction between the roles of patient and client. Isn't it implied in the word "patient" that you need to *be patient*, to be passive, to *wait* until you are told what to do or have done to you? Being a patient *vis-à-vis* a doctor, for example, places you in the "one-down" position— you are not an equal in any way. Yes, the medical doctor has more knowledge and experience than you do in their field. They should be respected for their knowledge and skill and accomplishment in the same way that a musician, a tailor, a plumber, a chef, a professor, and an experienced hauler of trash (a "garbologist") need to be respected. Is there an extra aura due to the fact that doctors may be involved in life or death decisions in their work? Yes, this needs to be acknowledged. However, in a similar way, the captain flying a 747 on a transoceanic flight and the driver of a tourist bus in mountainous terrain also have the potential of life and death decisions in their skilled hands.

Think of the relationship this way: a *client* is someone who *hires* the services of a professional. The professional (doctor, lawyer, plumber, electrician, car mechanic) works *for* the client on a fee-for-service basis. **If you can hire a professional, you can also fire them, and you can do this without giving reasons—this is your prerogative as the purchaser, the client.** One of the functions of support groups is to give support to a member who reports unsatisfactory medical services. You are under no obligation to continue with a particular doctor if you are not satisfied with them for whatever reason. Out of politeness, you may tell them that you are considering switching physicians and why. Common reasons, in my experience, are: a doctor who will not answer questions; a doctor who is cold or remote; a doctor whose examination is perfunctory; or a doctor who is inaccessible. Generally, you have choice in your physicians—there are some health plans where this is not the case. If you can't change to another more open plan, then you are stuck and need to work defensively within that system.

My friend Elaine was in her seventies when she was diagnosed with breast cancer. Her first surgeon/oncologist worked in a nearby hospital. It might have been a plus for Elaine that the hospital was local and that the physician was a woman. Yet, Elaine found her to be cold and unresponsive and overly "professional." This physician was "fired." Friends then helped Elaine research physicians within a reasonable area. In the big city which was 70 minutes away by car, Elaine found her perfect physician. On the initial interview, accompanied by her husband, Elaine said this wonderful doctor spent two and one-half hours doing an examination, answering all of their questions, and describing options. This surgeon did a lumpectomy and nodal dissection and Elaine is still under her care. You have choices.

It is always a good practice to research your disease, and to be prepared with knowledgeable questions at your appointments. Write out the questions and concerns in advance of the appointment. There is nothing wrong with reading them aloud and giving a copy to your doctor. Let them know that it is your expectation that the questions will be answered. Sometimes, a knowledgeable nurse can provide most of the answers. Studies have been carried out on what doctors hear their patients say, and what the patients hear and recall of their physicians' statements. These studies have shown that what the doctors recall and what the patients recall are both rather faulty. You can take notes. Better still, you can audiotape the session for later listening. Meichenbaum and Turk (1987) have reviewed the literature on *adherence*, that is, how well do patients carry out their doctors' instructions. Adherence or compliance is surprisingly low, and is mainly due to improper recall. The treatment for diabetes mellitus, for example, is very well-known and the regimen is conducive to leading a near-to-normal life. The regimen is not burdensome given the benefits. Yet, according to Meichenbaum and Turk, compliance by diabetics is typically less than fifty per cent. Take notes, make audiotapes, and ask for written instructions.

My surgeon for some recent minor surgery had provided printed hand-outs that were quite comprehensive. His nurse explained what was in the hand-outs. The trend toward "defensive" medicine is producing more of this kind of information.

It is your choice as to your attitude towards your physician. Let me tell you a personal story. A few years ago I had to change physicians. A knowledgeable friend highly recommended a Dr. George Jones (fictitious name). He took a personal history in his office prior to the initial physical examination. I suggested that we work together on a first-name basis. "After all," I said, "if you insist on my addressing you as Doctor, then I can insist on your addressing me as Professor." George was very open to this way of being friends and working collaboratively. About one year later, we happened to be chatting about the distinctions between patient and client, and George commented that he was certain that none of the other six physicians in his group practice would be open to being called by their first name. In his office, I do not overdo the first-name thing, and am sensitive to office protocol.

One of the things I really like about George is that I always have the sense that I have his undivided attention when I am with him. I am also certain that he will sit with me and answer all my questions, no matter how long it takes. I do not take undue advantage of his way of being with patients. The level of mutual respect and trust that we feel for each other is healing in its truest sense.

On the other hand, the most common complaint about doctors that arises in our support group has to do with doctors not listening, or being too busy and rushed to answer questions. You can confront your doctor directly about unanswered questions and what you do not like in their behavior. Since your relationship with your doctor can have a powerful effect on the course of your disease, then be direct with them on what they do that is helpful or harmful in your interactions. For example, if hugs are important to you, then ask your doctor for a hug. Also, tell your doctors what you do like about the way they interact with you—this is a two-way relationship.

Oncology nurses are generally well-informed about all aspects of their doctor's work. They also may have more time to sit with you and explain the treatment, preparation for the treatment, side effects, what to expect after the treatment, and how to care for yourself or a significant other. They, too, can be asked for hugs. We all know of people, who as patients are aggressively demanding, rude, or simply nasty. In principle, the medical establishment should treat these people no differently than a courteous or undemanding person. The aggressive patient *may* be able to influence the system and get things out of it that others cannot. But, given human nature, these pushy patients generally get short-changed by the system. This doesn't mean that you should fawn over your doctor and be a wimp. It is possible to be assertive *and* polite, demanding *and* courteous, firm *and* respectful. People respond to politeness. There is a major difference between deference or awe and respect. I happen to think that medicine works best, both for curing and healing, when it is done cooperatively and collaboratively. Does your doctor work *on* you or *with* you? If the former, you should consider switching after sharing your feelings about how you have been treated.

Remember, as a client and consumer you have choices. These choices are not just about the physician—they include treatments, tests, and facilities. Norman Cousins wrote about his heart attack (1984). A few days after the attack he was scheduled for a stress test. Upon entering the test facility he found it cold, mechanical, and intimidating. He canceled the test. His physician reacted with concern, and told him how important this test was for designing his treatment protocol. Cousins agreed, and told his doctor that he would take the stress test if his favorite music was played, and if some paintings (reproductions) were hung in the room. This was done and Cousins proved to be a very cooperative patient. There are many things like this which are under your control.

You have the right, perhaps even the obligation, to seek out second and third opinions. The big city in my area (Dayton) has a number of good hospitals and oncologists. Yet, sixty miles away there is one of the major cancer hospitals and research centers in the country, the James Hay Cancer Hospital of the Ohio State University. When a second or third opinion is necessary in my area, I recommend a trip to the Hay. The physicians there are more likely to be aware of experimental protocols, and may even be doing research in one's specific type of cancer.

Have your doctors communicate with each other. It is useful to have your personal physician or oncologist serve as the central person for coordinating your tests and treatments and follow-ups. Otherwise, you can get lost in the system between all of the specialists. You can also use a family member or friend as a coordinator of services.

My mother was fond of saying, "One hand washes the other." Work cooperatively with your medical helpers. If you are involved in alternative therapies, do not forget that traditional scientific western medicine also has a lot to offer, and you should hedge your bets by availing yourself of *all* modes of help.

16.3 Helplessness, Hopelessness, and Control

Somewhere in their training many medical people were cautioned about the dangers of giving false hope. There was an unspoken implication that such "false hope" would somehow harm the recipient. After all, if a patient expects too much from a given treatment, they are then being set up for disappointment. And, it is that disappointment which is presumably harmful, that might lead to depression or a sense of hopelessness. So, doctors are told:

- Don't promise more than you can deliver.
- Be honest and accurate and scientific in your prognoses and predictions.
- Tell the truth, no matter how devastating it may be.
- The principle of informed consent means that you have to inform patients about possible side-effects and predicted outcomes based on your experience and knowledge and the literature.

This approach may be mechanically and legally correct, but it is not compassionate. It ignores the folk wisdom of, "Where there is life, there is hope." This common-sense statement is the driving force for exploring alternative therapies. So, what is wrong with hope? Is there some formula that combines giving hope with informed consent?

The first devastating statement by a physician is, "You have cancer," (or some life-challenging disease). It is still probably true that most people who hear these words take them as a sentence of imminent death. There is also a fear that the progress of the disease necessarily involves not only pain, but unbearable pain. Is there some way to present a diagnosis of cancer that is less crushing? "The test results indicate that you have a kind of cancer that is treatable." "You are lucky that we caught this cancer at such an early stage." "Most people with this kind of cancer lead normal lives with treatment." It would be cruel to present the diagnosis in any other way if it is at all possible, given the type of cancer and its stage, to speak in these hopeful ways. The lay person does not generally know that there are many different kinds of cancer, and that each one has its own typical course of development. There are several dozen different kinds of breast cancer, although a few predominate. The patient is entitled to this kind of information.

What if the cancer is a particularly malignant type that is fast-growing, or may have already metastasized? Can the doctor still hold out hope? The second kind of devastating statement a doctor can give is, "Your cancer is too advanced for treatment." or "We've done everything known to modern medical science. I'm sorry." These are direct no-hope statements that imply that you should immediately make out your will, tidy up your affairs, and say your goodbyes. An alternative compassionate statement might be, "I am not sure what else to do at this time. Let's continue working together. I'll keep checking the literature. We'll do whatever we can to keep you comfortable. I'll certainly help you in whatever you wish to do or try. You can always call upon me to talk or for advice. We're in this together. You know, I'd like a hug now." [Caution: some patients will not want to be hugged.]

For some people, offers to pray together are important. Since hope is such an important part of healing, hope should always be offered. No matter how adverse the circumstance, the person with the disease *always has the choice about how to respond* to what the doctor says. Feeling hopeless can have profound physical effects—so can feeling hope.

Our modern efficient medical delivery systems (isn't that a mouthful!) are typically designed for the convenience of medical personnel and their associated health management colleagues. There are seemingly endless forms to fill out, many of them incomprehensible. The system almost appears to be Kafka-esque in design, and is structured more like an assembly line than a healing relationship between one human being and another. Hospital and office routines can engender a sense of helplessness in the patient. This feeling of helplessness can be harmful to health, and patients need to develop empowering skills, ways of taking control over their passage through the medical system. One example of doing this was cited earlier—the way Norman Cousins approached taking a stress test. The rest of this section is devoted to ways of being in control of your medical experiences.

a. *Medical Records*—What is written about you is written about *you*, and you have the right to both read and obtain copies of all of your medical records. Although there may be things written in your records that you do not understand, they are still yours. You can always ask some knowledgeable person, perhaps a medical reference librarian, to "translate." Your doctor and his/her nurse should be willing to explain what is in your records. You can also request that copies of records (or the records themselves) be sent to another physician or clinic. Be persistent since you can encounter resistance in obtaining or reviewing your medical records.

b. *Ombudsman*—Almost all hospitals now have an ombudsman or patient representative/advocate on their staff. You can use these people to represent your interests with the hospital. They can expedite procedures and obtain answers quickly. They are paid to be *your* advocate within the system, and their knowledge of procedure and protocol works for you. A member of your family or a friend can sometimes serve the same function. (They may need to have a written authorization.)

c. *Pastoral Staff*—Most hospitals employ, or have available, pastoral staff (hospital chaplains) to help patients with religious and spiritual concerns. The chaplain can also serve as an advocate, and as someone with "inside" information on the workings of a hospital. They will pray with you and spend time with you and listen to you. Chaplains generally have links with community resources such as support groups, social aid, and legal aid. The medical social services department is also a good source for information and community resources. You do not need to be religious your-

self, or of the denomination of the chaplain, to request their services. Of course, you can also ask your own minister to visit.

d. *Clothing and Room Decor*—The clothing issued to patients in hospitals is designed for the convenience of the staff. By all means,
bring your own pajamas or night gowns, bathrobe, and slippers.
Leisure clothing like sweat suits or work-out clothes may also be
worn. Be comfortable in your own familiar clothing. You can add
your own pillow, and cover your bed with your own bedspread,
quilt, or afghan.

Personalize the decor of your room. An artist friend could not
stand the institutional art in her room and covered the picture with
a favorite colorful shawl. You could also hang (with permission)
personal artwork.

It appears to be the case that patients in rooms with views of
sky and greenery do better than those in interior rooms with no
views, or views of other buildings. At the minimum, you have
contact with the weather. Visual vistas do something for inner
peace. Ask to get a room with a view of the outside world, preferably one that looks out on greenery.

It is not only children who are comforted by stuffed animals.
For some reason, having a special stuffed animal or toy can be
comforting. Many nursing homes, for example, encourage the
practice of residents having dolls or stuffed animals. There are
even hospitals that permit visits of pets, or have their own visiting
pet program.

You never know how much of your physical environment is
under your control until you test the system. If the first response is
"No," being insistent may get results.

e. *Examinations*—You can refuse to be examined or take a particular test. You may be able to modify the conditions of the test, as
Norman Cousins did. Some examination conditions may be under
your control. Let me relate three stories.

The following story was told to me by a mutual friend of
Harriet's. (I later checked this story with Harriet who told me that
it wasn't true, but could have been true since she was certainly
capable of that behavior. So, here is her apocryphal story.) Harriet
was hospitalized with an abdominal problem. One morning the
chief resident was making rounds, followed by his gaggle of students. When he got to Harriet's bed, he consulted her chart and

began to discuss her "case." He was interrupted by a loud "ahem" from Harriet. He made his first eye contact with Harriet, where-upon she said, "Did I give you permission to talk about me?" After a longish pause the chief resident said, "May I have your permission to talk about your case?" Harriet looked at him and the students and simply said "No." The doctor, dutifully followed by his students, had to move on. Harriet was not a "case" or a "possible gall bladder." Examinations and discussions of your disease need your permission.

Bernie Siegel tells the story of a woman who was an artist and who was hospitalized for a while. She had a friend bring an easel, a large pad of newsprint, and a collection of colored felt-tipped pens. This woman would not let anyone examine her or do anything in the room without first paying her "fee" of doing a drawing. This worked well until an intern came to examine her. She explained the procedure. He said that he didn't have the time and that he couldn't draw. She said, "No examination." They were log-jammed until she said, "Do you have any money?" At first he was non-plussed, then he looked in his pockets. "I have thirty five cents." She said, "That's enough. Put the money on my tray and you can examine me." He did.

A twelve year old boy with cancer didn't like some of the hospital staff who came to him in his room. His mother gave him a gun. Well, it was a pistol. In fact, it was a water pistol. The boy could then "shoot" anyone who gave him a hard time. The boy died a few weeks after he received his gun. An intern who really cared for the boy saved the water pistol to give to other patients. (This story was told by Bernie Siegel.)

It is a common complaint, almost a cliché, that hospital food is awful. The menus may be nutritionally correct for you at that time, but there is a large leeway in diets. There is no sense to a "correct" meal if you find it unpalatable and do not eat it, or selectively eat a portion. Talk to the food staff about your likes and dislikes. Friends and relatives can bring in hot dishes that you like. If you have trouble feeding yourself, then a friend or relative may (or may not!—your choice) make this easier. Many Hospice facilities have kitchens so you can prepare your own food or have someone prepare a favorite food on the spot. Some even have smoking rooms for those patients who are smokers—a level of compassion and consideration that is commendable. In one Hospice, all patient rooms look out on a green area with a bird feeder. Ducks from a nearby pond walk that area. Most Hospices have an armchair in the room that is convertible to a single bed, and a separate toilet and shower facility for family. All of this is thoughtful and helpful.

There are lots of ways to empower yourself. For example, if there is a particular technician or nurse who makes you feel uncomfortable, or whom you dislike for *any* reason, you can request that a different person work with you. There is no reason to tolerate a brusque or rude technician in the radiation facility, for example. Bernie Siegel has commented that the patients that the staff complain about as being uncooperative, or even too demanding, appear to be the survivors. On the other hand, the overly compliant and docile patients appear not to survive as well. Remember, again, that there are great differences between being abusively demanding, politely assertive, and passively compliant. I recall a friend who always got what she wanted and needed from medical personnel because she was so undemandingly loving that the staff just wanted to be in her presence, even hang out in her room when they had a spare minute or two. Her special healer was a personal angel. I believe she was an angel herself. It was a great privilege for me to share in her and her husband's life, and her death.

16.4 "Mechanical" Matters, Wills, etc.

By "mechanical" matters I mean all of those practical considerations that need to be attended to with some urgency by people who have life-challenging diseases, and their families. Of course, prudence dictates that many of these matters should be taken care of when you are well and there is no urgency. My wife and I made these arrangements many years ago. Our most recent update was done before an extended trip overseas—what if the plane fell from the air? Each of several items will be separately discussed.

a. *Wills*—A legally binding will gives directions about the disposition of your worldly possessions after death. Most couples will everything to the survivor, with further provisions for both dying at the same time or within a short time of each other. It is generally best to consult a lawyer for the writing of a will. If your estate is simple, there are clever computer programs available at nominal cost which will help you write your will with specific provisions to make it legal within your state (in the U.S.). You must also comply with provisions for notarizing or witnesses. Copies of your will can be deposited with your bank, your lawyer, your children, friends, and the designated executor of your will. The will can be sealed or open.

When my mother was nearing the end of her life she gave herself the pleasure of giving away cherished items to her children, grandchildren, and friends. There's a way now to donate assets to a charitable organization that lets you, for example, keep the dividends of stocks until your death, when the assets belong to the charity. Estate planning is important, period. There are specialists who can help you with this for a fee.

b. *The Living Will*—The living will is your way to give instructions to your family and to your medical personnel about your medical care if you become incapacitated and can't directly convey your wishes. The living will specifies just what care and interventions you are willing to have in the last stages of your life. For example, you can specify that no extraordinary measures or resuscitation methods be used. Living wills need to be properly executed and witnessed and filed with relevant people, according to the laws of your state. For your information, a sample living will (valid in Ohio) is included as Appendix D. At the end of the living will form I have indicated my personal choices taken from my living will— these are *my* choices and you need to discuss these matters with your spouse, family, doctor, minister, or friends. A living will is a *personal* statement. (A Christian Affirmation of Life is in Appendix F and a Christian Living Will is in Appendix G.)

The written contract that you sign when you are eligible for a Hospice program (six months or less prognosis for life) contains agreements that are similar to a living will. This contract is to be carefully studied. You typically agree that no extraordinary measures will be used to prolong life. Since "extraordinary measures" are open to interpretation, you need to be as specific as possible in this area. Again, it is well to execute a living will when you are in good health. It is always possible to change a living will as your circumstances change.

c. *Durable Power of Attorney for Health*—A power of attorney gives another person or an institution the legal authority to represent your interests. The *durable power of attorney for health* document comes into force by a conscious act if you are sentient and can communicate, or automatically if you can no longer make decisions for yourself. (A court may be involved in such a decision.) Among other matters, it empowers your executor to make decisions about medical treatment on your behalf. These instructions need to be legally written and witnessed and filed. Different states have different requirements. For your information, a sample Durable Power of Attorney for Health (valid in Ohio) is included as Appendix E. Again, my own choices are indicated at the end of the form—please make your own considered choices.

You also need to be aware that some doctors, nurses, and hospitals will not be willing to honor your choices in a living will or of your executor for a Durable Power of Attorney for Health. Always check in advance with your personal physician and any specialists whose services you can anticipate using. Also check on the policies in these matters of your area hospitals. All these medical people and institutions should give you clear and easily understandable responses. You can change doctors and specify particular hospitals. This is one reason to execute these documents in advance.

d. *Medical Insurance*—The one area that seems to get people hotter under the collar than any other is medical insurance. There are a variety of coverages: Medicaid, Medicare, personally paid for private plans, supplemental plans, and employer contracted plans. However, some individuals fall through the cracks in the system because they have no medical coverage whatsoever. With the prevalence of managed care, despite all of the fine print and PR flummery, it is frequently difficult to know what is covered by a particular plan, and to what extent. The paperwork for an outpatient procedure or an office visit can continue for months and months before it is resolved. For example, I had an inguinal hernia repair done in February 1998, and the final resolution occurred in March 1999. You need to be persistent, keep all paper records, and document each step. There are 800-numbers to call for almost everything. Once you have persisted through the "if this, press that," you may get some answers and some satisfaction.

A major difficulty with managed care arises if there is a conflict between what your doctor recommends for your care and what the system permits. I can recall a friend whose oncologist recommended a particular course of chemotherapy that my friend's insurance company refused to authorize. This refusal was despite the doctor's recommendation and the citation of literature studies indicating that this course of treatment was 25–35% effective for his cancer. My friend died before we had exhausted all of the channels within the insurance company. One recourse that many insured people take, who have been denied a particular treatment, is to seek legal counsel and to sue the insurance company. Legal maneuvers take time and effort and energy and money that would best be spent on yourself and your healing. If it is too draining for you to pursue these matters relating to medical insurance, you need to recruit an advocate from family or friends. The old advice of "sue the bastards" might be your last recourse.

e. *Financial Matters*—A will meets legal requirements for disposing of your estate after you die. But, the complexity of inheritance laws and probating a will means that you need to do estate planning well before you die. There are books and computer programs and financial advisers to help you in these matters. One friend has taken care of all the details in his estate and each of his children has a loose-leaf binder with all of the information. In fact, he has already made his funeral arrangements and paid for them. Even though we may feel immortal as a teenager, no one gets out of this world alive! Plan accordingly. There are ways to minimize inheritance taxes and shorten probate. It is not considerate to dump this on your children.

f. *Suicide and Euthanasia*—A friend of mine recently told me about his brother-in-law Charles' death. Charles had cancer and was in the last stages of his life. There was a surprise gathering of Charles' friends at a cook-out for him. As Charles entered the room, he exclaimed, "Aha, the Last Supper!" A man with a sense of humor and much spirit. After two days, he needed life support to breathe. A week after "the Last Supper," and with his family about him, Charles asked his doctor to pull the plug. The doctor did. Was this suicide? Euthanasia? Illegal? Moral? Murder? Although there are legal constraints and legal definitions that differ widely, the answers to these serious questions are ultimately personal in my judgment. My wife and I have certain private agreements about various life contingencies. It is wise to think about these issues before circumstances force such considerations upon you.

Do you have a right to die with dignity? Are all parts of the process under your control? Can you guarantee no harm to others if you make such a choice? There is a vast literature on this subject now, and much debate. There are also groups like the Hemlock Society (PO Box 101810, Denver, CO 80250-1810. 800-247-7421) that provide information about these things. For a person with a life-challenging disease and their family, these questions are no longer theoretical. Consider them with care and concern.

16.5 Communicating with Others—Relationships

If you do have cancer, how do you communicate? How much do you share of your treatment? Your feelings? Your fears? Your concerns? With whom do you share and when? All of the time? Rarely? Only when they ask?

All relationships seem to change once you've been diagnosed with a life-challenging disease. It is not unknown, cruel as it may appear, for the healthy wife or husband to seek a divorce. This decision may be opportunistic, financially the only recourse, or it may be that they just do not know how to cope with such a catastrophic event in their partner's life. Some gay partners remain together when one is diagnosed with AIDS, others separate, some flee. A wedding service may include the words, "In sickness and in health," and, "Till death do us part," but these solemn vows may not survive events like an auto accident that causes quadriplegia. How well do you (and can you) know your life's partner? Relationships evolve through time and circumstance, but life-challenging and debilitating diseases can and do wreak havoc on relationships. Who do you turn to? What can you do?

Since medicine is their *chosen* profession, you can presumably say anything to your doctors, and also ask them anything. Some aspects relating to this were discussed above. Yet, you will find many doctors who are uncomfortable when you want to share personal feelings, when you become emotional, or when you show signs of "hysteria" or depression. If you can't communicate with your doctor, then a counselor or psychotherapist, social worker or minister may be your next choice. You can get medication only through a medical doctor or psychiatrist. Some psychoactive drugs can be quite helpful to get you over the initial shock and distress of a diagnosis. Used wisely, a relaxant or sleeping pills can get you to the point where you are thinking more clearly, and are ready to take charge of your life and make choices. Some people avoid prescription drugs on principle, but when taken for a specific purpose and in a time-limited way, they can be most beneficial in a tough spot. By all means get the effects and side-effects explained to you.

Almost everyone I know who has a life-challenging disease has told me or the support group about friends who no longer call, and relatives who become remote. On an overt level, being in the presence of someone who has cancer or AIDS, for example, is a forceful reminder of mortality. People who can't handle that thought in themselves, or who can't acknowledge the mortality of someone they love, cut themselves off to deny the idea of possibly imminent death. You will most likely experience the shock of losing some close friends and relatives, and the surprise of new supportive relationships. You can give short shrift to the morbidly curious, those strange people who want to know all of the "details." Your life is none of their business. A friend who grew tired of well-meaning queries about his health simply states, "I'm fine; there are just some parts of me that are not."

You will need to calibrate relationships in terms of your own needs. You can say in a support group things you could never say to your family, for example. There may be one friend you can "dump" on in the sense of falling apart, crying, and giving voice to your deepest fears. The networking and friendships that develop within support groups are very helpful, but you need to be assertive about using this resource. They are *your* people, and you can be comfortable with them since they have been through or are going through your experiences. I can be a very sympathetic listener to your experiences surrounding chemotherapy treatments, but I have not lived myself with the hospital, the staff, the chemo room, the needle sticks, and the hours of waiting. There is an instant rapport with sisters who have had lumpectomies, with brothers who have had radical prostatectomies, and anyone who has lived through a series of radiation treatments. You become part of another culture with all of its rites, rituals, ceremonies, and secret words.

16.6 Support Networks
A single person with cancer can be quickly overwhelmed by the demands put on them, but so can the family of a married person.

If you are employed, there are all the arrangements that have to be made about time off, insurance, etc. If you are a homemaker, your spouse will end up with employment concerns. The family's life gets disrupted; new routines need to be established. The person who is ill may need changing degrees of home care depending on where they are in their treatment, and the progress of the disease. How do you manage your changed life? One way to do this is to set up a support network. There are similarities and differences as to how this is done depending on whether you are single or married.

If you are single, call a meeting of concerned friends to set up your support network. The organization of this meeting may best be done by a friend who has the time and is willing to serve as your support network coordinator. Before the meeting prepare a list of specific things that you need from your supporters. This list may include some or all of the following items:

(1) *Co-ordinator*. Who will be the coordinator? This service may be performed in rotation by several people.

(2) *Transportation*. Who will drive you to your different appointments when you cannot do this by yourself?

(3) *Food*. Who will buy food for you? Who will prepare meals? Meals can be brought in, or you may go to that person's house.

(4) *Cleaning*. Who will make arrangements for cleaning your house and coordinate volunteers to do this?

(5) *Laundry*. Who will handle the laundry?

(6) *Garden and Yard*. If you live in a house with a garden and/or yard, who will take care of this, e.g., mow the lawn, rake the leaves and weeds?

(7) *House/Apartment Maintenance*. Who will be available to fix things that need repair, to find servicepeople, or to move furniture?

(8) *Financial*. Do you need assistance financially to pay for your treatments? Do you need financial advice? Can someone raise money for you?

(9) *Legal*. Do you need help with a will, or a living will, or a Durable Power of Attorney for Health?

(10) *Medical Insurance*. Do you need someone to check your coverage and to be your representative/advisor with your medical insurance provider?

(11) *Hospitals*. Who will help you deal with your hospital(s) and their paperwork and bills and appointments?

(12) *Medical Care*. Do you have *one* doctor who is in overall charge of your treatment? Ideally, all medical services and reports should be channeled through this one physician. You may also need a lay person who helps with communicating with doctors, and who is willing to research options for medical care.

(13) *Counseling*. Do you have a trusted mental health worker in whom you can confide and with whom you can divulge your innermost feelings?

(15) *Fun*. Do not forget to party, to socialize, to have fun, to go out—someone may be able to coordinate fun activities.

Remember one of Rabbi Hillel questions, "If you are not for yourself, who will be?"

Let me expand on this last sentence. Most of us were brought up to be selfless, to think of the other person first, to do good deeds. But, in this world, by and large, you will not get things if you do not directly ask for them. Wishing and dreaming and praying may work, but asking is better. The worst thing than can happen is that you encounter a "No." Ask again. Ask someone else. In this sense you need to be somewhat selfish to get your needs met. This is not only okay, it is in effect demanded by the circumstances. My mother used to admonish, "Ask nicely." So, ask nicely, but ask!

For a person with a family, a family member may serve as the convener and organizer of your support network. This network would include both family and friends. You still need to do the homework of preparing a specific list of needs. It may be harder to be "selfish" within the family—it still needs to be done to get needs met.

You may be part of a religious or social group that already has mechanisms in place to establish a support network for you. Contact them, and use them. There are professional helping services available that can provide most of what you need. Some charge, and some do not. You may need to hire a cleaning person or a private duty nurse.

If you become part of a Hospice program, they have professional staff who care for your needs in many categories. In areas where they do not directly provide a service, the social worker can direct you to relevant resources.

You do not have to go through this alone—reach out and someone will take your hand.

16.7 Counseling and Psychotherapy

When you're stuck and emotionally up against a wall, you can consider going to a counselor or psychotherapist for emotional support and understanding. They will help you find ways of coping with your situation. This *may* be a good time to work through unfinished business from the past. The choice is yours. If the disease is creating difficulties in the relationships with your spouse, your family, with significant others, or at work, then therapy can be helpful. There are therapists who specialize in working with couples, with families, and with those who have life-challenging diseases. It is important to get a good match. If the therapist is not helpful, find another one. There are also ministers who specialize in this kind of work. If you think that medication will be helpful, then approach your doctor or a psychiatrist. "If I am not for myself,…"

16.8 Prayer and Religious Support

There are a number of interesting studies (see Dossey, 1991, 1993, 1996, 1997 for details; also see Section 4.6 for more details on this subject) indicating the power of prayer in healing. This is prayer by the affected person, their family, their church, and by groups who are (apparently) unconnected with the person. If praying is important to you, then by all means pray, and make arrangements for others to pray for and with you.

I know people who have benefited mightily from religious retreats, personal support from their minister, and support from their church. I also know others who felt that they got no support from the same activities. One friend would no longer let her minister visit since he was so obviously uncomfortable in her presence—this was painful to her. Again, you need to calibrate this kind of support to find out what is helpful to you.

16.9 Helping Others

Even though you may be distressed, uncomfortable, and in pain, there may still be ways in which you can help others. Just like you cannot touch without being touched, you can't help others without being helped yourself. At the minimum you are not giving up, giving in, or being helpless. There are still useful things you can do. If you are in a hospital, there may be fellow patients who are less mobile than you are. Can you visit with them, read to them, listen to them? If you are bed-ridden, then perforce you are a captive audience to whoever visits you. Can you listen and respond in ways that are helpful to your visitors, the nurses, the staff, your doctors? No matter the circumstances, there are always choices. You can decide to be a passive lump or an active participant. Remember, the best gift you can give is being receptive to gifts, letting or *asking* others to do things for you. If you are mobile, then there are many ways you can help others. The more you help, the more you are helped.

16.10 Massage

One of the great joys in life can be a full-body massage, preferably for sixty minutes. For a number of years I have treated myself to a biweekly massage. My masseur is knowledgeable about all sorts of bodily aches and pains and knows just where to press or smooth to ease discomforts and release muscle strains. He has also heard, somewhere, that you shouldn't massage people who have cancer, and he doesn't. But, I think he is quite wrong in this regard. Of course, you need to be careful where you massage, and just how much pressure to use. With care and caution, massage can do wonders for people who have life-challenging diseases. Check it out.

You should also be aware that there are many schools of massage—some are quite gentle, while others may use a great deal of pressure. Shiatsu, for example, uses much pressure on particular acupressure points. I am sure this pressure can be adjusted. Some facilities have their own massage people. Some hospitals permit non-staff practitioners to do massage on their premises.

16.11 Information Sources

When people find out you have cancer they all want to give you advice and information. Have you tried this? Have you read that? Have you consulted with...? My brother/mother/uncle had the same thing and they.... How much information do you want and need?

The desire for information is culturally based. In Japan, for example, it is considered proper to tell the cancer patient essentially nothing about their condition and treatment. Euphemisms are frequently used like, "You have extreme stomach distress," rather than say outright, "You have pancreatic cancer." Within the United States we have come a long way from my youth when the word "cancer" was only whispered, or not said out loud at all. Some people want all the information they can possibly get about their disease and its treatment, including technical information. Others wish to eschew information, do not want to participate in their treatment, and turn over all decisions to their doctors and/or family. I think that hugs and information are wonderful, but I also recognize that some people do not like being hugged or want information. Their wishes in this regard must be respected. Hugs should be offered *tentatively*, and be ready to back off gently.

If you do desire information, it is readily available from a variety of sources. There is so much information available that you may not have the time or energy to explore it, let alone study and evaluate it. Your partner or a friend may be asked to take over the role of screening available information and provide you with a limited amount of material. The Worldwide Web or Internet is now the primary source of information on the disease itself, and treatment options. Some good sources are the National Cancer Institute of NIH, Medline, American Cancer Society, and the National Center for Complementary and Alternative Medicine (NCCAM) of NIH. A friend who is adept at searching the Web can be of great help. So can medical school librarians and hospital reference librarians. Your doctors and their staff can usually direct you to sources and provide you with relevant materials. For your guidance, a number of the principal Web sites are listed in Appendix H.

Once you have studied the information, what then? How do you choose between which source to believe when there is conflicting information? If you decide to try alternative therapies (in addition to standard medical treatment), which one or ones do you pick? Where and who are the providers? How much do they charge? How long is the treatment? Is it possible to check their background and success rates? Do they accurately describe their treatment protocol or shield it behind proprietary claims? Is their literature full of glittering generalities? Do they insist that you stop all other treatments and do theirs alone? Consult with your doctor before leaping; also consult with trusted friends. For alternative cancer treatments, Lerner's book (1996) is a good starting place for evaluation.

16.12 Controlling Medication

You may recall Arthur Shapiro's comment, cited in the chapter on the placebo effect, that the story of medicine up through the 1950s was in fact the history of the placebo effect. Since the 1950s many medications have been put on a more scientific footing, albeit with the ever-present placebo effect. (Remember that a major purpose of double-blind studies is to separate out the placebo effect from the material or procedure under test.) Some medicines work better in combination, some do not, and may even have antagonistic effects on each other. Are we over-medicated? Perhaps. There are some precautions that you can take.

First, have your doctor and/or their nurse explain the purpose of the medication, the dosage and regimen, the predicted useful effects, and the potential side-effects. If an information leaflet does not come with your medication, ask your pharmacist for one. Check the PDR (*Physicians' Desk Reference*) for the drug you are taking—your local library should have a copy in its reference section. Ask the doctor or pharmacist about potential difficulties with taking *other* drugs, even non-prescription over-the-counter drugs, at the same time. Do you take the drug before eating? With food? After the meal? When and with what time lapses? Should you increase your intake of fluid, and to what extent? Should you avoid or restrict alcoholic beverages? Are there special foods you should take with the drug? It is a good idea, for example, to eat a small container of yogurt each day you are on an antibiotic to re-populate your large colon with "good" bacteria.

If you are on multiple medications, make a list of all of the drugs that you take, their dosage, when and how you take them, and note the color and shape of the drug (they are all distinctive). This is especially important if you are hospitalized and drugs are administered by the nurses. Knowing the color and shape, for instance, can help you know at a glance if you are getting the correct medication. It is useful to review your list of medications periodically with your doctor—they may have forgotten all of the prescriptions, some of which may no longer be needed, some of which may have been prescribed by other physicians, or which work synergistically or antagonistically with each other. You may even need to consult a specialist on medication. Every once in a while I hear of someone whose doctor took them off all medication to start afresh.

Above all, be sensitive to your own bodily reactions to a given drug. Common adverse side-effects are: nausea, diarrhea, constipation, dizziness, rashes, and dry mouth. Immediately consult your doctor about these side-effects and whether you should stop the medication or alter the dosage or switch to an alternative one. Since some medical insurance plans restrict the brand of the drug doctors may prescribe, or insist on generic drugs, you need to be sensitive to the source of the drug. In principle, generic drugs should have the same beneficial effects and side-effects of name-brand drugs, but differences have been noted. We all react to drugs differently. The doctor prescribes a "standard" dose for your age, weight, and condition. But, some people require significantly different doses—higher *or* lower—than the standard amount. You and your doctor may need to calibrate the dosage.

Modern drugs are often amazingly effective. They can also cause harmful reactions, as in *adverse drug reactions* (ADR). The paper by Lazarou, Pomeranz, and Corey (1998) in the respected *Journal of the American Medical Association* points out the enormous number of ADRs the researchers found in a study of the literature. They looked solely at hospital ADRs. There are even ADR caused fatalities—in fact, there are so many of these that the authors list ADR fatalities as the fourth to sixth (depending on how assessed) cause of death in the United States. The number was estimated to be 76,000 to 137,000 for 1994. This is indeed scary. You need to be very alert about the medications given to you in hospitals, and in general.

16.13 Nutrition

Nutrition appears to be high on everyone's list of lifestyle changes that are needed when you are confronted by a life-challenging disease. Unfortunately, there appears to be little consensus about the best diet for any given condition, except, perhaps, for diabetes mellitus. There are major dietary regimens like macrobiotics and vegetarian (which has many variations). Book after book has been published lauding the virtues of some particular diet of which the author is convinced got rid of their cancer or cured lupus, for example. The truth of the matter is that each and every one of these special diets has probably helped someone, or some small group of people attain freedom from their particular disease. On the other hand, there appears to be no scientifically controlled double-blind studies that point clearly to a particular diet to cure cancer or a specific cancer, for example. How much of these dietary successes are due to the placebo effect? Probably, a significant amount, but only a proper study will say how much. Otherwise, the evidence is anecdotal and word-of-mouth.

Are there particular diets or dietary guidelines that are effective? In the next chapter, H. Ira Fritz, Ph.D., who is a specialist in nutrition, gives his considered opinion on diets for those with life-challenging diseases. Are his views the last word? No. But, they are a reasoned set of recommendations based on his study of the literature. Andrew Weil has written (1972, 1995, 1996) sensibly about nutrition. I believe that the common sense approach towards nutrition is the one to follow. This means eating a balanced diet with plenty of fresh fruits and vegetables, and a minimum of processed or fried or fatty foods. The odds are on your side if you do not smoke, over-eat, over-drink, or vegetate as a couch potato.

Most of the special diets start with a "body cleansing" routine that involves lots of water and/or fresh fruit juices, fasting, and something like a brown rice diet for a week or two. Coffee enemas are sometimes recommended as a way of "detoxifying" the body. You should consult your physician before attempting a cleansing/detoxifying regimen.

Under the heading of "nutrition" we need to add a seemingly endless array of food supplements. Antioxidant combinations are rather popular now. It is not clear how much of which antioxidant or combination it makes sense to take. Essiac tea and the Hoxie herbal solution and amino acids and B complexes and coenzyme Q10 and vitamin C all have their adherents. If the side-effects are minimal, you may wish to explore these supplements. The discipline required to follow a particular diet or set of supplements may be too restrictive or uncomfortable for you and your lifestyle. I always feel cautionary about dogmatically promoted dietary regimens that must be followed to the exclusion of other approaches. Before you commit to a dietary/supplement regimen, check and double-check.

If you are what you eat, be careful about what you eat.

16.14 Physical Exercise

The book entitled *Biomarkers* by Evans and Rosenberg (1992) summarizes much exercise physiology research that was actually carried out with and for older people, rather than attempting to extrapolate the results of experiments made with college students as subjects. Their message is simple—it is never too late to change your diet and/or the amount and kind of exercise. Evans and Rosenberg (1992, p. 42) indicate that there are 10 biomarkers of vitality that *you can alter*. They are:

1. Your muscle mass
2. Your strength
3. Your basal metabolic rate (BMR)
4. Your body fat percentage
5. Your aerobic capacity
6. Your body's blood-sugar tolerance
7. Your cholesterol/HDL (high-density lipids) ratio
8. Your blood pressure
9. Your bone density
10. Your body's ability to regulate its internal temperature

Each of these ten items is discussed extensively. Their book gives a detailed program for these ten biomarkers that is specifically designed for the older population. Nutrition is covered briefly in this chapter and in more detail in Chapter 17 by H. Ira Fritz, Ph.D. Exercise falls into three categories: aerobic, anaerobic, and weight-bearing.

Aerobic exercises are done at a rate that allows sufficient oxygen to get to tissues. They are fast-paced activities that make you huff and puff. They place demands on your cardiovascular apparatus. Anaerobic exercises are so strenuous that the tissues end up with an oxygen deficiency. Anaerobic activities are those like sprinting where the body can do "without oxygen" for a short period of time. You should exercise in only the aerobic range. Covert Bailey (1991) points out that exercises like jogging need to be done at such a rate that you have sufficient wind to talk with a fellow jogger. Exercises that involve the large muscles in the legs are more effective than upper body exercises that involve smaller muscles. Thus, jogging, biking, fast walking, stepping machines, and cross-country skiing (or ski machines) are more useful than swimming, which is mainly an upper body exercise. Three to four sessions per week of aerobic exercise that last at least thirty minutes appear to be the minimum to maintain fitness. For older people, probably the best exercise (less strain on joints) is vigorous walking. Start with what you can do now, even if it is only 100 feet, and extend your range and speed a little bit each day. Consistency is important. Stretching before *and* after exercising reduces strain. Start your exercise session with a five to ten minute low-intensity aerobic warm-up, followed by five minutes of stretching. End your activity with five to ten minutes of an aerobic cool-down, slowing down gradually, and followed by stretching.

Working out in a weight room has two effects: building muscle mass and increasing bone density. The authors of *Biomarkers* point out that muscle improvement is highly specific. An exercise to strengthen your right biceps will strengthen only your right biceps. So, a weight room regimen involves a variety of machines or free weights so that all principal muscle groups are exercised. You work with a particular muscle group and weight doing up to twelve repetitions (reps) before fatiguing. If you can do only a few reps with a particular weight, then go to a lower weight. When it is easy to do twelve or more reps, go to the next highest weight. Do not exceed 80% of your maximal capacity to lift. Avoid locking elbow or knee joints when lifting. Recent research suggests that one set of twelve reps done two to three times each week is sufficient to maintain and even extend fitness. Muscles grow in a particular pattern in response to stressing them. They increase in mass over a 24 to 36 hour period. So, exercise a particular muscle group no more frequently than every *other* day. If you wish to use the weight room daily, then alternate muscle groups each day.

The way the body increases bone mass works differently than for muscle mass. Apparently, according to the *Biomarkers* researchers (see pp. 77–81), weight-bearing exercises for *any* bone or bone group in the body signals the body to uniformly increase bone mass in *all* of the bones in the body. So, *any* kind of weight-bearing exercise is important for older people to strengthen their bones *throughout* their bodies, that is, there is a whole-body effect. These exercises can begin, even for bed-ridden people, by doing something simple like raising a paperback book a dozen times, two to three times each day. They can then progress to heavier paperbacks and other objects.

The important thing is to get people to do some form of weight-bearing exercises regularly, no matter what their age or condition. They also get an almost immediate feedback from aerobic and weight-bearing exercises which encourages them to do more. Recommending some kind of regular exercise of the two types is part of my multi-modal approach to working with people who have life-challenging diseases. When I suggest exercise, a frequent reaction is, "How can I do that when I am so sick/when I have cancer?" An unspoken objection is, "Why bother when I am going to die soon?" The "bother" is worth it for giving them some hope, some sense of control, and the feedback they feel in their muscles and bodies.

16.15 Acupuncture

We have written earlier in this book about acupuncture and that many people do get relief from such treatments. The paper by Melzack, Stillwell, and Fox (1977) provides a potential scientific basis for the use of acupuncture. When seeking an acupuncturist, consult with knowledgeable people, and work with someone who has been in the field for a significant length of time, like ten years or more. This is a treatment where the years of experience of the practitioner are important. There are licensed acupuncturists.

16.16 Pain Management

Western medicine has come a long way from the time when doctors were afraid to give too much pain medication because they feared that their patients would become addicted. (Certainly, morphine, the preferred drug for controlling severe pain, is addictive.) The practice of pain control has changed due to two considerations. First, it makes no sense to worry about addiction for cancer patients in their last days, weeks, or even months. For the people (I know several) who have "graduated" from a Hospice program, the problem of beating the addiction appears to be small with respect to the problems concerning re-entering the world of people with normal life expectancies. The second factor is that doctors and particularly Hospices now know a great deal more about the control of pain, and have better devices for controlling the delivery of pain medication. Many hospitals have pain clinics which specialize in the control of all kinds of pain. These clinics are staffed by a variety of professionals including medical doctors, psychiatrists, psychologists, hypnotists, and social workers.

There is now no reason to be uncomfortable or in severe pain for any significant length of time. Following Melzack's lead (Melzack, 1990) administering pain-control medication only on demand, which causes the yo-yo or see-sawing effect, has diminished. The goal is to keep the patient as comfortable *and* as sentient as possible. This is best done by administering lower doses, but sufficient for sustained comfort, by slow-release pills, patches or implants, by metering pumps, or by a regularly timed delivery. These approaches minimize the peaks of pain and the almost comatose valleys. The metering pumps also have an over-ride to help control break-through pain by self-administering an extra controlled dose. Since you are the only judge of your comfort level, you need to be assertive to get what you want. People respond differently to the same dosage, and their needs change with time. Ask and you shall be succored.

One of the most feared consequences of cancer is the severe pain which comes with *some* cancers, particularly in the last stages. All cancers are different, and many do not involve major pain or disability. Remember Frankl's advice—we may not be able to control what happens to us, but we always have the choice of how we respond. Being held by someone you love may be the medication of choice.

16.17 Hypnosis

Hypnosis has much to offer in a variety of ways. For example, hypnosis is well-established as a method of pain control. There are no side-effects, and the patient can generally be quite sentient. Hypnosis can be used to control the nausea that often accompanies chemotherapy treatments. It can also help to minimize the side-effects of radiotherapy treatments. Hypnosis generally has a calming and relaxing effect. Guided imagery work can be considered to be a kind of hypnosis since hypnotic language skills are needed for effective work. Earlier in this book we have written about the use of hypnosis for preparation for surgery or other invasive treatments.

Many hospitals now have a hypnotherapist on staff, or on their list of consultants. It is my hope that there will be more use of hypnosis to help people with life-challenging diseases. At the worst, hypnosis will be little help; at the best, significant help; and there are also no side-effects.

16.18 Talking to a Comatose Patient

Just as there is evidence that people under the surgical plane of anesthesia can hear and understand what is said to them (see Section 10.3), there are also strong indications that people in comas can hear and respond on some level to what is said to them. At the minimum, this helps the person doing the talking—they can express their concern and love and feel that they are communicating with a loved one. Physical contact, like holding a hand, appears to help this communication. It is similarly important to talk to people who have had strokes and who are limited in the ways they can respond. You can read poetry, favorite passages, or entire books. You can ask for responses like eye blinks or hand squeezes. Although it is sometimes hard to do this kind of communicating, I have always found it to be worthwhile.

16.19 Grieving

Your survivors will grieve for you—there is also grieving to be done by you before that time. To grieve is to acknowledge a loss, that loss can be of a person, a pet, a favorite object, and missed opportunities. Saying goodbye to life and all it has meant to you can be helped by consciously grieving over your losses. This is not something that is done to excess with great wailings and gnashings of teeth. It is generally done with some sadness, some nostalgia, and many good memories. If this kind of grieving and letting go makes sense to you, then do it privately or with someone you trust. As discussed earlier in the section on ceremonies, you may wish to devise a ceremony for grieving. We are all somewhat saddened by losses, even anticipated losses, and buoyed up by happy memories. Brooks (1985) has written a remarkable book on grieving the loss of her husband—the book is in the form of a monthly journal. (See Section 15.3 for a structured writing workbook for grieving.)

16.20 Ideomotor Signaling

One way to cope with the changes going on in your body and all the new sensations is to use ideomotor signaling to query your body's inner sense of what is going on (see Section 13.12). If you are good at this technique, it can be of great use to you in assessing what goes on in your body. It does take practice, and an experienced hypnotherapist can get you started and teach you what you need to know. Alternatively, you may just go to a hypnotist and have them guide you through this kind of body scan.

It has been said, "The body never lies." and "Who knows your body better than you?" Ideomotor finger signaling is one way to put these two observations together.

16.21 Meditation and Relaxation

How do you relax given the continuing stress and interruptions to your life that a serious disease brings about? If you are already adept at meditation or doing self-relaxation, then you need to *schedule* one or two fixed times each day for this purpose. The word "schedule" is emphasized since for healing—and curing—relaxation may be as important as treatments. It is said, for example, that the *panic reaction* which accompanies a heart attack kills more people than the physical damage to the heart. In this regard it is enlightening to read how Norman Cousins (1984) handled his heart attack. To lower his tension level, and the tension level of those around him, he told jokes to by-standers and the paramedics who took him to the hospital!

There are many relaxation/meditation tapes available. There are courses in how to meditate and relax. Your therapist or a friend could make a relaxation tape for you. You can make such a tape for yourself by taping one of the many available scripts, or favorite passages from the Bible, Koran, Torah, Vedas, books of poetry, etc.

Most people find a long soak in a hot bath, or a long shower, to be very relaxing. You know the things that you do that are most relaxing for you. This may be music or a good book or watching television or going out with friends or the theater or the movies. Recall that the effectiveness of your immune system is enhanced when you are in a relaxed state.

16.22 Simplicity

The *simplicity* movement has been growing in the U.S. The goal is to simplify your life. In a consumer society driven by advertising we are continually urged to buy more and more things. A personal computer which was state-of-the-art three years ago is considered to be obsolete technology today—too slow and too little memory. How often do you replace your car, your washing machine, your vacuum cleaner, your stereo equipment, etc.? Do you really need another pair of shoes? Can you share a lawn mower with your neighbor? With several neighbors? How much "stuff" do you really need?

When you are diagnosed with a life-challenging disease or have some catastrophic event in your life, you suddenly get a different perspective on what things are really important. These are your health and your relationships. "Objects" no longer have the same value. That promotion you were "killing yourself" for is literally not worth dying—or living—for. Don't wait for cancer for permission to find meaning in your life. Don't wait for that catastrophic disease to begin simplifying your life. Don't wait.

There are books (Elgin, 1981; St. James, 1994; Andrews, 1997; Luhrs, 1997) on simplicity. The titles of these four books, respectively, are illuminating: *Voluntary Simplicity. Toward a Way of Life that is Outwardly Simple, Inwardly Rich*; *Simplify Your Life. 100 Ways to Slow Down and Enjoy the Things that Really Matter*; *The Circle of Simplicity. Return to the Good Life*; and *The Simple Living Guide*. Many communities have simplicity circles and study groups.

16.23 Laughter

The *Reader's Digest* has a long-standing feature whose title is, "Laughter—the Best Medicine." When was the last time you had a *belly* laugh, one of those fits of laughter that brings tears to your eyes, a stitch in your side, and has you fighting for breath? Laughter is an excellent medicine. Norman Cousins (1979) literally used laughter to cure himself of ankylosing spondylitis (rheumatoid arthritis of the spine where the connective tissue progressively disintegrates—no known cause or cure). (He did this in collaboration with medical advice.) Laughter will probably not have such a dramatic effect on your disease, but we do know through David Spiegel et al.'s work (1989) that mental attitudes can have profound physical effects.

At our support group meetings there is a lot of laughing. This may surprise some, but not our members. There is occasional "black" humor related to disease or treatment—it is really only occasional. We simply enjoy laughing together. People bring in jokes and cartoons to share. The world outside of the support group is too serious. Aside from Patch Adams (1998), how many doctors are willing to clown it up? Families frequently feel it is inappropriate to laugh or do fun things—he's got cancer, you know. If what you are doing isn't FUN, what is it? If you can't laugh, can you be alive? Laugh and the world laughs with you. Crying alone is sad. The studies probably haven't been done yet, but I am willing to bet that the immune system is enhanced by laughter. Since you can't physiologically be panicked and relaxed at the same time, which one will you choose?

I heard a joke the other day….

16.24 Dying Well

I know I am going to die sometime, that this life, this consciousness, this inner sense of who I am, the uniqueness of me, will end. I know this and I don't really believe it or expect it. When I was young I could not conceive of what it would be like to be 68 years old. Too far away, too remote. My image of old people—those in their fifties or sixties—was formed by my older relatives and people I saw in the street. I grew up, age three to twenty one, at 1932 Crotona Parkway in the Bronx. That building has long been demolished. We lived on the first floor and the living room windows looked out on Crotona Parkway. This street was separated by a small strip of park, perhaps sixty feet wide, from the main parallel thoroughfare of Southern Boulevard with its trolley cars and businesses. Looking to the right, our block ended on the main cross street of Tremont Avenue with its trolleys. But, we had that grassy strip, that park, that extended for perhaps ten blocks in total. The side of the park facing our tenement was lined with benches. Old people sat on the benches. They talked, they snoozed, they read the newspaper, and they minded children. The "old" people I knew were those who sat on the benches, tired, waiting for death, way past the prime of their lives. Being old was being a bench person. Or, maybe, being like Mrs. Sousi who lived below us, right off the sidewalk, and who seemed to spend her life looking out her window. This window was open in the summer and closed in the winter. She was a woman who studied life from her privileged perch. What did she see? What did she think? What did she make of the children, the mothers, the bench sitters? She was old, too.

Due to a strange circumstance I saw my father for the last time on the afternoon of the day he died. He was 94 years old and living in the Sephardic Home in Brooklyn. I had planned on visiting my sister in California for a week. Lillian was twelve years older than I, and her breast cancer had returned after her husband's sudden death due to an aneurysm. The least expensive flight I could get from Dayton to San Diego was actually to go to New York City first. So, I took this opportunity to see Pop. He looked weak and fragile and asked me to help him go to the toilet. I assisted him. When he finished, he asked me to wipe him since he could not do this for himself. I did. He died that night, peacefully, simply from old age, literally passing away. I knew that he probably never changed my diapers when I was a baby. Yet, for me, there was something especially powerful in the last service I did for him. A circle, a cycle, was completed. My father died well.

My vision of dying well is being at home in my own bed, surrounded by family—my wife, my sons and their wives, my grand children, maybe their spouses and great grandchildren, and close friends. We laugh and tell stories and touch and hug. Perhaps we all hold hands in a large circle. Maybe, someone sings one of the songs I sang to my children and their children at bedtime— *Hush little baby, don't say a word, papa's gonna buy you a mocking bird ... —* or— *Hush-a-bye, don't you cry, go to sleepy little baby ...* Maybe, in the background I can hear Pete Seeger on my favorite album (*Goofing Off Suite*) singing, "Oh, had I a golden thread with needle so fine, I would weave a magic cloth of rainbow design, of rainbow design." There would be sunshine and birds singing. I would look at everyone for the last time. Close my eyes, and die. My ashes would be spread in the blueberry patch where all of the family pets are buried. I would die well.

Dying well takes some planning, some thinking, much coopera-tion, and a great deal of luck. Have you thought about your last days? What you would like them to be like? How to bring that dream about? Yes, we may have no control over that event, but we can dream and hope and plan. This is a natural event, and can be joyous, a celebration of life, of accomplishments, of love. Horace Mann left us with the legacy, "Be ashamed to die until you have won some small victory for humanity." I feel that I have already done so. I know that I will win some more small victories. It is suf-ficient to know that I have two sons whom I like as well as love, that I've known a wonderful life with my wife, and that in many small ways my being here has made a difference in the lives of oth-ers. You have, too. We can all die well.

16.25 Summary

The "system" may not be out to get you, but it frequently seems that way. This chapter gives information on the many ways you can cope with the system and take care of yourself. You always have the choice about what you think and feel about a situation. There is much more that is under your control than you think. The extremes are being a passive lump that things are *done to*, or an active agent that things are *done by and with*. The more control you have over your life and treatment, the better the odds for a good outcome. Enjoy!

Chapter 17

Nutrition and Life-Challenging Diseases
H. Ira Fritz, Ph.D.

17.1 Introduction: Lifestyle and an Integrated Approach

In our modern society, nutrition is viewed differently by different segments of the population. This variation of opinion is also found among health professionals. Nutritional approaches to disease should neither be taken for granted nor considered to be panaceas. Also, nutrition cannot be considered just by itself, nor should it be focused on a specific disease. When considering a dietary lifestyle, a person should target an eating pattern that is easy and natural to maintain, but also one that adheres to generally accepted and researched guidelines and principles. The last several years have produced much evidence indicating the importance of both integration and balance in nutrition. I use the term *integration* to mean the use of nutrition as a part of a total lifestyle program. This includes regular exercise of both the aerobic and resistance type, some attention to group support or social network, some attention to relaxation, and a balanced approach to an eating pattern. I use the term *balance* to mean a style of eating consistent with an individual's cultural context, but a pattern which includes a wide variety of primarily whole foods.

17.2 Prevention

One example of this idea of integration is the research on diets and the prevention of heart disease. This work began out of studies done by Pritikin and McGrady (1979, p. 5). He anecdotally reported that diets which contained less than 10% of their calories from fat seemed to decrease the risk for heart disease (Pritikin, 1983).

These pioneering general studies were refined and further developed by Ornish (1991). Ornish's work is critical for a number of reasons. First, he extended the work on dietary principles. Ornish uses a vegetarian diet with limited amounts of skim milk and egg white. This diet prohibits fried foods and sharply decreases total fat intake (20% or less of energy from fat). Patients were given angiograms, placed on the Ornish program, and then given follow up angiograms 12–24 months after starting the diet. The second angiograms indicated that *compliant* patients *reversed* the size of the atherosclerotic lesions present in their arteries. This would suggest that nutrition has a major role to play in the prevention and reversal of coronary heart disease and, by implication, occlusive stroke. Although the preceding statement is very likely true, it is incomplete, since Ornish uses a *whole* lifestyle intervention program. This program includes altered eating patterns, *and* an exercise program (primarily walking), *and* daily relaxation (centered around meditation), *and* group interaction and support. This *total* intervention program includes deep and consistent lifestyle changes. Ornish has suggested that the most compliant patients show the most complete and systematic reversal of the disease process. The notion of a multi-modal approach is important for our discussion on nutrition, just as it is a central theme of this book.

Low-fat diets generally decrease blood lipids and cholesterol, in particular. The lowering of blood cholesterol decreases one of the major risk factors for cardiovascular disease. However, there have been some suggestions that very low cholesterol levels may be associated with increased cancer risks (Sharp and Pocock, 1997; Zureik et al., 1997). In addition, low-fat diets tend to be low in the essential fatty acids. Essential fatty acids are defined as those fatty acids which the body cannot synthesize and therefore must be present in food or otherwise ingested. These polyunsaturated compounds fall into two general families. They are the omega-3 fatty acids which include alpha-linolenic acid and eicosapentaenoic acid (EPA) and docosahexaenoic acid (DHA). These essential fatty acids are found in specific plants and fish oils. The second family is the omega-6 fatty acids which include linoleic acid, gamma linolenic acid and arachidonic acid. Because these two families of fatty acids are different and have different and sometimes competing biological effects, it is necessary to have an appropriate ratio of omega-3 to omega-6 in our diets. The original Ornish program, because of its low-fat nature and its emphasis on legumes and the usually consumed vegetables, was also low in omega-3 fatty acids. The best sources of omega-3 fatty acids are animal products, especially fish oils. An additional value of consuming omega-3 fatty acids is their useful effects regarding decreased platelet aggregation (blood clotting) and increased vasodilation (blood vessel diameter). There are also potential problems with central nervous system function with low levels of essential fatty acids (Whitney et al., 1998). This may have implications for degenerative central nervous system diseases such as Parkinson's, Multiple Sclerosis and Amyotrophic Lateral Sclerosis (Simonian and Coyle, 1996).

There is an extensive literature (World Cancer Research Fund/American Institute for Cancer Research, 1997) on the chemoprevention of cancer. Although there are many points that are not clear, it appears safe to recommend a varied diet that is consistent with the United States Department of Agriculture's *Food Pyramid*. Those recommendations suggest 3–5 servings of vegetables and 2–4 servings of fruit each day. The work of Ames et. al. (1993) supports this idea. In a meta-analysis, Bloch (in Helzlsouer et al., 1994) reviewed 200 different studies. She suggests that the consistent consumption of fruits and vegetables is protective against cancer. Of the studies reviewed, 128 showed the preventative effects of 3–5 servings (usually defined as about 3 oz) each of fruits and vegetables. There is an extensive literature (e.g., Whitney et al., 1998, pp. 126–127) indicating that fiber consumption reduces the risk of both cardiovascular disease and gastrointestinal cancers. The results vary with the type of fiber. Soluble fiber (i.e., oat bran, fruit pectins, and legumes, etc.) seems to be involved with cardiovascular health; while insoluble fiber (i.e., wheat bran, whole grain breads and cereal, and vegetables, etc.) seems to be preventative for colon cancer.

Currently there is much interest in the concept of chemoprevention. That interest centers around the use of various nutrients to decrease the probability of contracting some form of cancer. This research is generally focused on the use of plant-derived materials or phytonutrients. Some of these are well-defined antioxidants, i.e., vitamin E, vitamin C, selenium, and beta-carotene. Others of these compounds are more chemically varied and generally fall in the classification of polyphenols or flavonoids. This research is still in its early stages. Comstock et al. (1991), in an epidemiological study, indicated that there was a correlation between low levels of specific antioxidants (beta-carotene, vitamin E, selenium, and vitamin A) and susceptibility to cancer at specific sites, the sites being different for the different antioxidants.

When discussing the chemoprevention of cancer there are a number of specific substances that should be considered. Phytonutrients are being examined carefully in a number of ways. (A whole issue of *Nutrition Reviews*, 57, No. 9, part II, 1999, is devoted to these studies.) Polyphenols in general (Balentine, Albano, and Nair, 1999; Ursini et al., 1999), and particularly those in green tea (Ahmad and Mukhtar, 1999), are being examined as powerful chemopreventative tools. These studies grow out of epidemiological considerations and are attempting to examine specific compounds and their mechanisms. The review by Ahmad and Mukhtar (1999) is particularly useful because it examines the characteristics of an "ideal" chemopreventative agent. It is one which should be inexpensive, have high acceptability, no or low toxicity, and be effective with some well-defined mechanism.

The antioxidant nutrients have also been examined as possible chemopreventative agents. Current evidence regarding vitamin C is inconclusive (Koo, 1997; Barth et al., 1998). The evidence regarding beta- carotene suggests caution based on the Finnish smokers study (The Alpha-Tocopherol, Beta-carotene Cancer Prevention Study Group, 1994). In this study those smokers who consumed beta-carotene supplements had an increased risk of cancer. Other antioxidants have been suggested as being useful. Folate, sometimes called folic acid, has been found to reduce the risk of pancreatic cancer in men and breast cancer in women at intake levels of around 400 μg per day (Kim, 1999). (μg = microgram) However, the best example of an antioxidant would be selenium. The suggested intake of selenium is 70 μg per day. In a recent study (Clark, et al., 1996), the evidence suggested that oral supplementation of 200 μg per day had a preventative effect on certain types of cancer. These studies and others are developing into a discussion and examination of recommended levels of intake.

The Recommended Dietary Allowances (RDA), currently being renamed as Reference Daily Intakes (RDI), were developed to insure adequate levels of intake to prevent deficiency disease. Various researchers (Bloch in Helzlsouer, et al., 1994; Diplock in Helzlsouer, et al., 1994; Ursini et al., 1999) propose the concept of an optimal level of intake which would be both safe and useful in a curative or preventative mode in addition to protection against deficiency disease. A recent example of this kind of study is the work of Levine (1999) with vitamin C. He suggests that doses of 200 mg per day saturate the systems in the body and represent optimal or near optimal intake. It should be noted that the RDI for vitamin C is 60 mg. Recent studies (Visioli and Galli, 1998; Ursini et al., 1999; and Ahmad and Mukhtar, 1999) have examined a variety of polyphenols as preventative agents for both cardiovascular disease and for cancer. This common approach is based on two ideas. In cancer, there is damage to cellular DNA that can result in mutation and uncontrolled growth. Oxidation may also be the cause of this damage, either directly or indirectly. If this oxidative damage can be prevented, then the probability of cancer is markedly decreased.

For cardiovascular disease the story is somewhat more complicated. There are a number of risk factors for cardiovascular disease. When a person has one or more of these factors, the probability of their developing the disease is higher than if they did not have the factors. The well-defined risk factors for cardiovascular disease which *cannot* be changed are: genetic history, male gender, age and race/ethnicity (Suter and Vetter, 1999). There are a series of risk factors which are modifiable. They are: high blood pressure, obesity, diabetes, blood lipids (including cholesterol), compulsive personality, sedentary lifestyle, and smoking. (It is interesting to note that smoking is the major causative factor for lung cancer as well as some other cancers of the upper respiratory and digestive tracts.) Cardiovascular disease prevention, whether focusing on heart attack or on stroke, is aimed at preventing or controlling the size of atherosclerotic lesions. These lesions are composed of cholesterol and other fatty substances. These substances accumulate on the interior arterial wall. There are two factors which are major contributions to these lesions. The first and most easily modified factor is elevated homocysteine, an amino acid. Homocysteine can be controlled by using folic acid in the range of 400–1000 μg per day. Vitamins B12 and B6 also help in the metabolism of homocysteine and can keep levels under control (Cooper, 1996, pp. 24–36). (B12 should be consumed in the range of 50–200 μg per day depending upon the intake of folate. B6 levels should be no more than 50–60 mg per day because of the potential for nerve damage.) The other factor is one of the serum lipoproteins, low density lipoprotein or LDL. The problem is caused when LDL is in an oxidized state. LDL can be maintained in more reduced forms through the use of vitamin E supplements. The levels quoted in the literature range from 300–600 I.V. per day (Cooper, 1996, p. 210). In addition to the protective effect on LDL, this level of vitamin E seems to inhibit the aggregation of blood platelets caused by atherosclerotic plaque (Steiner, 1999). Vitamin E may also antagonize vitamin K. This antagonism results in an inhibition of blood clotting, one of the immediate causes of myocardial infarction or occlusive stroke. Aspirin, which is commonly recommended as a preventative for both first and second heart attacks, acts to keep platelets inactive, thus decreasing the likelihood of a blood clot. These two approaches are additive. The potential problem of this decrease in clotting capacity is the increased probability of hemorrhagic stroke. This underlines the need for balance.

When discussing the prevention or delay of cardiovascular disease, there is one other factor that needs to be mentioned. It is a controversial one. Low and consistent intake of alcohol at the level of one-half to one drink equivalent for women, and one to two drinks per day for men, has a protective effect. A drink equivalent is 3–5 ounces of wine, 12 ounces of beer or 1.5 ounces of distilled spirits. Higher consumption is harmful and does not have additional benefits. The problem with this, and one that has caused heated debate, is whether a recommendation should be made concerning alcohol consumption. The potential problem of addiction or alcoholism is one that needs to be considered as well as general family/cultural beliefs regarding the use of alcohol. My personal approach has been to inquire whether alcohol is a part of an individual's lifestyle, and then to proceed to specific recommendations. The protective effect is related to both a low level of intake and of intake consistency (Suter and Vetter, 1999).

The various studies reported above were all accomplished using what is considered to be the "gold standard" for biomedical research. They used randomized, double-blind, placebo-controlled methodology. This approach is important and has led to much of the dramatic increase in medical knowledge that we currently have. However, it is designed to examine carefully the effects of a highly controlled factor in some specific situation. For our discussion here, these methods have allowed us to write about the preventative effects of various nutritional factors. As we begin to think about the role of nutrition in curing or limiting a disease, this methodology is not as useful as we might want it to be. I would like to argue here for the use and consideration of a different approach, that of *outcomes research*. As mentioned in the beginning of this chapter, when we look at nutrition we need to use both a balanced and an integrated approach. That means we are using a number of factors at the same time, and what matters is the final outcome—increased longevity, loss of tumor, reversal of heart disease, etc. For instance, if we reexamine Ornish's (1991) intervention program for reversal of heart disease, there are a number of factors in the intervention. There is a low-fat vegetarian diet, an exercise program (walking), programmed relaxation, and group interaction and support. It is difficult to determine which of these factors contributes the most to the reversal of heart disease. There is also another factor which needs to be considered. How big an effect occurs simply because the individual is involved in an intervention program and everyone including the individual *expects* there to be improvement? This may be another example of the placebo effect (see Chapter 4). From the perspective presented here, neither the number of factors operating, nor the relative contribution of any specific factor is important. The critical issue is the overall, final outcome. Certainly, that is what is most important to the affected individual. In my opinion, not enough is being done to develop outcomes research as a useful and useable paradigm.

17.3 Nutrition for Controlling or Curing a Disease

In cardiovascular disease, there is a clear and viable path for reversing atherosclerotic lesions. The work of Ornish (1991) has dramatically shown that lesions can be reversed, and that the risk for occlusive cardiovascular disease can be decreased. His approach is described above, but he suggests that for reversal one needs to *adhere rigorously* to his suggested diet *and* include the other lifestyle changes. As mentioned above, it isn't clear what role each segment of his program has in this reversal. Importantly, the *system* works and should be used by those people who can effect the total lifestyle changes. The National Cholesterol Education program (Connor and Connor, 1989) recommends a less severe diet than the one Ornish uses, and that diet would appear to be useful for control if not also effective in reversal.

The picture with cancer is less promising at the present time. There are a number of eating patterns that various people recommend with *no* substantive evidence to support their use. Although there have been some limited reports (Pauling, 1976, p. 188) that large doses of vitamin C are effective in prolonging the lives of terminally ill cancer patients, there are no well-controlled studies that support this idea. The traditional medical literature (Bloch, 1994) approaches nutrition for the cancer patient in a conservative and somewhat discouraging way. Bloch suggests that we have insufficient knowledge and limited success in using nutrition as an adjunct in cancer treatment. Her editorial is in part a response to a review by Klein and Koretz (1994) which finds no convincing evidence of a positive nutritional effect. Others (Ottery, 1994; Ottery, 1995; Seligman, Fink and Massey-Seligman, 1998) suggest that supporting nutritional status, maintaining body composition, and maintaining functional status will improve the patient's quality of life. This becomes particularly important for the patient with poor appetite. This controversy is still in progress. A recent review (Davis and Dickerson, 2000), proposes a four-step anorexia treatment ladder for cancer patients to decrease the negative effects of cancer-related anorexia and cachexia.

This is where outcomes research would be quite useful. As discussed above, if a person uses an integrated approach, then positive outcomes—cure, remission, and increase in quality and/or quantity of life are the goal. In my judgment that means that a person should not reject standard medical treatment, but should also not be afraid to use the various alternative and complementary regimens that are available. A former friend and colleague of mine died of colon cancer. He outlived his physician's predictions by several years. He did not even quit smoking. His approach was simply to *ignore* his disease. Until near his death, he seemed to have a reasonable quality of life. Although I am not endorsing denial (which can have positive aspects), I do suggest that both quality and length of life can be improved by working on one's eating pattern *and* the rest of one's lifestyle.

I have deliberately chosen not to discuss some popular and widely used patterns (e.g., macrobiotics) because I could find nothing in the literature to support those approaches. However, I do not disagree with an individual who wishes to implement one of these plans as a part of an integrated approach to disease control. I truly believe in an outcomes based approach. I would never suggest that standard medical treatment be rejected, but the *addition* of other alternatives to that treatment seems to have been beneficial to a number of individuals.

17.4 Eating Pattern

It is clear to me and others (Connor and Connor, 1989; Willett, 1994; Gifford, 1998) that the way we eat in America leaves much to be desired. We eat too many convenience foods, too many high-fat fast-foods, and we spend very little time enjoying our food. Most other countries eat less processed food and more whole food. That is a place to begin. Ornish's (1991) eating plan is a severe one, and one that I would find difficult to follow. However, there are a number of steps that can be taken in the direction of the Ornish program (Connor and Connor, 1989) that would improve quality and length of life. I advocate an eating pattern based on what is called (Oldways Preservation and Exchange Trust) *The Traditional Healthy Mediterranean Diet Pyramid* (Gifford, 1998). There is some evidence (Trichopoulou and Lagiou, 1997; Trichopoulou, Vasilopoulou, and Lagiou, 1999) that the Mediterranean style diet may decrease the risk for cardiovascular disease. As may be seen in figure 17.1, the base of this pyramid is wholegrains and other starches. Fruits, vegetables and legumes are the next level, followed by olive oil, cheese and yogurt (I would recommend the low-fat varieties of these materials). Animal protein is represented by fish and poultry, with limited amounts of eggs and sweets, and very limited amounts of red meat. This approach is consistent with what is the practice in many parts of the world where red meat, and frequently any animal protein, is used as a condiment and not an entrée. There are many useful aspects to this approach. It means that most calories will be in the form of plant products which will increase the variety of phytonutrients as well as the fiber. The other part of this approach is a philosophical one, but one that is very much lifestyle related. That is, food should be prepared and enjoyed with enthusiasm and caring. If what Battino has said in earlier chapters is correct, then one's *attitude* toward one's life and disease can have an enormous impact on the outcome. Putting an effort into food preparation and serving it in an atmosphere of family and friends should have several beneficial effects—better portion control, more enjoyment, and more relaxation. "Slow food" is in the mouth long enough to be both tasted and savored. This eating style will also reduce saturated fat intake. An attempt should be made to reduce the intake of trans-fatty acids by reducing the intake of partially hydrogenated plant fats. This is not a low-fat diet, but it certainly can meet the U.S. dietary guidelines of no more than 30% of calories from fat. In addition, as with all the other pyramid guides, a family can use foods that are culturally and personally favored.

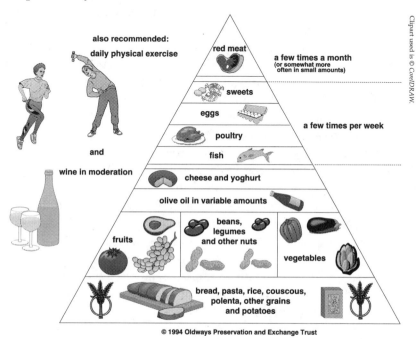

Clipart used is © CorelDRAW.

© 1994 Oldways Preservation and Exchange Trust

Figure 17.1
The Traditional Healthy Mediterranean Diet Pyramid.

I believe that, in addition to this basic eating style, there are a number of supplements that can be useful. Some source of omega-3 fatty acids (fish oils or flaxseed oil) should be included. Antioxidants, I believe, are critical. Vitamin E should be used at around 300–600 IU per day. A cautionary note here: synthetic vitamin E is not as effective as the natural form and the synthetic form promotes the loss of vitamin E from the body. Vitamin C (Johnston, 1999) appears to be safe up to 1.5–2 grams per day. Based on where one lives, a low level (50 μg per day) of selenium supplementation could be considered. Selenium content of soils, and consequently the plants that grow in that soil, can vary considerably. Older adults may wish to consider calcium supplementation. Willett (1994) has a useful discussion of calcium and dairy products, noting that many populations consume few dairy products and still may have low fracture rates on modest calcium intakes. Where protein consumption is high, calcium losses are increased. Calcium supplements are inexpensive and effective. The RDI for calcium is 1000 mg per day (adults ages 19–50). The recommended dose increases to 1200 mg per day for those over 50. Postmenopausal women, particularly those susceptible to, or with a history of osteoporosis, should probably be taking a minimum of 1500 mg per day. A note regarding balance must be added here. These high levels of calcium consumption can antagonize magnesium intake. Magnesium then needs to be adjusted upwards to stay in balance with calcium. The ratio of calcium to magnesium should be somewhere between 2.25 and 3 to 1. These minerals are generally best taken with food. A multivitamin-mineral supplement at RDI levels is worthwhile.

Many of the references used here are to review articles as a means of allowing the reader an easy entry into the literature. There are some sources which I would like to recommend strongly as places for the interested reader to obtain nutrition information. *Nutrition Reviews* is an excellent place to begin. Reviews found there tend to be critical and interpretive. As sources for original research, I recommend the *American Journal of Clinical Nutrition* and the *Journal of the American College of Nutrition*. I have frequently recommended the *Nutrition Action Healthletter* to my undergraduate students. The two Web sites I find most useful are www.veris-online.org and www.arborcom.com. The Veris Web site and newsletter deal primarily with antioxidants. The Arbor nutrition site has more general reviews of various nutrition topics.

17.5 Summary

Nutrition can be an important part of the disease process. It should be integrated into programs of prevention and treatment. There are regimens which decrease the risk for heart disease and cancer. It is also possible to reverse existing heart disease. Eating patterns are not the only part of one's lifestyle that need attention. Exercise, relaxation, and group interactions are also important. Although the current scientific literature does not offer much to the cancer patient, a nutritional program is probably a reasonable addendum to the treatment approach. There is not enough information from outcomes research to be a useful tool. However, this method should offer much hope in the future. *The Traditional Healthy Mediterranean Diet Pyramid* is recommended as an eating pattern. Supplements have a place in this eating pattern.

Chapter 18

Growing Up as a Non-Full-Blooded
Native American Healer

Helena Sheehan, Ph.D.

It has been almost ten years since my stepfather heard the dreaded words, "Yes, you have cancer. Right now, it is localized to the prostate and if we are lucky, surgery will be able to get it all." That was not the case. It took him three years to have the disease metastasize to his bones, and for him to die a slow, painful death. Mama prayed, chanted, and used herbs to lessen his pain. I used my hands. He died August 1989.

Statistics state that one in four is the expected number to have cancer. Just three years after Pop died, Mama was diagnosed with cancer. She had small cell carcinoma. It metastasized to her brain in the form of five tumors. Her initial reaction was one of stunned disbelief. Then she contacted an old Indian healer. When she learned there were no options, her heritage, her quiet acceptance and overall attitude to her own impending death gave even more strength to her years of practice. Once again I used my hands to help lessen the pain and move the clots.

Mother was Choctaw Indian from Oklahoma. She married a Cherokee man from North Carolina.

During my growing up years Indian traditions and cultural activities were not talked about. I have always believed that was because we were not full-bloods. There was a difference in treatment. Non-full-blood children were basically ignored and adults were just overlooked. However, Mama did what was expected of her. She even ran for chief of our tribe. She made sure that my brother (who was killed in the line of duty 18 years ago) and I did not become a statistic. She quietly instructed in the healing and herbal usage of the old ways. She was considered to be an *old one* even when she was young. The traditional ways were not talked about, they were lived and demonstrated. As a child I would be taken places to *be* with those who were ill and often asked to touch them on their feet and ankles. I find it difficult to write about the healing ways as I learned them. Today healing is viewed as an alternative form of medicine. It is from that perspective that I will write this chapter.

18.1 Introduction

Alternative medicine is a big health issue today. Why? It is my belief that the idea of alternative medicine is being treated as something new. But, how short the memory is. It was in just the last century that all medicines came from plants and most were administered without a doctor or pharmacist. Now, for the most part, medicines are synthetic and come from laboratories, must be prescribed by a doctor and filled by a pharmacist. However, as *alternatives* become accepted into social practice, the meaning could change. They will no longer be viewed as nontraditional or optional, but will be connected to mainstream medicine. They will not be in competition with conventional medicine, but will work in cooperation (Hammerschlag and Silverman, 1997). It will become an accepted as well as expected practice. Just look at the number of commercials that are on television for across-the-counter herbs and brand-name vitamins and minerals.

Today's conventional medicine is considered to be bio-analytical and is used primarily as interventions. For the most part, conventional medicine relies on drugs, surgery and technology. It excels at symptomology and diagnosis. It is most often the preferred *choice* for treatment of infectious and life-challenging diseases, organ failure, injuries, acute pain and emergencies. In other words, if you have a broken leg, it would be in your best interest to seek medical attention for treatment.

If you are suffering from chronic fatigue, hypertension, digestive or immune disorders, colds, headache, back pain, and any ailments that can be related to stress, like eating junk food, being overweight, substance abuse or lack of exercise, chances are you may manage your own health care at home.

According to the *New England Journal of Medicine* (Campion, 1993), about 144 million people made visits to alternative practitioners during 1990. They spent nearly 14 billion dollars on health services not covered by medical insurance during that year alone. About 104 million of those people did *not* tell their regular physicians of their decision to seek alternative approaches. Could this indicate a crisis of confidence in the medical establishment? The United States government thought so. They formed a special National Center for Complementary and Alternative Medicine at the National Institute of Health to look into some of the alternative practices.

One aspect of alternative medicine that has received much attention is the healing used by Native Americans. The rest of this chapter will review one non-full-blooded Native American's approach to healing.

18.2 About Healers

Healers and medicine men are among the world's oldest professions. They are thought to be religious specialists. They were the world's first doctors and priests and go back as far as the Stone Age (Baldwin, 1970, p. 106). Even Cro-Magnon man had a "sorcerer" and used art and magic for healing. Today there is scarcely a society without a medicine man or healer.

The Native American people have medicine men or healers that counsel, heal wounds and disease. They are called on to predict the future, assure success with planting and harvesting, influence the weather, and witch for water. They also conduct birth, burial and sporting ceremonial feasts and dances for tribes and individuals.

18.3 History

There is not an American Indian in North America who has not been exposed to or affected by the Anglo world. Yet to be *an Indian* carries a sense of honor, homeland, commitment to one's tribe, reservation or community, and a duty to one's people no matter where a person lives. American Indians often practice two contrasting ways of life. They grow up with a two-track cultural background and find themselves participating in the Indian world as defined by tribal affiliation, and the white man's world as determined by personal need. The term "white man" is to be interpreted as to how it relates to the concept that it is the government which determines the quality of life for *all* Americans, male, female, Indian and non-Indian.

Identifying, developing and utilizing human resources has often been a concern of this nation. Although Indians have been written about since the time of John Smith, it has been during just the last few decades that education, family life, attitudes, values, counseling and medicine have been dealt with effectively in the literature. Yet, Native Americans are not often seen as a valuable human resource. (Ferguson, 1981)

From a *medical* standpoint healing traditions have been handed down from generation to generation. Often, the Native American's only source was to draw on things they had been taught or believed for their personal and physical well-being. Because of their social structure and beliefs they gathered herbs, bark, and roots to keep themselves healthy.

It is sometimes difficult for non-Indians to identify with Native culture and tribal values. While there is much literature available about the Native American, the topics indicate a preference for traditional subjects (art, language, living conditions).

To many people, the term "Indian"—referring to the native inhabitants of North America—generally brings to mind one of four stereotypes. They are: a handsome brave with a feather and riding a painted pony; a regal Pocahontas Indian Princess; a downtrodden, hunched over burden-bearing "squaw" drudging behind her warrior husband; or an aged medicine man whose deep-set eyes hold knowledge of the world's mystic secrets. (Ferguson, 1981)

Throughout history tribes have called the healer by many names. These include medicine man, prophet, shaman, doctor, medicine giver, conjurer, wizard, Kahuna, or healer. The healer could be male *or* female. They have knowledge about the use of herbs and roots in various forms that could be for emetics, cathartics, sweats, wounds, sores, baths, and drawing out.

Medicine men and women have played an important role in the daily lives of many native peoples. It is believed by followers of Native American medicine that the medicine man has power, spirit, and energy that can be of help in times of need. They are the *healers*.

Not all tribes have the same kind of medicine people. For example, the Yurok of California have only medicine women. Some tribes have only men healers. And others, such as the Apache and Hopi, have men and women, each with their own specialty areas.

Rena Swentzell (in *Native Peoples*, 1998, p. 62) has written that the Native American connectedness to life is undeniable and that Native peoples have distinctive qualities and personalities because they are part of the cosmos. It has been believed by many for centuries that Native Americans have been sensitive to wood, clay, and rocks. This has made them aware of the clouds, of rain, and the mountains. This sensitivity has allowed an in-depth look at the nature of the physical, emotional and spiritual complexities of a person. A similar sensitivity has given people like Carl Hammerschlag and Howard Silverman (1997) the opportunity to look at and write about the plethora of information regarding the harmony that Native Americans have with the earth. This harmony is necessary for individuals to achieve wholeness and as a way to be in *balance* with one's surroundings.

Furthermore, it is believed that because Native Americans venerate the earth, that creativity and spiritualism is the extension of that which flows through the earth and permeates those creating harmony and balance. (Native American Center, 1999.)

All existence, as Native Americans know it, was created by the sky and the earth—to man and woman. All parts of places between earth and sky were interconnected. Since separation from nature did not happen before the European/Christian influence, it is the psychology of living *with*, rather than separate *from* nature that gives different life meanings in the Indian culture. It is from this perspective that harmony and balance are maintained and healing can occur, according to Native Americans. Healing is believed to be comforting, and is accepted by the Indian *because* its purpose is to restate culturally accepted relationships at all levels. It is necessary to focus on relationship qualities and to confirm the human place in the natural world. To do this one must not focus on the individual, because every one and every thing is *connected*. *All parts of the whole are believed to be interrelated.* (*Native Peoples*, 1998, p. 62)

So, what does all of this mean? Are there questions? Is there confusion? Confusion arises from the idea that it is not possible to write outside the context of the belief system. One person cannot sit down and write or pass on the way a healer heals for all the Native tribes in the United States. That is not what I am trying to do. And yet, the questions are basically: how and who?

Philosophically, the healing path is walked alone, is revered, and even thought to be somewhat scary and mystical at the same time. In today's society and times, because so many are taught to hold on, to be greedy and to be jealous, the way of the healer is sometimes difficult. Yet, becoming a healer can be a choice and a lifestyle. Training can begin at an early age. Selection can be from a specific family, or because of devotion and dedication, wisdom and honesty. Sometimes it is considered an honored position and passed down from generation to generation. It can be passed from father to son, father to daughter, mother to daughter, or mother to son. It is the healer who is trusted with secrets, rituals, habits, and legends, and who is at *all* celebrations and critical meetings. (Baldwin, 1970, p. 110)

Some children who follow the traditional ways are encouraged to seek a "vision" which is given as a gift from the Great Spirit. The vision can reveal the purpose of the person's life. It can serve as the motivation to keep them on a particular path. It can give a message that is passed on from the "Old Ones" that help them to survive or adapt to a situation they may find themselves in. If, during this quest, one chooses to practice the ways of the healer, then a spiritual connection is made. It is necessary to meditate or have a quiet time every day. It is necessary to spend time outside. It is during this connection time that one is working to establish a personal relationship with the Creator, and the sense of awe that comes from learning to appreciate nature. Prayers and chants are ways to talk to the Creator, and an opportunity to share views, frustrations, hopes, and dreams with the Great One. Meditating is listening for the voice of the Creator to come through. Making this connection a part of your life can bring about a sense of peace and tranquility that can not be found in other work and with other people. It makes a bond between you and the Creator and allows a strengthening of the spirit within. This becomes a personal defense against disease and is a very important part of healing (Liptak, 1992, p. 16).

After the spiritual connection has been made, it is possible to notice an attitude change. This should not come as a surprise. After all, it is this attitude that is necessary for preventing illness and for healing others from illness.

In many Native American tribes it is believed that healing powers are mysterious and come from spirits, and that strength is acquired through fasting, dreams, and visions. The healer is able to summon a spirit that can perform tasks beyond the capability of ordinary people. These spirits may be the souls of dead medicine men, or the spirits of sundry plants or animals. A healer can have two, three, or more spirits. The more spirits, the more powerful "the medicine." It is healers that become the interpreter or the medium between the human and the spirit world. They communicate and can help or appease anger.

Some healers are born, others are made, and some are even made by an acquired healing power. Some healers require a long period of initiation and training, which can be very arduous. The person not only receives instructions in everything related to becoming a healer, but is isolated, conducts fasts, observes severe restrictions and taboos, goes without sleep and undergoes ordeals. After completing the required course of study and paying with time and money, the person is admitted to the profession by a ceremony, yet still has to prove themselves worthy of being a healer.

No matter how one becomes a healer, in most tribes the healer's job is to diagnose and cure disease. He or she can be a jack-of-all-trades, serving as a soothsayer, hypnotist, teacher, prophet, scientist, lawyer, and priest. They may even specialize in fortune telling, ghost chasing, rainmaking, making of charms, or finding a lost object. It is believed that the most common way to become a healer is to be guided by a vision. This is believed to be the path with the most strength.

Once one has become a healer, it is *attitude* that determines one's strength. Attitude is one of the most important factors in healing serious disease. (Moondance, 1994, p. 7) The healer recognizes this by the fact that many times people become overwhelmed by the seriousness of the disease. A healer also recognizes that an appropriate attitude is necessary for preventing disease and for healing disease. If one worries about getting sick, there is a greater chance of becoming ill. There are positive and negative factors in all life. The positive represents everything good that happens and the negative represents the bad. Although the negative is definitely a part of life, it does not have to be given power over life by focusing on it. This causes a negative attitude to develop.

Studies have shown that those with negative attitudes are more likely to lead chaotic lives. They are also more likely to become ill, or have debilitating or life-challenging diseases. Many people have had a hard time focusing on the positive side because they have allowed their negative side to consume them.

People talk about becoming healers and practicing the "old ways." They often ask how they can become a healer. There are many books that have been written on how to follow the medicine path or medicine wheel and become a healer.

Healing is often ceremonial in nature. Herbalism, which is used ceremonially, is a gift still used today. It is believed that physical health often fails because the spirit is weak. Dancing and chanting are used depending upon the severity of the disease and the debilitation of the spirit. It is the ceremony and ritual of healing that can help harness the power to deal with the change in life. When dealing with physical disease, it is the ceremony that complements traditional medicine and therapy. A healer can guide the ill person to enhance their own healing process by using paths and sensations that are unique to them. Remember, the Native American believes for the most part, that if your body, mind and spirit are healthy, you are in *harmony*. And being in *harmony* puts you in balance or *at one* with the universe. This means that the ups and downs of everyday life will not bother you, if your overall attitude lets you live in peace, in harmony with the world. What this can mean in a nutshell is that you "kick back" (relax and take it easy) or that you won't "wig out" (lose control or your temper, go on a tirade) at the least little thing. It becomes a personal choice in determining how and on what you choose to expend your energy.

Native Americans believe there are two causes of disease: natural and unnatural. *Natural disease* comes from violating a taboo or treating a sacred object with disrespect. *Unnatural disease* comes from forces outside the body. They affect a person whose spirit is too weak to fight. They believe that when disease strikes something foreign invades the body. If this happens, special "medicine" is needed. The special medicine comes from the healer. Sometimes just knowing the healer is on the way helps the person feel hopeful and can speed recovery. (Liptak, 1992, p. 15)

From this perspective it becomes necessary to recognize that medicine men and healers perform a ceremony. Perhaps Hammerschlag and Silverman said it most succinctly when they wrote (1997, p. 22),

> ... ceremonies and rituals can be powerful tools (medicine) that help us harness the power to deal with important transition events in our lives. When dealing with physical illness [these] ceremonies can and should serve as complements to standard medical diagnostic and therapeutic practice. Even current medical procedures can be viewed as ceremonial: from hospital rounds to ceremonial instruments used to perform specific procedures to office visits. By ceremonializing medical procedures it expands them into events that invite participation and responsibility for the healing process.

It is important to remember a time in life or in our dream life when anything is possible. There are dreams that good things will happen, and these dreams are a way to recapture your spirit. The dreams actually allow you to become the principal agent in your own healing.

Remember, again, that to be healthy to the Native American is to be in *balance*. This balance occurs when what is known is the same as what is said, and when what is said is how you feel. It is *harmony* when balance occurs between knowledge, feeling, and action.

Native people believe a person is *out* of harmony when sickness or misfortune results. It is necessary to recognize that to Native Americans life symbols move with the sun. When the sun sets, it is the ending; and this, in and of itself, is the process for a new beginning. This beginning is a place beyond where we are at present and this beginning takes place every day.

18.4 Stories

As I wrote earlier, healing was not something that was talked about when I was growing up. I was told by one side of the family it was passed from male to female, and by members of the other side that it was passed from oldest female to oldest female, and that it could be learned and should be treasured. But most importantly, I was told it was a gift, something that was not to be abused or used for money or power. Because of this, I did not talk about what I did (healing) as a child or as an adult, nor what I was expected or have been asked to do.

When I was asked to write this chapter, I put it off, thinking it was because it was not right to *talk* about healing. I recently saw a movie on television that in my mind gave me permission to write. The movie (*Resurrection*, a TV drama shown on March 15, 1999) had many truths in it. I believe that what I have been allowed to do comes from a rich heritage in my family that has been passed down through both sides for many generations. There are many homeopathic remedies and survival strategies that are considered a part of our healing. I believe all of us are capable of using such healing strategies.

My maternal great-grandmother (non-Indian) died when I was five years old. She was a very tiny person and a very special person. She taught me not to fear death and not to fear helping other people when I was asked to. Her husband, who worked with all races, was a healer. People came from miles around to have him heal. He could stop bleeding, remove warts, and discolor blemishes. I was just a little girl when he took the numerous warts that I had on my fingers and hands away. I remember how scared I was sitting on the front porch when he removed them. I later asked lots of questions and wanted to do what he did. He said I could do what he did, and probably was already doing it. At the time I did not realize this.

My earliest memories are of being taken to houses where the people were sick and asked to put my hands on their feet and legs.

Although I could feel temperature changes, I did not really know that I was doing anything. Many times there were elders at the head and upper body of the person. As I got older, I moved to the upper body of the person. Most of the time I was not told what was wrong with the person or even where they were hurting. Sometimes I did not see their faces. Talking was not necessary, although there were times when talking became a part of the process for the person who was ill. There were no ceremonies and rituals to speak of. The whole process seemed to be less public and very private. There was a great quiet in the house, and great respect for the ill. The idea was that the person wanted to get well.

Now I look back and wonder. I think the energies that come from a child are so open, giving, and pure. The strength that can be shared by a child is amazing.

And I was called upon to work on animals that were sick. I did not understand, but did as I was asked. I remember stopping the bleeding of cats, dogs and baby calves. I worked on animals with bad cuts, sprains, and bites from spiders, and animals that would not eat.

As I grew older, when someone at school would get hurt, I would be asked to hold them. Oftentimes there would be blood and it would stop flowing. If there were burns, they would not blister. This was all but one time when a boy in my school was burned so badly I could not take the burn. But, I worked to keep him cool so he would not feel the pain.

After I had children of my own, I found that I could be of help to them almost weekly. They did not understand, but knew that I could help them when they hurt. I had to be extremely careful. Sometimes I could burn them if I kept my hands on them too long. I worried about that. Oftentimes I would not have to touch them. Once, when our youngest son fell down the stairs and needed stitches in his head, they put him on a cradle board in the emergency room. I had already stopped the bleeding. Of course, he screamed and kicked because he did not understand what was going on. The doctor told me I could not stay in the room. I told him that I could. I just needed to touch my son on his ankle and he would lie quietly and they could administer the stitches. I told him that I would not talk. The doctor finally gave in, I put my hand on his ankle and he quietened right down.

Another time my friend's house burned down. There were nine children and mom and dad. They all got out, but nothing could be saved. My friend had burned her feet trying to get her books. At school she asked me to put my hands on her feet and make them cold. I did.

When our older son was about three, he was outside helping his father in the yard. He put his hand on the top of the tiller motor and had a white hot burn. When I saw what happened, I cupped his hands in mine and put his fingers in my mouth. I held him for a few minutes, pulling the burn into my body. The fire of the burn was removed. His hand was cool to touch and he did not blister. I was able to take the burn from him. For some reason, I did not *pass* the burn on and his little hand print blistered on my back. I called Mama and she told me I would have to carry the burn for a while. It took almost two weeks for the burn to disappear from my back. I always believed it was because I was reacting as a mother, and not paying attention to what I was doing.

While I was writing the above, I just had a young man come in and tell me his throat was raw and he had a "lump" when he swallowed. He was cold to touch. I had him turn around and I put one hand on his throat and another at the back of his head. I asked him what he felt. He said some pressure. I lifted my hands so he could feel the heat—and asked him what he felt then. He said, "This was too weird. My throat is not sore and the lump is gone." I asked him if he wanted me to clear his nose. He said "no," he liked the nasal sound.

I have worked with numerous adults and children throughout my life. Much of the time the work centers around some kind of pain. I do not need a lot of time. A few months ago I was visiting a friend I had not seen in a few years. When she opened the door I sensed she was not feeling well. Before we left the house she asked me if I would "work" on her back. We went into the house. I put my hands on her back and she felt changes. When we went outside I told her husband how he could help her and what to do. When I am working with someone who has a spouse I will teach that spouse how to do what I do when I am not there and additional help is needed. I just received a letter from a friend who told me that her husband has been able to be a terrific help by doing what I showed him.

When our sons played football they used to have an exercise called "bleeders"—also known as "marauders." Our older son was most affected by the exercises. He used to get cramps that you could actually see in his legs. He would come home from practice and I would use my hands to work on the cramps. He would practice the next day.

Recently, our younger son had two very bloodshot eyes. He had what looked to be blood spots in his eyes from broken blood vessels. Yet, they did not seem to be breaking up or moving. This was causing pain and pressure. This particular son does not like to ask for help, yet he wants to heal and even has a "medicine stick." Finally, the pressure was so bad he allowed me to put my hands on his eyes and head. The blood spots began to break up. One even moved to the bottom of his eye. The pressure lessened and pain went away. While he was sleeping I put my hands over his eyes a couple of times more. His eyes cleared.

Sometimes things do not change. A woman I know came to me and asked me to remove the fungus from under a nail. I couldn't do anything. I had the same feeling when I held her thumb that I got when I touched Mama's head where the tumors were. However, the woman said she felt a difference. There was less pressure and a change in color. Recently my son had a fungus. I could not get it to dry either—I could not get any energy to go through.

We were at a party and the person next to me seemed to be favoring his one hand. Because he was not someone I knew, I asked my husband if it would be okay if I approached him about his pain. Suffice it to say, I did, and I asked him if I could touch him on his wrist and hand. The joint at the thumb was swollen badly. He could not bend his thumb. The joint had heat. I put both of my hands over the joint, took out the heat, then sent it back through the joint. He asked me how I did that. By the time we left he was using his thumb and hand comfortably and freely.

Once there was a young girl taking a test. I was watching her, and her eyes kept rolling back into her head. I walked back to her and asked if she was okay. She told me they had just discovered a tumor in her brain, and the pressure and pain were very bad. She grabbed my hands and put them on her head, and held them there. Then I put my hands over the top of her head without touching her. I could feel a mass, but the pressure lessened. And, instead of going to sleep, she completed her test.

Recently my husband was working on the car. The engine was still hot and he burned himself. When I came outside he had put his hand over the burn. I could see the red skin and the beginning of a blister. I asked him how long since the burn. He said about two minutes. I moved his hands, and put my hands over the burn. He felt the cold from my hands. He felt the fire of the burn leave his arm. He continued to work after I removed my hands. There was still some sensitivity to touch, but by morning the redness, blister, and sensitivity to touch were not there. It was like it never happened.

I have also worked with people over long distances. People have phoned and asked for help. If I have worked with them before in person, I ask them just to recall when I was there and work from that aspect. If I have not worked with them before, we will talk a while and I will work from a different perspective. It seems to be more effective if I have worked or lived with them before, even if it was for a different reason.

I have worked with people who are having earaches or headaches. In extreme cases of pain, I have asked their permission to put my hand above their head or beside their ear. I do not need to touch them.

18.5 Self-Healing

So how can one heal? After reading the concepts of Native American traditions, it comes down to five parts that make up the traditional steps of healing. You must identify the purpose, find someone to facilitate, prepare, perform, and close.

In identifying the purpose, it is necessary to share hopes, dreams, and fears openly. This part of the ceremony becomes necessary as a way of telling a story. It provides structure for getting in touch with what is inside and allows something good to happen because old things are viewed in a new way. It helps people feel connected. It recognizes how wants change or what one wants to happen changes. This is just *one* way.

For Mama, once she was told that she had cancer, her first response was, "I need to contact someone stronger than I am." To my knowledge she did. There was a ceremony, and it was determined that she was nearing death. Her time was limited. For Mama I could just listen. I heard what I was asked to do, then rephrased it to be sure I understood. I worked with her pain.

For her, facilitation provided the structure and kept the attention focused on the purpose. In the case of Mama's cancer, it was an event that had occurred and had to be allowed to continue. Because there was respect for the man she contacted, she learned the projected outcome of the problem. It could not be fixed. However, she was better able to prepare. It was therapeutic and revealing and it gave her a chance to reconnect with the community.

The preparation phase was an important part of her healing process. It was needed to develop connections before the ceremony. It served as a means for providing joy, comfort, and healing. It provided insight of things that were to come. It posed and answered questions. Remember, healing does not always mean there will be a cure.

When performing a healing it is necessary to choose a place that will support the purpose. Think about the work that needs to be done and the space in which it will be done. Please understand, from my perspective, it is the actual performance of the healing that is the most crucial part.

If particular materials are needed, it is important to gather them before the ceremony. They can consist of things that can be used as symbols during the ceremony. For every person and every healing, this is different. It can include sacraments or things which affect the senses. There can be music, drumming, candles, fire, oil, clothes, foods, wine, tobacco, cedar, sage, or sweetgrass. Objects can be used that reflect the Native heritage and allow one to focus on the purpose. This can also include books, antlers, feathers as well as pictures, a special stone, or something handed down. The purpose is to feel the spirit. (I have a friend who often brings sweetgrass into my room throughout the year. What a delight!)

In the Native culture of healing, closure is important. Everyone involved must recognize that there will be closure. This can be as simple as a cleansing breath, or as elaborate as a review of the sequence of events, story or trance. It is important to remember that things are not *made* to happen. They just happen on their own. An example of improper closure was described when the hand print came upon my back.

A healing ceremony can be used as alternative medicine. But, in reality, for many it is the only medicine. So, whatever thoughts and preoccupations keep you or hold you back can be taken away. Prayer and chants are seen as a part of the ceremony that asks for something good, and the intrinsic healing forces will act as a guide. This type of healing can be in conjunction with other medicines.

It is important that one recognize that healing is not always a cure—as in getting well. This happened with Mama. It became inevitable that her disease was terminal and death was imminent. When this happens you must deal with the uncertainty that comes. All we know and have experienced can come from the questions that we face at the end of life on this earth. Dying does not mean that we have to ask why we are here. Instead it becomes a personal responsibility for each of us to manage the dying process. It becomes necessary to die with dignity, to be aware and content and be connected. We want death to mean something—a healing.

Perhaps Mama summed up the teachings and the process best when on the day of her death, only 12 weeks after diagnosis, she looked out the window, the curtains were blowing in the early morning spring breeze, and said, "Oh, it is such a beautiful day to die." She turned her head, sighed and that was her last breath. She was *connected*. What a beautiful and profound transition. Healing for Mama served as a guide to enhance her own process by using the paths and sensations that were unique to her. She was able to use all but one of her senses. I believe it was the ceremony, rituals, and the way she viewed and lived her life that helped her to harness the strength to deal with the change that was coming into her own life. They complemented the medical and therapy practices that she was experiencing, and let her die with the dignity that she so deserved.

Remember, when healing, you are the *tool* that is receiving health and help through your relations on earth. Keeping this in mind will give you the perspective that you will need.

18.6 Conclusion

We like to figure things out and make sense of them. More often than not, things are more comfortable to live with after they have been categorized and put in their proper place. Our need to provide closure and completeness is not a new concept in the thinking process, but something that has been around for as long as people have existed. A way to explain the unexplainable is the means by which we control our own fate. The words in this chapter do not fit nicely into one category. To some readers they could make very little sense. This chapter is intended as an attempt to reveal the potential for good. The ability to heal is a by-product of the life being lived. The healing abilities are believed to be related to emotions and feelings coming from the *old ones,* that are rooted deep in a heritage that is taught by example. Does it make sense? It is all I know, and I do not question.

Ritual and healing abilities can be expressed in different ways. They are a natural part of being alive and are a part of each and every one of us. These abilities can also be passed on, learned or inherent. As individuals, we need only to recognize the abilities to be able to release them for the good of humanity.

From my perspective, it is necessary to understand that *helping* is the purpose of *healing*. The work is done humbly, without bragging, and the ego is not involved. It is okay to not fully understand or grasp the meaning of what is written here.

The good and bad in each of us is a given; the presence of these coupled with free choice make us human and binds us as people, regardless of race, belief or physical impairment. Allowing the expression of the good, or the bad, or not allowing either to express itself fully, gives us the diversity seen in humanity. It is with this in mind that most will find what it is they can take away from this writing and call their own. A comfort can be found and a good can be felt. What it comes down to is that we all have different healing ability levels. It is what we do with the ability that we have that provides us with the capability to move to a different level. I think Black Elk said it best when he wrote, "A person who has a vision is not to use the power of it until after he has performed the vision on earth for people to see." Perhaps this is the way of the healer (Neihardt, 1961, p. 172).

Chapter 19

Some Beginning Words

19.1 Inspirational Words

Words can be so meaningful—a particular phrase catches our ear, makes some connection with who we are at that moment, and transforms us. The world appears differently, we see it through different eyes. We feel different from the inside out. Is this why magicians use special words to change the world? And, they have to be said in just the right pattern. Words are magic and can transform us, help us transcend from wherever we are. Think of phrases like: I love you; to be or not to be; you make me so happy; God loves you; cancer is just a word, it is not a sentence; hold me; one hand washes the other; all we ever have is now. Words are magic (See de Shazer, 1994). In this section I include many passages that have been particularly meaningful for me by several authors that I repeatedly turn to. I find their words comforting and inspiring.

In one context or another, I think of Rabbi Hillel's summary of his life's wisdom. I first heard these three questions when I was a teenager attending weekly discussion groups under the tutelage of Joe Goldberg at the Ethical Culture Society of New York.

If I am not for myself, who will be?
If I am only for myself, what am I?
If not now, when?

19.2 Bernie Siegel's Words

Bernie Siegel's writings (1986, 1989, 1993, 1998) were the initial impetus that got me into this work. I also have a large collection of his audiotapes, some videotapes, and have attended several of his workshops and presentations. The following is a selection of some of his writings (the citation is given at the end of each portion):

Physicians must stop letting statistics determine their beliefs. Statistics are important when one is choosing the best therapy for a certain illness, but once the choice is made, they no longer apply to the individual. All patients must be accorded the conviction that they *can* get well, no matter what the odds.

Exceptional patients have the ability to throw statistics aside—to say, "I can be a survivor"—even when the doctor isn't wise enough to do so. (1986, p. 39)

Unexpected healing happens often enough that physicians must learn to project hope at all times, even in what seem to be the final hours. Patients are not looking for results of a medical Gallup poll. They're looking for a success-oriented relationship. They're looking for someone to say, "Hold on, you can make it. We'll help you"—as long as the patient wants to stay alive. (1986, p. 41)

Hope comes about largely as a result of the patient's confidence and trust in the healer. (1986, p. 44)

Nobody's going to sue a doctor for accenting the positive, and the physician doesn't have to make any guarantees. All that's necessary is to change the emphasis: "A lot of good things can happen with this treatment. It is possible the following adverse effects may occur, but I don't expect them." ... Patients should also be reminded that normal cells can recover from the strong medicines better than the weak, sensitive cancer cells. (1986, p. 132)

Visualization takes advantage of what might almost be called a "weakness" of the body: it cannot distinguish between a vivid mental experience and an actual physical experience. (1986, p. 153)

You only have to remember that you cannot change anyone. You can only change yourself. But remember you create the other person by what you're like. ... Taking care of unfinished business may someday come to be recognized as the most effective pain reliever and preparation for surgery. (1986, p. 197)

Finding the ability to love requires giving up the fear, anguish, and despair that many people nurture. Many people have a lifetime of unresolved angers circulating through their minds and causing new stress with each recall. Confronting them and letting go of them involves honestly facing your own part in the problem, and forgiving yourself as well as others you've resented and feared. If you do not forgive, you become like your enemy. (1986, p. 199)

Spirituality, unconditional love, and the ability to see that the pain and the problems are opportunities for growth and redirection—these things allow us to make the best of the time we have. Then we realize that the present moment is all we have, but it is infinite. (1986, p. 201)

Today I see that even death can be a form of healing. When patients whose bodies are tired and sore are at peace with themselves and their loved ones, they can choose death as their next treatment. They do not have pain because there is no conflict in their lives. They are at peace and comfortable. (1986, p. 207)

God has given us free will to make love and life meaningful. This creates a critical risk because we now have the ability to destroy our universe if we choose not to love.

However, it is only in this critical time that the archetype of the miracle can appear. When one believes in love and miracles divine intervention occurs.

We have an infinite number of choices ahead, but a finite number of endings. They are destruction and death or love and healing. If we choose the path of love, we save ourselves and our universe.

Let us choose love and life. (1986, p. 225)

Feelings are chemical and kill or cure. As a doctor I believe it's my responsibility to help my patients use them to cure and heal themselves. While placebos can be useful, because as symbols of hope they activate expectations, my reputation, my training, my belief in my patients and my own hopeful-ness have symbolic value, which I can use to guide my patients into health. When some of my patients get better despite the odds against them, you may say that these are people I have deceived into health. But I don't see that as a crime. I will always use all the tools at my command, because all healing is scientific. If I'm accused of offering false hope, my answer is that there is no false hope—only false *no* hope—because we don't know the future for an individual. (1989, p. 16)

Like most doctors, I have to try to remember that I am merely a facilitator of healing, not the healer himself—a fre-quent source of confusion for doctors! That's why I've asked my patients to call me by my first name. As Bernie, I'm a human being whom my patients and the people I work with can relate to; they will accept my being perfectly imperfect. When no one expects the impossible of me, including me, that's an immense burden off my shoulders. But "Dr. Siegel" is a label that assigns me a fixed role and means I'm sup-posed to be perfect. I will inevitably be a failure at being per-fect. (1989, p. 125)

There is a path to your own heart, your own treasure chest, and I would like you to follow it. When people follow it, I hear them say, "I have a disease, but it doesn't have me." ... When we find our way of contributing love to the world, we are in harmony with the world. (1993, p. xv)

Once you literally accept that you could die on the way home, you begin to free yourself to act in a way that says, "This is me. This is how I feel like contributing." Again, this is not selfish. When you accept your mortality, more humor and love come into your life.... I ask people to live in small time segments, because I see over and over again that happy people are living in the moment ... (1993, p. 23)

Think about what you would say if God told you, "I want you to be happy for the rest of your life." What would you do to be happy? This is difficult for most adults to answer. (1993, p. 29)

"What is true is, if you have someone who truly cares about you, when you do not have your health, you have everything. It is easier to buy good health than to buy good love." (1993, p. 56. Quoted from a letter to Bernie from Anita.)

When you have a child, make sure that child knows that you are imperfect. Don't be afraid to share your inadequacies and emotions. Let children know that it is all right to get angry at you, and let them feel safe doing so. (1993, p. 59)

"Hi, I'm writing at the request of Dr. Bernie Siegel and your brother's fiancee. I'm also writing to you because I want to. I understand that you have liver cancer. I was told over a year ago that I would probably die in six weeks. I didn't die. I don't plan to die for a long time. The advice I can offer you is what worked for me.

"*One*, don't believe anyone who tells you when you will die. *Two*, nobody knows when another person will die. *Three*, liver cancer does not mean death, necessarily. *Four*, if you want to live, fight for it. *Five*, get away from anyone who does not support whatever action you decide to take for yourself, and that even includes family. *Six*, find something, anything, that you truly love to do and throw yourself completely into this activity. It will become a form of meditation for you. It will take your mind off of your illness and allow your body to heal itself. *Seven*, if the doctor offers you a treatment and you believe in it, do it. *Eight*, believe in yourself. *Nine*, death is not a failure. Everyone dies. Just give life your best shot. I have been on different forms of chemotherapy for over two years. The drugs I believed in worked, the drugs I didn't like not only didn't work, but the tumors grew." (1993, pp. 67–68. A letter from Fay Finkelstein cited by Bernie.)

But my feeling is that life is absolutely fair. It's just that we need to redefine the rules. Difficulties, problems, pain and losses come with life. And so our question becomes, how do we deal with these things? Can we use them as redirections and even look at them as gifts?... I learned many years ago that the genuinely happy people I meet are not happy because they have had only good fortune. I know that they are choosing their attitude. (1993, p. 182)

If you want to live forever, love someone. (1993, p. 219)

19.3 Rachel Naomi Remen's Words

Rachel Naomi Remen's *Kitchen Table Wisdom* (1996) is full of personal stories illustrating her life changes from a scientifically trained physician to a caring healing collaborator and medical director of the Commonweal program. Here are a few quotes:

> I listened to human beings who were suffering, and responding to their suffering in ways as unique as their fingerprints. Their stories were inspiring, moving, important. In time, the truth in them began to heal me.... Everybody is a story.... Sitting around the table telling stories is not just a way of passing time. It is the way the wisdom gets passed along. The stuff that helps us to live a life worth remembering.... The stories we tell each other have no beginning and ending. They are a front-row seat to the real experience.... Real stories take time. We stopped telling stories when we started to lose that sort of time, pausing time, reflecting time, wondering time. (1994, p. xxv)

> All real stories are true.... Stories are someone's experience of the events of their life, they are not the events themselves. Most of us experience the same event very differently.... Truth is highly subjective. (1994, p. xxvii)

> All stories are full of bias and uniqueness; they mix fact with meaning. This is the root of their power. Stories allow us to see something familiar through new eyes.... Facts bring us to knowledge, but stories lead to wisdom. The best stories have many meanings; their meanings change as our capacity to understand and appreciate meaning grows. (1994, p. xxviii)

> If we think we have no stories it is because we have not paid enough attention to our lives. Most of us live lives that are far richer and more meaningful than we appreciate. (1994, p. xxix)

Perhaps every "victim" is really a survivor who does not know it yet. (1994, p. 28)

Things that I have hidden from others for years turn out to be the anchor and enrichment of my middle age. What a blessing it is to outlive your self-judgments and harvest your failures. (1994, p. 38)

Of course love is never earned. It is a grace we give one another. Anything we need on earth is only approval. Few perfectionists can tell the difference between love and approval. Perfectionism is so widespread in this culture that we actually have had to invent another word for love. "Unconditional love," we say. Yet, all love is unconditional. Anything else is just approval. (1994, p. 47)

The bottom line is that grieving is not meant to be of help to any particular patient. You grieve because it's of help to you. It enables you to go forward after loss. It heals you so that you are able to love again. (1994, p. 54)

For a long time, I had carried the belief that as a physician my love didn't matter and the only thing of value I had to offer was my knowledge and skill. My training had argued me out of my truth. Medicine is as close to love as it is to science, and its relationships matter even at the edge of life itself. (1994, p. 65)

... we may become as wounded by the way in which we see an illness as by the illness itself. Belief traps or frees us. Labels may become self-fulfilling prophecies. (1994, p. 66)

In my experience, a diagnosis is an opinion and not a prediction.... The diagnosis is cancer. What that will mean remains to be seen. (1994, p. 67)

But life never comes to a closure, life is process, even mystery. Life is known only by those who have found a way to be comfortable with change and the unknown. Given the nature of life, there may be no security, but only adventure. (1994, p. 67)

What we believe about ourselves can hold us hostage.... According to Talmudic teaching, "We do not see things as they are. We see them as we are." (1994, p. 77)

If we fear loss enough, in the end the things we possess will come to possess us. (1994, p. 87)

I suspect that the most basic and powerful way to connect to another person is to listen. Just listen. Perhaps the most important thing we ever give each other is our attention. And especially if it's given from the heart. When people are talking, there's no need to do anything but receive them. Just take them in. Listen to what they're saying. Care about it. Most times caring about it is even more important than understanding it. Most of us don't value ourselves or our love enough to know this. It has taken me a long time to believe in the power of simply saying, "I'm sorry," when someone is in pain. And meaning it. (1994, p. 143)

As a friend with HIV/AIDS puts it, "I have let go of my preferences and am living with an intense awareness of the miracle of the moment." Or in the words of another patient, "When you are walking on thin ice, you might as well dance." (1994, p. 171)

Joy seems to be a part of an unconditional wish to live, not holding back because life may not meet our preferences and expectations. Joy seems to be a function of the willingness to accept the whole, and to show up to meet whatever is there. (1994, p. 171)

The less we are attached to life, the more alive we can become. The less we have preferences about life, the more deeply we can experience and participate in life.... Embracing life may be more about tasting than it is either about raisin toast or blueberry muffins. (1994, p. 172)

Freedom may come not from being in control of life but rather from a willingness to move with the events of life, to hold on to our memories but let go of the past, to choose, when necessary, the inevitable. We can become free at any time. (1994, p. 199)

I have come to suspect that the subjective world is probably a hologram and the pattern of our most fundamental beliefs is reflected in the smallest of our behaviors. If this is so, breaking up that pattern at any point may eventually free us from it. The way in which we go to the grocery store may tell us everything about the way in which we live a life. The way we tend the life force in a plant may be the way we tend our own life force. We are exquisitely coherent. Healing requires a certain willingness to hear and respond to life's needs. (1994, p. 214)

Expertise cures, but wounded people can best be healed by other wounded people. Only other wounded people can understand what is needed, for the healing of suffering is compassion, not expertise. (1994, p. 217)

Our listening creates sanctuary for the homeless parts within the other person.... Listening creates a holy silence. (1994, p. 220)

Yet any of our daily habits can awaken us. All of life can become ritual. When it does, our experience of life changes radically and the ordinary becomes consecrated. Ritual doesn't make mystery happen. It helps us to see and experience something which is already real. It does not create the sacred, it only describes what is there and has always been there, deeply hidden in the obvious. (1994, p. 284)

19.4 Sharp and Terbay's Words

The title of Sharp and Terbay's book (1997) says it all, *Gifts. Two Hospice Professionals Reveal Messages From Those Passing On*. These "messages" are from people in their last stage of life. This book needs to be read for full impact. An anonymous Hospice patient submitted the following under the heading of "Dying With Dignity." (pp. 279–282) I have left out some of the material to reproduce her fifteen guidelines for living.

When I was forty-seven years old, my doctor told me I had incurable cancer of the colon with metastasis to the surrounding lymph nodes and ovaries. The prognosis was six months. If I lived longer than six months, the doctors told me my quality of life would be very poor.

Here I am, at fifty-seven, without my colon, ovaries, spleen, and many lymph nodes. I have had three series of chemotherapy, four surgeries and countless experimental treatments. Still I go on....

After much thinking, crying and re-evaluation, I have tried my best to live by the following guidelines:

1. Life isn't always fair, so I don't waste time saying "why me?" And, no, I'm not being punished for anything. My God doesn't punish.
2. I am determined to live my life as fully as possible. I don't let "cancer" control my life. I have never gotten up in the morning thinking, "Oh, I have cancer." I get up and go on with my day as if I didn't have cancer.
3. I've planned my life. I travel. I go out shopping. I go to dinner. I entertain. And when my body made me change this lifestyle, I created another lifestyle. I'm not going to quit living.
4. I refuse to be a "Pitiful Pearl." If I acted that way, I believe people would turn away from me. I let people tell me about their aches, pains and problems. I'm interested in other people. I smile a lot. I say, "I'm doing as well as I can."
5. I believe it is harder for my loved ones watching me die, than what I am going through. I hate to see the pain, the helplessness and fear in their eyes. I try to make it as easy for them as I can.
6. I've never lost my sense of humor. And I would recommend to people "If you don't have a sense of humor, get one." Laughter is the best possible medicine. There are lots of funny things out there if you look.
7. I've forgiven people—those who say the wrong things and those who don't know what to say. I know that sometimes being with me frightens them. I think it makes them think of their own mortality.
8. I took charge of my illness. I demanded to be part of my treatment. I asked questions. I know what medications I'm taking and why. I refuse to be intimidated by the medical community. By the same token, I don't blame my doctors. They are doing their best to help me. I try to help them

help me by doing as I'm supposed to do and by being a nice person instead of a pesky patient.

9. Every pain isn't cancer. When I get a new ache or pain, I wait a week or two and if it doesn't go away, then I go to the doctor. I don't spend my life worrying.
10. I've taken care of business. I have my affairs in order. I've left instructions for my family. I have a will, a living will. I refuse to leave a mess for my family to clean up.
11. I try to have a project going on to keep myself busy when I'm not feeling well.
12. I've written notes to my loved ones. It was difficult to do, but I know they will be happy when they read my notes.
13. I read. I keep myself informed about what is going on in the world because there is more to conversation and life than cancer.
14. I try to put other people first. I don't waste my energy feeling sorry for myself. Everyday, I count my blessings—and I have so many!
15. Lastly, if I've had a rotten day and I've failed at everything on this list—I forgive myself. I apologize and go on— determined to do better tomorrow. I try not to beat myself up because I know I'm entitled to a bad day every now and then.

I realize I am nearing my last days. I hope that I will be able to be brave. I want to die with dignity and I never want to forget the blessings I have had along the way. I have been blessed with excellent care and for that I am eternally grateful. I am counting on God to help me in this final journey.

My favorite line is "Men make plans and God smiles." I wonder if He was smiling the day I rented the beach house for next August?

19.5 Stephen Levine's Words

Stephen Levine (1979, 1982, 1984, 1987, 1991, 1997) has been working for a long time with people who have cancer and people nearing their deaths. His writings are healing and helpful.

The more you open to life, the less death becomes the enemy. When you start using death as a means of focusing on life, then everything becomes just as it is, just this moment, an extraordinary opportunity to be really alive. (1982, p. 30)

If you can participate in this moment openly, then you'll more likely be present for the next. If that next moment turns out to be on your deathbed, then you'll be open to that too. There is no other preparation for death except opening to the present. If you are here now, you'll be there then. (1982, p. 33)

The Zen master Suzuki Roshi said, "One should live their life like a very hot fire, so there is no trace left behind. Everything is burned to white ash." (1982, p. 77)

... when two people are pulling on either end of a rope, it takes only one of them to let go of his end to release all of the tension between them. (1982, p. 80)

If our only spiritual practice were to live as though we were already dead, relating to all we meet, to all we do, as though it were our final moments in the world, what time would there be for old games or falsehoods or posturings?... Only love would be appropriate, only the truth. (1982, p. 99)

Healing is the title we give to the phenomenon of the mind and heart coming back into balance. (1982, p. 199)

As long as we are thinking of healing as opposed to dying, there will be confusion. (1982, p. 200)

Death is not the enemy. The "enemy" is ignorance and love-lessness. (1982, p. 203)

In fact, death is not what happens when you leave your body. Death is what happens when we live our lives in confusion and close-heartedness, in anger and fear. (1984, p. 32)

And remember when you ask for something in a prayer you are really just praying to yourself, but when you sit in prayer with a willingness to listen, you receive God, you receive deeper and deeper levels of yourself. (1984, p. 108)

It was those who were against themselves, at odds with themselves, trying to "beat their illness," who seemed to have the hardest time and the slowest healing, if healing was present at all. But those who seemed to meet their illness in their heart instead of in their mind appeared to have a radically different experience. Not all those who embraced their illness survived in the body, but we observed a healing which occurred beyond our previous definition or understanding. Unfinished business melted in the loving kindness with which they met the pain in their body and the confusion in their mind. (1987, pp. 8–9)

... so it is evident that the choice to live or die *affects* the course of an illness but does not *determine* its outcome. (1987, p. 270)

But all of those who seemed to make the best use of a terminal prognosis began to change their relationship to relationship itself.... But almost all said that they would have slowed down and stopped to smell, if not plant, the roses. (1997, p. 6)

When we begin to respond to discomfort instead of reacting to it, an enormous change occurs. We begin to experience it not as just "our" pain but as "the" pain. And it becomes accessible to a level of compassion perhaps previously unknown. When it's "the" cancer instead of "my" cancer I can relate to others with the same difficulty, and I can send compassion into the cancer rather than helplessly avoiding it and turning its pain to suffering. (1997, p. 19)

19.6 Joan Borysenko's Words

Joan Borysenko (1988, 1990, 1994) is one of our leading healers. Her books and presentations are inspirational.

The following are twelve brief reminders from the epilogue (1988, pp. 207–211)

1. You cannot control the external circumstances of your life, but you can control your reactions to them.
2. Optimal health is the product of both physical and mental factors.

3. You could think of yourself as healthy.
4. Things change. Change is the only constant in life.
5. Your beliefs are incredibly powerful.
6. The only escape from stress, fear, and doubt is to confront them directly and see them for what they are.
7. Emotions fall into two broad categories, fear and love.
8. Would you rather be right or would you rather experience peace?
9. Accept yourself as you are.
10. Practice forgiveness (letting go).
11. Stay open to life's teachings.
12. Be patient. Patience means mindful awareness.

Forgiveness is the exercise of compassion.... Through the attitude of forgiveness, we attain happiness and serenity by letting go of the ego's incessant need to judge ourselves and others. (1990, p. 174)

... forgiveness is up to us. *Forgiveness is not conditional on someone else's behavior.* (1990, p. 177)

As with forgiving ourselves, the process of forgiving others begins with the recognition that we are holding onto something and that, despite any others person's role in creating the situation, we are the one responsible for what we do with our hurt. (1990, p. 184)

A wound with meaning is much easier to heal than a wound that is meaningless or that, worse, is interpreted as divine punishment or other evidence of personal unworthiness. (1994, p. 93)

19.7 Viktor E. Frankl's Words

Viktor E. Frankl's life and writings have inspired several generations of people worldwide. His most widely read book has been *Man's Search For Meaning* (1959, 1962, 1984 3rd ed.). You may also wish to read *The Doctor And The Soul* (1986) among his many writings, and especially his autobiography *Recollections* (1997).

Don't aim at success—the more you aim at it and make it a target, the more you are going to miss it. For success, like happiness, cannot be pursued; it must ensue, and it only does so as the unintended side-effect of one's personal dedication to a cause greater than oneself or as the by-product of one's surrender to a person other than oneself. Happiness must happen, and the same holds for success: you have to let it happen by not caring about it. I want you to listen to what your conscience commands you to do and go on to carry it out to the best of your knowledge. Then you will live to see that in the long run—in the long run, I say!—success will follow you precisely because you had forgotten to think of it. (1984, pp. 12–13)

We who lived in concentration camps can remember the men who walked through the huts comforting others, giving away their last piece of bread. They may have been few in number, but they offer sufficient proof that everything can be taken from a man but one thing: the last of the human freedoms—to choose one's attitude in any given set of circumstances, to choose one's own way.

And there were always choices to make. Every day, every hour, offered an opportunity to make a decision, a decision which determined whether you would or would not submit to those powers which threatened to rob you of your very self, your inner freedom; which determined whether or not you would become the plaything of circumstance, renouncing freedom and dignity to become molded into the form of the typical inmate. (1984, p. 75)

If there is meaning in life at all, then there must be a meaning in suffering. Suffering is an ineradicable part of life, even as fate and death. Without suffering and death, human life would not be complete.

The way in which a man accepts his fate and all the suffering it entails, the way in which he takes up his cross, gives him ample opportunity—even under the most difficult circumstances—to add a deeper meaning to his life. (1984, p. 76)

As we said before, any attempt to restore a man's inner strength in the camp had first to succeed in showing him some future goal. Nietzsche's words, "He who has a *why* to live for can bear with almost any *how*," could be the guiding motto for all psychotherapeutic and psychohygienic efforts regarding prisoners. (1984, p. 84)

What was really needed was a fundamental change in our attitude toward life. We had to learn ourselves and, furthermore, we had to teach the despairing men, that *it did not really matter what we expected from life, but rather what life expected from us*. We needed to stop asking about the meaning of life, and instead think of ourselves as those who were being questioned by life—daily and hourly. Our answer must consist, not in talk and meditation, but in right action and right conduct. Life ultimately means taking the responsibility to find the right answer to its problems and to fulfill the tasks which it constantly sets for each individual.

These tasks, and therefore the meaning of life, differ from man to man, and from moment to moment. Thus it is impossible to define the meaning of life in a general way. (1984, p. 85)

During no moment of his life does man escape the mandate to choose among possibilities. Yet he can pretend to act "as if" he had no choice and no freedom of decision. This "acting as if" constitutes a part of the human tragicomedy. (1986, p. 76)

Love is not deserved, is unmerited—it is simply grace. But love is not only grace; it is also enchantment. (1986, p. 133)

In some respects it is death itself that makes life meaningful. Most importantly, the transitoriness of life cannot destroy its meaning because nothing from the past is irretrievably lost. Everything is irrevocably stored. (1997, p. 29)

I do not forget any good deed done to me, and I carry no grudge for a bad one. (1997, p. 35)

I can see beyond the misery of the situation to the potential for discovering a meaning behind it, and thus to turn *an apparently meaningless suffering into a genuine human achievement*. I am convinced that, in the final analysis, there is no situation that does not contain within it the seed of a meaning. (1997, p. 53)

Power schmower. I agree with John Ruskin who once said: "There is only one power: the power to save someone. And there is only one honor: the honor to help someone." ... As the Talmud says: "He who saves but one soul is to be regarded as one who has saved the whole world." (1997, p. 55)

As early as 1929 I had developed the concept of three groups of values, of three possible ways to find meaning in life— even up to the last moment, the last breath. The three possibilities are: 1) a deed we do, a work we create; 2) an experience, a human encounter, a love; and 3) when confronted with an unchangeable fate (such as an incurable disease), a change of attitude toward that fate. In such cases we still can wrest meaning from life by giving testimony to the most human of all human capacities: the ability to turn suffering into a human triumph. (1997, p. 64)

Live as if you were already living for the second time, and as if you had made the mistakes you are about to make now. (1997, p. 124)

The preceding quotations are ones that have been especially meaningful to me. I am sure that you have your own collection.

19.8 Closing Healing Imagery Script

Find a place where you are completely comfortable, a quiet place, a place where you will not be disturbed. This is your time, now, with nothing to bother you, and nothing to disturb you. Your own special quiet time. If you need to move a bit to be even more comfortable, please do so. I may not be saying these words in just the right way, or even using just the right words for you, now. Feel free to change what you hear and how you hear it so that you get exactly what you need at this time.

You can start with paying attention to your breathing, noticing each breath as it comes in ... a kind of healing and energizing breath. And then the exhale, a cleansing and clearing breath. Feeling the air fill your lungs and raise your belly. And then, exhaling, chest softly falling and belly gently moving. Just one breath at a time. Gently, easily, naturally. Your time, your quiet time, an internal time, peaceful.

And there are beginnings and endings, places to start and places to stop, times to start and times to stop. How close are you to closing this chapter of your life? How ready are you to venture out and explore, moving into the next phase? Testing, and tasting, and exploring, and doing new and interesting things. Some of them may be old dreams, and some may be new dreams ... The sum of the somethings that you always wanted to do, a way of adding up your life with one thing after another. Experience upon experience, breath upon breath, this now leading to and becoming that then. One more and one more and one more ... all within our mortality. This life, this moment, lasting and everlasting. Testing, tasting, trying, venturing, exploring ...

And, how new and how old, and how bold? And, will you be bowled over or roll over or bowl over and move over to something surprising? How surprised will you be? Life is change, changing, and you can change with it, finding new meanings in old things and old meanings in new things. Will it be fine to find a different feeling? A new feeling? Another way of being in the world, being another way, ways of being, and ways to be that are not weighty but light and easy, where you no longer wait, and the weights that weighed you down are lifted, feeling lighter, finer, finding, opening, exploring. What wonderful feelings of adventure and excitement and openness. Always safely, yet safely daring. Always safe, yet the anticipation, the change, the variety, carry with them a different kind of being, a different kind of security. Safely, easily, naturally, normally. Continuing to breathe easily and softly, safely, exploring, believing, finding, being ...

Your time. A quiet time. A time for exploration and joy. And, when you are ready, you can just take a deep breath or two, stretch, smile, and come back to this room, here and now. Thank you.

Appendix A

Questions for People in Their Dying Time

Lawrence LeShan has compiled a list of 33 significant questions for people in their dying time to consider (1989, pp. 161–165). These are good questions to ponder at any time of your life. You may wish to make a selection of these questions for a particular client.

1. As you look at your whole life from the viewpoint of where you are now, what was it all about? Was it a good life? Was it a lonely life? Was it a frustrating life?
2. If your whole life had been designed in advance so that you would learn something from it, what would be the lesson you were supposed to have learned? Did you really learn it? What else would you have needed in order to have learned it?
3. What was the best thing that ever happened to you? What was the worst? (These are separate questions and, as a general rule, seem to be the most helpful when asked in this order.)
4. What was the best thing you ever did? What was the worst?
5. What was the best period of your life? What was the worst?
6. How would you finish these statements: "Out of my childhood I love to remember ..." "Out of my childhood I hate to remember ..."?
7. Do you believe it is true that "It is better to have loved and lost than never to have loved at all?" What led you to this conclusion?
8. If you were asked by a child you love, to tell him or her the one most important thing that you have learned in life, what would you reply?
9. There is an old Greek legend about the three Fates who govern all lives: Clotho, who weaves the thread of a person's life; Lachesis, who colors it; and Atropos, who cuts it and the person dies. How did Lachesis color *your* life? Did Atropos cut it off too soon? Too soon for what? Can you still do what you have unfinished so far?
10. In each symphony (ballad, folksong, popular song) there is a central theme. It has many variations, these appear in the different sections (verses), but underlying them all is the theme. What has been the theme of your life?

11. If you could change *one decision* of your life, what would it be? Why did you make it the way you did? What does this tell you about how you saw yourself and the world at that time? Can you forgive yourself for making that decision the way you did? For feeling the way you did? If not, why?

12. For the things you did, what do you now need to do in order to be able to forgive yourself?

13. For the things that others did to you, what do you need to do in order to forgive them? For the things that happened to you, what do you need in order to forgive yourself?

14. If you were to overhear your friends talking about you at your funeral, what would you most like to hear them say about you? Like least to hear?

15. As you look back on your life, what were the moments when you were most yourself? What helped you to do this? What were the moments you were least yourself? Why do you think this was so?

16. What was the best time of your life? Tell me about it? What was the worst time of your life? Tell me about it.

17. How were you the same all your life, as a child, a youth, an adult, now? How were you different at those different times of your life?

18. What do you need to finish your life, to complete it? Can you do it from this hospital room?

19. During this time, what is the longest time of the day for you? What do you mostly feel and think during this time?

20. In an ancient manuscript *The Book of Splendor* is the statement: "God's purpose is not to add years to your life, but to add life to your years." What do you think of this?

21. What is the thing in yourself that you have been most afraid to experience consciously? To think and feel about? Does it now seem as necessary to hide it from yourself as it did in the past?

22. What is it about you that you have most hidden from others? Does it seem as necessary to keep it hidden as it did in the past?

23. All our lives we try to change people to what we think they should be. At this time of life we can often see that love is accepting people as they are and letting them be while hoping and wishing for more for them. Can you do this with those you love? What in you keeps you from this?

24. The time of dying is the last learning time we have on Earth. What lesson is there for you to learn in your dying? What in you keeps you from being able to learn it?
25. What is the major role you have played in recent years? What masks have you worn most often in the presence of others? Are they roles you wish to play during these last times?
26. All our lives we try to *accomplish* something, to *do* something. What is it that you were trying to do in recent years? Is it still so important to you? How can you finish the attempt so that it ends with the most harmony and honesty?
27. Have you been mostly walking one road in recent years? Is there another road that you now need to walk in order to make your life journey more complete?
28. Is there someone you protected in recent years at a high cost in energy and time? Are you still trying to protect him or her? (Or be something for him or her?) Is it the best thing for this person for you to continue protecting him or her? For you?
29. What do you need to *finish* your life? Can you do it from this bed? How or why not? It is in *you* that we need to finish things and it is inside you that you can.
30. What is it that has happened to you that you have never been able to forgive God (or the Fates) for?
31. For what do you most need the forgiveness of God?
32. There is the story of one of the great Hasidic Rabbis named Zusya. His congregation asked him to do something, a particular political action. He refused. They said, "If Moses were our Rabbi, he would do it." Zusya answered, "When I die and rise and stand before the throne, God will not ask me why I was not Moses. He will ask me why I was not Zusya." Does this story in any way relate to you and your life? How?
33. What has been the best season of the year for you? Why?

LeShan adds (1989, p. 166)

The central and critical question with which we approach people in their Dying Time is something to the effect: "How do you feel about what is happening to you?" This says (if it is really meant as a question that you want an answer to) "We can talk about anything you wish. I am not afraid. I am not part of the conspiracy of silence that surrounds you unless you wish me to be."

Appendix B

Patient's Bill of Rights

Bernie Siegel (1986, pp. 127–128) gives the following as a patient's bill of rights. It is written as an open letter to physicians.

Dear Doctor:

Please don't conceal the diagnosis. We both know I came to you to learn if I have cancer or some other serious disease. If I know what I have, I know what I am fighting, and there is less to fear. If you hide the name and the facts, you deprive me of the chance to help myself. When you are questioning whether I should be told, I already know. You may feel better if you don't tell me, but your deception hurts.

Do not tell me how long I have to live! I alone can decide how long I will live. It is my desires, my goals, my values, my strengths, and my will to live that will make the decision.

Teach me and my family about how and why my illness happened to me. Help me and my family to live *now*. Tell me about nutrition and my body's needs. Tell me how to handle the knowledge and how my mind and body can work together. Healing comes from within, but I want to combine my strength with yours. If you and I are a team, I will live a longer and better life.

Doctor, don't let your negative beliefs, your fears, and your prejudices affect my health. Don't stand in the way of my getting well and exceeding your expectations. Give me the chance to be the exception to your statistics.

Teach me about your beliefs and therapies and help me to incorporate them into mine. However, remember that my beliefs are the most important. What I don't believe in won't help me.

You must learn what my disease means to me—death, pain, or fear of the unknown. If my belief system accepts alternative therapy and not recognized therapy, do not desert me. Please try to convert to my beliefs, and be patient and await my conversion. It may come at a time when I am desperately ill and in great need of your therapy.

Doctor, teach me and my family to live with my problem when I am not with you. Take time for our questions and give us your attention when we need it. It is important that I feel free to talk with you and question you. I will live a longer and more meaningful life if you and I can develop a significant relationship. I need you in my life to achieve my new goals.

Appendix C

The Wellness Community Patient/ Oncologist Statement

The effective treatment of serious illness requires considerable effort by both the patient and the physician. A clear understanding by both of us as to what each of us can realistically and reasonably expect of the other will do much to enhance the outlook. I am giving this "statement" to you as one step in making our relationship as effective and productive as possible. It might be helpful if you would read this statement and, if you think it appropriate, discuss it with me. *As your physician I will make every effort to:*

1. Provide you with the care most likely to be beneficial to you.
2. Inform and educate you about your situation, and the various treatment alternatives. How detailed an explanation is given will be dependent upon your specific desires.
3. Encourage you to ask questions about your illness and its treatment, and answer your questions as clearly as possible. I will attempt to answer the questions asked by your family; however, my primary responsibility is to you, and I will discuss your medical situation only with those people authorized by you.
4. Remain aware that all major decisions about the course of your care will be made by you. However, I will accept the responsibility for making certain decisions if you want me to.
5. Assist you to obtain other professional opinions if you desire, or if I believe it to be in your best interest.
6. Relate to you as one competent adult to another, always attempting to consider your emotional, social, and psychological needs as well as your physical needs.
7. Spend a reasonable amount of time with you on each return visit unless required by something urgent to do otherwise, and give you my undivided attention during that time.
8. Honor all appointment times unless required by something urgent to do otherwise.
9. Return phone calls as promptly as possible, especially those you indicate are urgent.
10. Make test results available promptly if you desire such reports.

11. Provide you with any information you request concerning my professional training, experience, philosophy and fees.
12. Respect your desire to try treatments that might not be conventionally accepted. However, I will give you my honest opinion about such unconventional treatments.
13. Maintain my active support and attention throughout the course of the illness.

I hope that you as the patient will make every effort to:

1. Comply with our agreed-upon treatment plan.
2. Be as candid as possible with me about what you need and expect from me.
3. Inform me if you desire another professional opinion.
4. Inform me of all forms of therapy you are involved with.
5. Honor all appointment times unless required by something urgent to do otherwise.
6. Be as considerate as possible of my need to adhere to a schedule to see other patients.
7. Make all phone calls to me during the working hours. Call on nights and weekends only when absolutely necessary.
8. Coordinate the requests of your family and confidants, so that I do not have to answer the same questions about you to several different persons.

Taken from Benjamin (1995, pp. 210–212).

Appendix D

Living Will Declaration (State of Ohio)

I,_____, presently residing at _____,
Ohio, (the "Declarant"), being of sound mind and not under or
subject to any duress, fraud or undue influence, intending to create a Living Will Declaration under Chapter 2133 of the Ohio
Revised Code, as amended from time to time, do voluntarily make
known my desire that my dying shall not be artificially prolonged.
If I am unable to give directions regarding the use of life-sustaining treatment when I am in a terminal condition or a permanently
unconscious state, it is my intention that the Living Will
Declaration shall be honored by my family and physicians as the
final expression of my legal right to refuse medical or surgical
treatment. I am a competent adult who understands and accepts
the consequences of such refusal and the purpose and effect of this
document.

In the event I am in a terminal condition, I do hereby declare and
direct that my attending physician shall:

1. administer no life-sustaining treatment;
2. withdraw such treatment if such treatment has commenced; and
3. permit me to die naturally and provide me with only that
   care necessary to make me comfortable and to relieve my
   pain but not to postpone my death.

In the event that I am in a permanently unconscious state, I do
hereby declare and direct that my attending physician shall:

1. administer no life-sustaining treatment, except for the provision of artificially or technologically supplied nutrition
   or hydration, unless in the following paragraph, I have
   authorized its withholding or withdrawal;
2. withdraw such treatment if such treatment has commenced; and,
3. permit me to die naturally and provide me with only that
   care necessary to make me comfortable and to relieve my
   pain but not to postpone my death.

❏ _____ IN ADDITION, IF I HAVE MARKED THE FOREGO-ING BOX AND HAVE PLACED MY INITIALS ON THE LINE ADJACENT TO IT, I AUTHORIZE MY ATTENDING PHYSICIAN TO WITHHOLD, OR IN THE EVENT THAT TREATMENT HAS ALREADY COMMENCED, TO WITHDRAW, THE PROVISION OF ARTIFICIALLY OR TECHNOLOGICALLY SUPPLIED NUTRITION AND HYDRATION, IF I AM IN A PERMANENTLY UNCONSCIOUS STATE AND IF MY ATTENDING PHYSICIAN AND AT LEAST ONE OTHER PHYSICIAN WHO HAS EXAM-INED ME DETERMINE, TO A REASONABLE DEGREE OF MED-ICAL CERTAINTY AND IN ACCORDANCE WITH REASONABLE MEDICAL STANDARDS, THAT SUCH NUTRI-TION OR HYDRATION WILL NOT OR NO LONGER WILL SERVE TO PROVIDE COMFORT TO ME OR ALLEVIATE MY PAIN.

In the event my attending physician determines that life-sustain-ing treatment should be withheld or withdrawn, he or she shall make a good faith effort and use reasonable diligence to notify one of the persons named below in the following order of priority:

1. (Name) _____, (Relationship)_____
presently residing at (Address) _____
_____, Phone _____

2. (Name) _____, (Relationship)_____
presently residing at (Address) _____
_____, Phone _____

For purposes of this Living Will Declaration:

(A) "Life-sustaining treatment" means any medical procedure, treatment, intervention, or other measure including artifi-cially or technologically supplied nutrition and hydration that, when administered, will serve principally to prolong the process of dying.

(B) "TERMINAL CONDITION" MEANS AN IRREVERSIBLE, INCURABLE, AND UNTREATABLE CONDITION CAUSED BY DISEASE, ILLNESS, OR INJURY TO WHICH, TO A REASONABLE DEGREE OF MEDICAL CERTAINTY

AS DETERMINED IN ACCORDANCE WITH REASON-
ABLE MEDICAL STANDARDS BY MY ATTENDING
PHYSICIAN AND ONE OTHER PHYSICIAN WHO HAS
EXAMINED ME, BOTH OF THE FOLLOWING APPLY:

(i) THERE CAN BE NO RECOVERY, AND

(ii) DEATH IS LIKELY TO OCCUR WITHIN A RELATIVELY
SHORT TIME IF LIFE-SUSTAINING TREATMENT IS
NOT ADMINISTERED.

(C) "PERMANENTLY UNCONSCIOUS STATE" MEANS A
STATE OF PERMANENT UNCONSCIOUSNESS THAT,
TO A REASONABLE DEGREE OF MEDICAL CERTAINTY
AS DETERMINED IN ACCORDANCE WITH REASON-
ABLE MEDICAL STANDARDS BY MY ATTENDING
PHYSICIAN AND ONE OTHER PHYSICIAN WHO HAS
EXAMINED ME, IS CHARACTERIZED BY BOTH OF THE
FOLLOWING:

(i) I AM IRREVERSIBLY UNAWARE OF MYSELF AND MY
ENVIRONMENT, AND

(ii) THERE IS A TOTAL LOSS OF CEREBRAL CORTICAL
FUNCTIONING, RESULTING IN MY HAVING NO
CAPACITY TO EXPERIENCE PAIN OR SUFFERING.

(D) [Note: The author (RB) added this section and the following
medical directive.] The attached Medical Directive gives
specific details of my wishes for four separate situations for
additional guidance. _____ (initials)

I understand the purpose and effect of this document and sign my
name to this Living Will Declaration after careful deliberation on

(Date) _____ at (City) _____, Ohio.

(Declarant's signature) _____
THIS LIVING WILL DECLARATION WILL NOT BE VALID
UNLESS IT IS EITHER (1) SIGNED BY TWO ELIGIBLE WIT-

NESSES AS DEFINED BELOW WHO ARE PRESENT WHEN YOU SIGN OR ACKNOWLEDGE YOUR SIGNATURE OR (2) ACKNOWLEDGED BEFORE A NOTARY PUBLIC.

I attest that the Declarant signed or acknowledged this Living Will Declaration in my presence, and that the Declarant appears to be of sound mind and not under or subject to any duress, fraud or undue influence. I further attest that I am not the attending physician of the Declarant, I am not the administrator of a nursing home in which the Declarant is receiving care, and that I am an adult not related to the Declarant by blood, marriage or adoption.

Signature: _____   Residence Address: _____

Print Name: _____

Date: _____

Signature: _____   Residence Address: _____

Print Name: _____

Date: _____

(OR CERTIFICATION BY A NOTARY PUBLIC.)
[NOTE: This document was prepared and distributed by the Ohio State Bar Association and their preparation of the document is gratefully acknowledged.]

* * * * * * * * * * * * * *

The following is a detailed *medical directive* which adds some specific directions to the Living Will Declaration preceding. There are four separate situations described and for each of these there are twelve interventions described. For a few choices NA means Not Applicable. Due to space considerations only *one* column of four choices is provided—you would actually have to fill out four such columns, i.e., one for each situation. After the introductory material for the medical directive, each of the four situations is given in detail, then the table.

My Medical Directive

This Medical Directive expresses, and shall stand for, my wishes regarding medical treatments in the event that illness should make me unable to communicate them directly. I make this Directive being 18 years or more of age, of sound mind, and appreciating the consequences of my decisions.

SITUATION A: If I am in a coma or a persistent vegetative state and, in the opinion of my physician and several consultants, have no hope of regaining awareness and higher mental functions no matter what is done, then my wishes regarding the use of the following, if considered medically reasonable, would be:

SITUATION B: If I am in a coma and, in the opinion of my physician and several consultants, have a small likelihood of recovering fully, a slightly larger likelihood of surviving with permanent brain damage, and a much larger likelihood of dying, then my wishes regarding use of the following, if considered medically reasonable, would be:

SITUATION C: If I have brain damage or some brain disease that in the opinion of my physician and several consultants cannot be reversed and that makes me unable to recognize people or to speak understandably, and I also have a terminal illness, such as incurable cancer, that will likely be the cause of my death, then my wishes regarding the use of the following, if considered medically reasonable, would be:

SITUATION D: If I have brain damage or some brain disease that in the opinion of my physician and several consultants cannot be reversed and that makes me unable to recognize people or to speak understandably, but I have no terminal illness, and I can live in this condition for a long time, then my wishes regarding use of the following, if considered medically reasonable, would be:

Type of Intervention.	Situation A I want.	Situation B I want treatment tried. If no clear improvement, stop.	Situation C I am undecided.	Situation D I do not want.
Cardiopulmonary Resuscitation: if at point of death, using drugs and electric shock to keep the heart beating; artificial breathing		NA		
Mechanical Breathing: breathing by machine				
Artificial Nutrition and Hydration: giving nutrition and fluid through a tube in the veins, nose, or stomach				
Major Surgery: such as removing the gall bladder or part of the intestines		NA		
Kidney Dialysis: cleaning the blood by machine or by part of the intestines				
Chemotherapy: using drugs to fight cancer				
Minor Surgery: such as removing some tissue from an infected toe		NA		
Invasive Diagnostic Tests: such as using a flexible tube to look into the stomach		NA		
Blood or Blood Products: such as giving transfusions				
Antibiotics: using drugs to fight infection				
Simple Diagnostic Tests: such as performing blood tests or x-rays		NA		
Pain Medication: even if they dull consciousness and directly shorten life		NA		

The author's choices were "I do not want" for all interventions except pain medications where he checked "I want"

In addition to the above, this Medical Directive includes a section on organ donation, as follows:

334

ORGAN DONATION

I hereby make this anatomical gift to take effect upon my death. (please check boxes and fill in where appropriate.)

I give: ❏ my body   ❏ any needed organs or parts
           ❏ the following organs or parts _____
to: ❏ the following person or institution

_____

❏ the physician in attendance at my death
❏ the hospital in which I die
❏ the following named physician, hospital, storage bank, or other
    medical institution: _____
    for the following purposes:

❏ any purpose authorized by law
❏ transplantation   ❏ therapy of another person
❏ research   ❏ medical education

MY PERSONAL STATEMENT

Add details here on anything else you wish using additional space as needed:

Name (printed) _____

Name (signed) _____

Witness 1 (signed) _____

Witness 2 (signed) _____

Dat _____

[Please note that each individual state in the U.S. and each country will have its own legal standards about these matters.]

Appendix E

Durable Power of Attorney for Health Care (Ohio)

1. **DESIGNATION OF ATTORNEY-IN-FACT.**

I,_____, presently residing at _____, Ohio, (the "Principal") being of sound mind and not under or subject to duress, fraud or undue influence, intending to create a Durable Power of Attorney for Health Care under Chapter 1337 of the Ohio Revised Code, as amended from time to time, do hereby, designate and appoint: (Name) _____

(Relationship)_____ presently residing at _____

Phone _____ as my attorney-in-fact who shall act as my agent to make health care decisions for me as authorized in this document.

2. **GENERAL STATEMENT OF AUTHORITY GRANTED.**

I hereby grant to my agent full power and authority to make all health care decisions for me to the same extent that I could make such decisions for myself if I had the capacity to do so, at any time during which I do not have the capacity to make informed decisions for myself. Such agent shall have the authority to give, to withdraw or to refuse to give informed consent to any medical and nursing procedure, treatment, intervention or other measure used to maintain, diagnose or treat my physical or mental condition. In exercising this authority, my agent shall make health care decisions that are consistent with my desires as stated in this document or otherwise made known to my agent by me or, if I have not made my desires known, that are, in the judgment of my agent, in my best interests.

3. **ADDITIONAL AUTHORITIES OF AGENT.**

Where necessary or desirable to implement health care decisions that my agent is authorized to make pursuant to this document, my agent has the power and the authority to do any and all of the following:

(a) If I am in a terminal condition, to withdraw or to refuse to give informed consent to life-sustaining treatment, including the provision of artificially or technologically supplied nutrition or hydration;

(b) If I am in a permanently unconscious state, to give, to withdraw or to refuse to give informed consent to life-sustaining treatment; provided, however, my agent is not authorized to refuse or direct the withdrawal of artificially or technologically supplied nutrition or hydration unless I have specifically authorized such refusal or withdrawal in Paragraph 4;

(c) To request, review, and receive any information, verbal or written, regarding my physical or mental health, including, but not limited to, all of my medical and health care facility records;

(d) To execute on my behalf any releases or other documents that may be required in order to obtain this information;

(e) To consent to the further disclosure of this information if necessary;

(f) To select, employ, and discharge health care personnel, such as physicians, nurses, therapists and other medical professionals, including individuals and services providing home health care, as my agent shall determine to be appropriate;

(g) To select and contract with any medical or health care facility on my behalf, including, but not, limited to, hospitals, nursing homes, assisted residence facilities, and the like; and

(h) To execute on my behalf any or all of the following:

  (i)   Documents that are written consents to medical treatment, Do Not Resuscitate orders, or similar other orders;
  (ii) Documents that are written requests that I be transferred to another facility, written requests to be discharged against medical advice, or other similar requests; and
  (iii) Any other document necessary or desirable to implement health care decisions that my agent is authorized to make pursuant to this document.

4. WITHDRAWAL OF NUTRITION AND HYDRATION WHEN IN A PERMANENTLY UNCONSCIOUS STATE.

❑_____ IF I HAVE MARKED THE FOREGOING BOX AND HAVE PLACED MY INITIALS ON THE LINE ADJACENT TO IT, MY AGENT MAY REFUSE, OR IN THE EVENT TREATMENT HAS ALREADY COMMENCED, WITHDRAW INFORMED CONSENT TO THE PROVISION OF ARTIFICIALLY OR TECH-NOLOGICALLY SUPPLIED NUTRITION AND HYDRATION IF I AM IN A PERMANENTLY UNCONSCIOUS STATE AND IF MY ATTENDING PHYSICIAN AND AT LEAST ONE OTHER PHYSI-CIAN WHO HAS EXAMINED ME DETERMINE, TO A REA-SONABLE DEGREE OF MEDICAL CERTAINTY AND IN ACCORDANCE WITH REASONABLE MEDICAL STANDARDS, THAT SUCH NUTRITION OR HYDRATION WILL NOT OR NO LONGER WILL SERVE TO PROVIDE COMFORT TO ME OR ALLEVIATE MY PAIN.

5. DESIGNATION OF ALTERNATE AGENT.

Because I wish that an agent shall be available to exercise the authorities granted hereunder at all times, I further designate each of the following individuals to succeed to such authorities and to serve under this instrument, in the order named, if at any time the agent first named (or any alternate designee) is not readily avail-able or is unwilling to serve or to continue to serve:

First Alternate Agent: (Name)_____

(Relationship) _____

presently residing at _____

Phone:_____

Second Alternate Agent: (Name) _____

(Relationship) _____

presently residing at_____

Phone:_____

Each alternate shall have and exercise all of the authority conferred above.

6. NO EXPIRATION DATE. This Durable Power of Attorney for Health Care shall not be affected by my disability or by lapse of time. This Durable Power of Attorney for Health Care shall have no expiration date.

7. SEVERABILITY. Any invalid or unenforceable power, authority or provision of this instrument shall not affect another power, authority or provision or the appointment of my agent to make health care decisions.

8. PRIOR DESIGNATIONS REVOKED. I hereby revoke any prior Durable Power of Attorney for Health Care executed by me under Chapter 1337 of the Ohio Revised Code.

I understand the purpose and effect of this document and sign my name to this Durable Power of Attorney for Health Care after careful deliberation on (Date) _____

at (City) _____, Ohio.

(Signature of Principal) _____

THIS DURABLE POWER OF ATTORNEY FOR HEALTH CARE WILL NOT BE VALID UNLESS IT IS EITHER (1) SIGNED BY TWO ELIGIBLE WITNESSES AS DEFINED BELOW WHO ARE PRESENT WHEN YOU SIGN OR ACKNOWLEDGE YOUR SIGNATURE OR (2) ACKNOWLEDGED BEFORE A NOTARY PUBLIC.

I attest that the principal signed or acknowledged this Durable Power of Attorney for Health Care in my presence, that the principal appears to be of sound mind and not under or subject to duress, fraud, or undue influence. I further attest that I am not the agent designated in this document, I am not the attending physician of the principal, I am not the administrator of a nursing home in which the principal is receiving care, and I am an adult not related to the principal by blood, marriage or adoption.

Signature: _____

Residence Address: _____

Print Name: _____

_____

Date: _____

_____

Signature: _____

Residence Address: _____

Print Name: _____

_____

Date: _____

_____

OR ACKNOWLEDGMENT BY A NOTARY PUBLIC.

[NOTE: This document was prepared and is distributed by the Ohio State Bar Association, and we gratefully acknowledge their work on the document.]

Appendix F

Christian Affirmation of Life

To my family, friends, physician, lawyer, and clergyman:

I believe that each individual person is created by God our Father in love and that God retains a loving relationship to each person throughout human life and eternity.

I believe that Jesus Christ lived, suffered, and died for me and that his suffering, death, and resurrection prefigured and made possible the death-resurrection process which I now anticipate.

I believe that each person's worth and dignity derives from the relationship of love that God has for each individual person and not from one's usefulness or effectiveness in society.

I believe that God our Father has entrusted me a shared dominion with him over my earthly existence so that I am bound to use ordinary means to preserve my life but I am free to refuse extraordinary means to prolong my life.

I believe that through death life is not taken away but merely changed, and though I may experience fear, suffering, and sorrow, by the grace of the Holy Spirit, I hope to accept death as a free human act which enables me to surrender this life and to be united with God for eternity.

Because of my belief:

I request that I be informed as death approaches so that I may continue to prepare for the full encounter with Christ through the help of the sacraments and the consolation and prayers of my family and friends.

I request that, if possible, I be consulted concerning the medical procedures which might be used to prolong my life as death approaches. If I can no longer take part in decisions concerning my own future and if there is no reasonable expectation of my recovery from physical and mental disability, I request that no extraordinary means be used to prolong my life.

I request, though I wish to join my suffering to the suffering of Jesus so I may be united fully with him in the act of death-resurrection, that my pain, if unbearable, be alleviated. However, no means should be used with the intention of shortening my life.

I request, because I am a sinner and in need of reconciliation and because my faith, hope, and love may not overcome all fear and doubt, that my family, friends, and the whole Christian community join me in prayer and mortification as I prepare for the great personal act of dying.

Finally, I request that after my death, my family, friends, and the whole Christian community pray for me, and rejoice with me because of the mercy and love of the Trinity, with whom I hope to be united for all eternity.

Signed _____

Date _____

[Note: This document was approved by the Board of Trustees of The Catholic Hospital Association.]

Appendix G

The Christian Living Will

To My Family, Physician, Clergy, Attorney, and Medical Facility:

First: I, _____ , as
a Christian, believe that "Whether we live or whether
we die, we are the Lord's" (Romans 14.8). If death is certain, so is the faithfulness of God in death as in life. With
this high hope to sustain me, I wish to be responsible in
dying as well as in living.

Second: To this end, I implore all those responsible for my care
and knowledgeable of my condition to be completely
honest with me in the event of a terminal illness, so that
I may make my own decisions and preparations as
much as possible.

Third: If there is no reasonable expectation of my recovery and
I am no longer able to share decisions concerning my
future, I ask that I be allowed to die and not be kept
alive indefinitely by artificial means or heroic measures.
I ask that drugs be administered to me as needed to
relieve terminal suffering even if this may hasten the
moment of my death. I am not asking that my life be
directly taken, but that my dying be not unreasonably
prolonged if my condition is hopeless, my deterioration
irreversible, and the maintenance of my life an overwhelming responsibility for my family or an unfair
monopoly of medical resources.

Fourth: This request is made thoughtfully while I am in good
health and spirits. Even if this document be not binding
legally, I beg those who care for me to honor its intent,
which is in part to relieve them of some of the burden of
this decision. In this way, I take responsibility for my
own death and gladly give my life back to God.

Date: _____

Signed: _____

Witness: _____

Reaffirmations: _____

Date: _____

Signed: _____

Copies given to: _____

Appendix H

Some Relevant Web Sites and Phone Numbers

Web Sites

The following are a few of the enormous number of Web sites that I have found to be useful. Searching the Web under the key words of imagery, guided imagery, and cancer, for example, will send you off on an exploration of many sources or information, as well as much vending of particular products and services. OncoLink is a very good place to start your search. The following list is in alphabetical order.

Academy for Guided Imagery, Inc.:
> **www.healthy.com/agi**

Alternative Therapies in Health and Medicine—This is the premier journal in the field:
> **www.alternative-therapies.com/select/currentmain.html**

American Cancer Society—Information in many categories including living with cancer and treatments:
> **www.cancer.org**

American Society of Clinical Oncology—People Living With Cancer Section—Special information by oncologists for those with cancer:
> **www.asco.org**

Arbor Nutrition Guide—An excellent source about nutrition in general which contains many categories, and has links to other sources. Of special interest may be the section on vegetarian and alternative nutrition, also with many links:
> **www.arbor.nutrition.com**

Cancer Care, Inc.—Information on specific cancers and clinical trials:
> **www.cancercare.org**

CancerGuide—Provides a helpful "tour" about obtaining information about cancer, including clinical trials:
www.cancerguide.org

CancerNet—An information service provided by the National Cancer Institute (NCI) of NIH:
www.cancernet.nci.nih.gov

CanSearch—A guide to cancer resources maintained by the National Coalition for Cancer Survivorship:
www.cansearch.org

Commonweal—A health and environmental research institute with several programs including a one-week cancer residency retreat:
www.commonweal.org

ECaP (Exceptional Cancer Patients)—Bernie Siegel's speaking schedule; resource materials; training opportunities:
www.ecap-online.org

Healthfinder—A service of the U.S. Department of Health and Human Services with information on and links to many health-related subjects:
www.healthfinder.gov

HealthWeb—Developed under contract with the National Library of Medicine and contains information on a large variety of health-related subjects:
www.healthweb.org

The Hemlock Society—Information on options for a peaceful death:
www.hemlock.org

IBIS—An informational link to many resources maintained by the Integrative Medical Arts Group, Inc.:
www.healthwwweb.com

Links to Cancer Institutes and Research Centers—Information about specific cancers as well as message boards and links to support groups:
> **www.seidata.com/~marriage/rcancer.html**

MEDLINE—This is the National Library of Medicine's premier bibliographic database:
> **www.nlm.nih.gov/databases/medline.html**

Merck—This gives you free access to the complete *The Merck Manual,* the most widely used general medical text:
> **www. merck.com**

National Cancer Institute (NCI)—This Web site connects you to all of NCI's services:
> **www.nci.nih.gov**

National Center for Complementary and Alternative Medicine (NCCAM)—This center supports basic and applied research and training and disseminates information on complementary and alternative medicine to practitioners and the public:
> **www.altmed.od.nih.gov**

National Institutes of Health (NIH)—The U.S. government's central research agency on health matters:
> **www.nih.gov**

Nutrition Navigator—The Tufts University Web site for those who seek reliable information on nutrition:
> **www.navigator.tufts.edu**

Office of Dietary Supplements (ODS)—They maintain an extensive international bibliographic database on information about dietary supplements:
> **www.odp.od.nih.gov/ods/databases/databases.html**

OncoLink—University of Pennsylvania Cancer Center—This is a superb Web site with up-to-date information in many categories to help cancer patients. Some of the information is available in Spanish:
> **www.oncolink.upenn.edu**

Simonton Cancer Center—Information about Dr. O. Carl Simonton's programs:
   www.lainet.com/~simonton

Toxicology Data Network (TOXNET)—Databases on toxicology, hazardous chemicals and related areas:
   www.toxnet.nlm.nih.gov/servlets/toxnet.pages.homepage

Veris Resource Information Service—A particularly good source for information on antioxidants:
   www.veris-online.org

Useful Phone Numbers

The following are some useful phone numbers in alphabetical order:
   American Cancer Society: 800-227-2345
   American Pain Society: 847-375-4700
   Association of Oncology Social Work: 410-614-3990
   Cancer Care, Inc.: 800-813-4673
   CancerFax: 301-402-5874
   Cancer Information Service (CIS): 800-422-6237
   Exceptional Cancer Patients (ECaP): 814-337-8192
   National Cancer Institute: 800-422-6237
   National Coalition for Cancer Survivorship: 888-650-9127
   National Family Caregivers Association: 800-896-3650
   Oncology Nursing Society: 412-921-7373
   Patient Advocate Foundation: 800-532-5274

References

Achterberg, J. (1985). *Imagery in Healing: Shamanism and Modern Medicine.* Boston: New Science Library.

Achterberg, J., Dossey, B., & Kolkmeier, L. (1994). *Rituals of Healing: Using Imagery for Health and Wellness.* New York: Bantam Books.

Adams, P. (1998). *Gesundheit! Bringing Good Health to You, the Medical System, and Society through Physician Service, Complementary Therapies, Humor, and Joy.* Rochester, VT: Healing Arts Press.

Ader, R. (Ed.) (1981). *Psychoneuroimmunology.* New York: Academic Press.

Ader, R. (1997). The Role of Conditioning in Pharmacology. In A. Harrington (Ed.), *The Placebo Effect. An Interdisciplinary Exploration.* (pp. 138–165). Cambridge, MA: Harvard University Press.

Ader, R.A., & Cohen, N. (1975). Behaviorally Conditioned Immunosuppression. *Psychosomatic Medicine, 37,* 333–340.

American Journal of Clinical Hypnosis (1982, 1983). Special Issue: *Hypnosis and Cancer. 25,* Nos. 2, 3.

Ahmad, N., & Mukhtar, H. (1999). Green Tea Polyphenols and Cancer: Biological Mechanisms and Practical Implication. *Nutrition Reviews 57* (3): 78–83.

Ames, B.N., Shigenaga, M.K., & Hagen, T.M. (1993). Oxidants, Antioxidants, and the Degenerative Diseases of Aging. *Proceedings of the National Academy of Science (USA) 90:* 7915–7922.

Andreas, S., & Andreas, C. (1987). *Change Your Mind and Keep the Change.* Moab, UT: Real People Press.

Andreas, S., & Andreas, C. (1989). *Heart of the Mind.* Moab, UT: Real People Press.

Andreas, C., & Andreas, T. (1994). *Core Transformation.* Moab, UT: Real People Press.

Andrews, C. (1997). *The Circle of Simplicity. Return to the Good Life.* New York: HarperCollins Publishers.

Bailey, C. (1991). *The New Fit or Fat.* Boston: Houghton Mifflin Company.

Baldwin, G.C. (1970). *Schemers, Dreamers and Medicine Men: Witchcraft and Magic Among Primitive People*. New York: Four Winds Press.

Balentine, D.A., Albano, M.C., & Nair, M.G. (1999). Role of Medicinal Plants, Herbs, and Spices in Protecting Human Health. *Nutrition Reviews 57* (9, II): S41–S45.

Bandler, R. (1985). *Using Your Brain for a Change*. Moab, UT: Real People Press.

Bandler, R., & Grinder, J. (1975). *The Structure of Magic*. Palo Alto: Science and Behavior Books.

Bandler, R., & Grinder, J. (1982). *Reframing: Neuro-Linguistic Programming and the Transformation of Meaning*. Moab, UT: Real People Press.

Bank, W.O. (1985). Hypnotic Suggestion for the Control of Bleeding in the Angiography Suite. In S.R. Lankton (Ed.), *Ericksonian Monographs* No. 1. *Elements and Dimensions of an Ericksonian Approach*. (pp. 76– 88). New York: Brunner/Mazel.

Barker, P. (1985). *Using Metaphors in Psychotherapy*. New York: Brunner/Mazel.

Barth, T.J., Zoller, J., Kubler, A., Born, I.A., & Osswald, H. (1997). Redifferentiation of Oral Dysplastic Mucosa by the Application of the Antioxidants Beta-carotene, Alpha-tocopherol, and Vitamin C. *International Journal for Vitamin and Nutrition Research 67* (5): 368–376.

Battino, R., & South, T.L. (1999). *Ericksonian Approaches: A Comprehensive Manual*. Bancyfelin, Carmarthen, UK: Crown House Publishing Ltd.

Benjamin, H.H. (1995). *The Wellness Community Guide to Fighting and Recovery from Cancer*. New York: Jeremy P. Tarcher/Putnam Books.

Benor, D.J. (1990). Survey of Spiritual Healing Research. *Complementary Medical Research*, 4:1 September. 9–33.

Benor, D.J. (1993). *Healing Research*. Munich: Helix Verlag GmbH.

Benson, H. (1975). *The Relaxation Response*. New York: William Morrow and Co.

Benson, H. (1984). *Beyond the Relaxation Response*. New York: Times Books.

Benson, H. (with Stark, M.). (1996). *Timeless Healing—the Power and Biology of Belief*. New York: Scribner.

Bloch, A.S. (1994). Feeding the Cancer Patient: Where Have We Come From, Where Are We Going? *Nutrition in Clinical Practice* 9: 87–89.

Borysenko, J. (1988). *Minding the Body, Mending the Mind.* New York: Bantam Books.

Borysenko, J. (1990). *Guilt is the Teacher, Love is the Lesson.* New York: Warner Books.

Borysenko, J. (1994). *Fire in the Soul.* New York: Warner Books.

Brody, H. (1997). The Doctor as Therapeutic Agent: A Placebo Effect Research Agenda. In A. Harrington (Ed.), *The Placebo Effect. An Interdisciplinary Exploration.* (pp. 77–92.) Cambridge, MA: Harvard University Press.

Brooks, A.M. (1985). *The Grieving Time: A Year's Account of Recovery from Loss.* Garden City, NY: The Dial Press (Doubleday & Co.).

Brown, W.A. (1998). The Placebo Effect. *Scientific American.* January, 90–95.

Campion, E.W. (1993). Why Unconventional Medicine? *New England Journal of Medicine.* Jan. 28. *328*, No. 4, Editorial.

Byrd, R.C. (1988). Positive Therapeutic Effects of Intercessory Prayer in a Coronary Care Unit Population. *Southern Medical Journal 81:7* (July): 826–829.

Cheek, D.B. (1959). Unconscious Perception of Meaningful Sounds During Surgical Anesthesia as Revealed Under Hypnosis. *American Journal of Clinical Hypnosis, 1*, 101–113.

Cheek, D.B. (1960a). Use of Preoperative Hypnosis to Protect Patients from Careless Conversation. *American Journal of Clinical Hypnosis, 3* (2), 101–102.

Cheek, D.B. (1960b). What Does the Surgically Anesthetized Patient Hear? *Rocky Mountain Medical Journal, 57*, January, 49–53.

Cheek, D.B. (1961). Unconscious Reactions and Surgical Risk. *Western Journal of Surgery, Obstetrics, and Gynecology, 69*, 325–328.

Cheek, D.B. (1964). Further Evidence of Persistence of Hearing Under Chem-anesthesia: Detailed Case Report. *American Journal of Clinical Hypnosis, 7*(1), 55–59.

Cheek, D.B. (1965). Can Surgical Patients React to What They Hear Under Anesthesia? *Journal American Association Nurse Anesthetists, 33*, 30–38.

Cheek, D.B. (1966). The Meaning of Continued Hearing Sense Under General Anesthesia. *American Journal of Clinical Hypnosis, 8*, 275–280.

Cheek, D.B. (1981). Awareness of Meaningful Sounds Under General Anesthesia: Considerations and a Review of the Literature. In H.J. Wain *Theoretical and Clinical Aspects of Hypnosis*. Miami: Symposia Specialists Inc.

Cheek, D.B. (1994). *Hypnosis. The Application of Ideomotor Techniques*. Needham Heights, MA: Allyn and Bacon.

Clark, L.C., Combs, G.F., Turnbull, B.W., Slate, E.H., Chalker, D.K., Chow, J., Davis, L.S., Glover, R.A., Graham, G.F., Gross, E.G., Krongrad, A., Lesher, J.L., Park, H.K., Sanders, B.B., Smith, C.L., & Taylor, J.R. (1996). Effect of Selenium Supplementation for Cancer Prevention in Patients with Carcinoma of the Skin. *Journal of the American Medical Association 276* (24): 1957–1963.

Clawson, T.A., & Swade, R.H. (1975). The Hypnotic Control of Blood Flow and Pain: the Cure of Warts and the Potential for the Use of Hypnosis in the Treatment of Cancer. *American Journal of Clinical Hypnosis, 17*, 160–169.

Comstock, G.W., Bush, T.L., & Helzlsouer, K. (1992). Serum Retinol, Beta-carotene, Vitamin E and Selenium as Related to Subsequent Cancer of Specific Sites. *American Journal of Epidemiology 135* (2): 115–121.

Connor, W.E., & Connor, S.L. (1989). Dietary Treatment of Familial Hypercholesterolemia. *Arteriosclerosis (Suppl. 1) 9* (1): I91–I105.

Cooper, K.H. (1996). *Advanced Nutritional Therapies*. Nashville: Thomas Nelson, Publishers,.

Cousins, N. (1979, 1981). *Anatomy of an Illness*. New York: W.W. Norton & Co.

Cousins, N. (1984). *The Healing Heart*. New York: Bantam Books.

Davis, M.P., & Dickerson, E.D. (2000). Cachexia and Anorexia: Cancer's Covert Killer. *Supportive Care in Cancer*. In press.

de Shazer, S. (1985). *Keys to Solution in Brief Therapy*. New York: W.W. Norton & Co.

de Shazer, S. (1988). *Clues. Investigating Solutions in Brief Therapy*. New York: W.W. Norton & Co.

de Shazer, S. (1991). *Putting Difference to Work*. New York: W.W. Norton & Co.

de Shazer, S. (1994). *Words were Originally Magic*. New York: W.W. Norton & Co.

Dilts, R., Halbom, T., & Smith, S. (1990). *Beliefs: Pathways to Health and Well-being*. Lake Oswego, OR: Metamorphous Press.

Dokay, K.J. (1993). *Living with Life-threatening Illness. A Guide for Patients, their Families, and Caregivers*. San Francisco: Jossey-Bass Publishers.

Dossey, L. (1991). *Meaning and Medicine. Lessons from a Doctor's Tales of Breakthrough and Healing*. New York: Bantam Books.

Dossey, L. (1993). *Healing Words. The Power of Prayer and the Practice of Medicine*. New York: HarperCollins Publishers.

Dossey, L. (1996). *Prayer is Good Medicine*. New York: HarperCollins Publishers.

Dossey, L. (1997). *Be Careful What You Pray For ... You Just Might Get It*. New York: HarperCollins Publishers.

Driver, T.F. (1991). *The Magic of Ritual. Our Need for Liberating Rites that Transform Our Lives and Our Communities*. San Francisco: Harper.

Dubin, L.L., & Shapiro, S.S. (1974). Use of Hypnosis to Facilitate Dental Extraction and Homeostasis in a Classic Hemophiliac with a High Antibody Titer to Factor VIII. *American Journal of Clinical Hypnosis, 17*, 79–83.

Elgin, D. (1981). *Voluntary Simplicity. Toward a Way of Life that is Outwardly Simple, Inwardly Rich*. New York: William Morrow and Company.

Erickson, M.H., Rossi, E.L., & Rossi, S.I. (1976). *Hypnotic Realities*. New York: Irvington Publishers, Inc.

Erickson, M.H., & Rossi, E.L. (1979). *Hypnotherapy: An Exploratory Casebook*. New York: Irvington Publishers, Inc.

Erickson, M.H., & Rossi, E.L. (1980). *The Collected Papers of Milton H. Erickson on Hypnosis. Vol. II. Hypnotic Alteration of Sensory, Perceptual and Psychophysiological Processes*. New York: Irvington Publishers, Inc.

Erickson, M.H., & Rossi, E.L. (1981). *Experiencing Hypnosis. Therapeutic Approaches to Altered States*. New York: Irvington Publishers, Inc.

Esterling, B.A., L'Abate, L., Murray, E.J., & Pennebaker, J.W. (1999). Empirical Foundations for Writing in Prevention and Psychotherapy: Mental and Physical Health Outcomes. *Clinical Psychology Review, 19*, 79–96.

Evans, F. J. (1985). Expectancy, Therapeutic Instructions, and the Placebo Response. In L. White, B. Tursky, & G.E. Schwartz. (Eds.), *Placebo Theory, Research, and Mechanisms.* (pp. 215–228). New York: The Guildford Press.

Evans, W., & Rosenberg, I.H. (1992). *Biomarkers. The 10 Keys to Prolonging Vitality.* New York: Fireside (Simon & Schuster).

Ferguson, H.J.S. (1981). *A Study of the Characteristics of American Indian Professional Women in Oklahoma.* Ph.D. Dissertation: The Ohio State University.

Fink, J.M. (1997). *Third Opinion. An International Directory to Alternative Therapy Centers for the Treatment and Prevention of Cancer and Other Degenerative Diseases.* Garden City Park, NY: Avery Publishing Group.

Frankl, V.E. (1959; 1962, Rev. Ed.; 1984, 3rd Ed.). *Man's Search for Meaning.* New York: Simon and Schuster.

Frankl, V.E. (1986). *The Doctor and the Soul. From Psychotherapy to Logotherapy.* (2nd ed.). New York: Vintage Books (Random House).

Frankl, V.E. (1997). *Viktor Frankl. Recollections. An Autobiography.* New York: Insight Books (Plenum Press).

Freedman, J., & Combs, G. (1996). *Narrative Therapy. The Social Construction of Preferred Realities.* New York: W.W. Norton & Company.

Gifford, K.D. (1998). The Mediterranean Diet as a Food Guide: The Problem of Culture and History. *Nutrition Today 33* (6): 233–243.

Gilligan, S.G. (1987). *Therapeutic Trances, the Cooperation Principle in Ericksonian Hypnotherapy.* New York: Brunner/Mazel.

Gilligan, S.G. (1997). *The Courage to Love. Principles and Practices of Self-relations Psychotherapy.* New York: W.W. Norton & Company.

Glaser, R. (1985). Stress, Loneliness, and Changes in Herpes Virus Latency. *Journal of Behavioral Medicine, 8,* 249–260.

Gordon, D. (1978). *Therapeutic Metaphors. Helping Others Through the Looking Glass.* Cupertino, CA: Meta Publications.

Gravitz, M.A. (1988). Early Uses of Hypnosis in Surgical Anesthesia. *American Journal of Clinical Hypnosis, 30,* 201–208.

Green, E., & Green, A. (1977). *Beyond Biofeedback.* New York: Delta.

Grevert, P., & Goldstein, A. (1985). Placebo Analgesia, Naloxone, and the Role of Endogenous Opiods. In L. White, B. Tursky, and G.E. Schwartz, (Eds.), *Placebo: Theory, Research, and Mechanisms.* New York: Guildford Press. pp. 332–350.

Grinder, J., & Bandler, R. (1976). *The Structure of Magic II*. Palo Alto: Science and Behavior Books.

Grinder, J., & Bandler, R. (1981). *Trance-formations; Neuro-Linguistic Programming and the Structure of Hypnosis*. Moab, UT: Real People Press.

Hahn, R.A. (1997). The Nocebo Phenomenon: Scope and Foundations. In A. Harrington (Ed.), *The Placebo Effect. An Interdisciplinary Exploration*. (pp. 56–76.) Cambridge, MA: Harvard University Press.

Hall, E.T. (1959). *The Silent Language*. New York: A Fawcett Premier Book (Doubleday & Co., Inc.).

Hammerschlag, C.A. (1988). *The Dancing Healers*. New York: HarperCollins.

Hammerschlag, C.A. (1993). *The Theft of the Spirit*. New York: Simon & Schuster.

Hammerschlag, C.A., & Silverman, H.D. (1997). *Healing Ceremonies*. New York: A Perigree Book.

Harrington, A. (Ed.) (1997). *The Placebo Effect. An Interdisciplinary Exploration*. Cambridge, MA: Harvard University Press.

Helzlsouer, K.J., Bloch, G., Blumberg, J., Diplock, A.T., Levine, M., Marnett, L.J., Schulplein, R.J., Spence, J.T., & Simic, M.G. (1994). Summary of the Roundtable Discussion on Strategies for Cancer Prevention: Diet, Food, Additives, Supplements, and Drugs. *Cancer Research (Suppl) 54:* 2044s–2051s.

Jacobson, E. (1938). *Progressive Relaxation*. Chicago: University of Chicago Press.

James, T., & Woodsmall, W. (1988). *Time Line Therapy and the Basis of Personality*. Cupertino, CA: Meta Publications.

James, T. (1989). *The Secret of Creating your Future*. Honolulu: The Profitability Group, Inc. & Tad James.

Kabat-Zinn, J. (1990). *Full Catastrophe Living. Using the Wisdom of your Body and Mind to Face Stress, Pain, and Illness*. New York: Dell Publishing.

Johnston, C.S. (1999). Biomarkers for Establishing a Tolerable Upper Intake Level for Vitamin C. *Nutrition Reviews 57*: 71–77.

Kempermann, G., & Gage, F.H. (1999). New Nerve Cells for the Adult Brain. *Scientific American*, May, pp. 48–53.

Kiecolt-Glaser, J.K. (1984). Stress and the Transformation of Lymphocytes by Epstein-Barr Virus. *Journal of Behavioral Medicine, 7*, 1–12.

Kim, Y.I. (1999). Folate and Cancer Prevention: A New Medical Application of Folate Beyond Hyperhomocysteinemia and Neural Tube Defects. *Nutrition Reviews 57* (10): 314–321.

Kirsch, I. (1997). Specifying Nonspecifics: Psychological Mechanisms of Placebo Effects. In A. Harrington (Ed.), *The Placebo Effect. An Interdisciplinary Exploration.* (pp. 166–186.) Cambridge, MA: Harvard University Press.

Klein, S., & Koretz, R.L. (1994). Nutrition Support in Patients with Cancer: What do the Data Really Show? *Nutrition in Clinical Practice 9*: 91–100.

Koo, L.C. (1997). Diet and Lung Cancer 20+ years later: More Questions than Answers? *International Journal of Cancer Suppl 10*: 22–29.

L'Abate, L. (1992). *Programmed Writing: A Self-administered Approach for Interventions with Individuals, Couples, and Families.* Pacific Grove, CA: Brooks/Cole.

L'Abate, L. (1997). Distance Writing and Computer-assisted Training. In S.R. Sauber (Ed.), *Managed Mental Health Care: Major Diagnostic and Treatment Approaches.* (pp. 133–163). Bristol, PA: Brunner/Mazel.

Lankton, S., & Lankton, C. (1983). *The Answer Within. A Clinical Framework of Ericksonian Hypnotherapy.* New York: Brunner/Mazel.

Lawlis, G.F. (1996). *Transpersonal Medicine. A New Approach to Healing Body-mind-spirit.* Boston: Shambhala.

Lazarou, J., Pomeranz, B.H., & Corey, P.N. (1998). Incidence of Adverse Drug Reactions in Hospitalized Patients. A Meta-analysis of Prospective Studies. *Journal of the American Medical Association, 279*, No. 15, 1200–1205.

Lerner, M. (1996). *Choices in Healing.* Cambridge, MA: The MIT Press.

LeShan, L. (1974). *How to Meditate. A Guide to Self-discovery.* New York: Bantam Books.

LeShan, L. (1977). *You can Fight for Your Life.* New York: M. Evans and Co., Inc.

LeShan, L. (1982). *The Mechanic and the Gardener.* New York: Holt, Rinehart & Winston.

LeShan, L. (1989). *Cancer as a Turning Point.* New York: A Plume Book (Penguin Books).

Letters to the Editor. (1989). Psychological Support for Cancer Patients. *The Lancet*, Nov. 18, 1209–1210; rebuttal letter, ibid., Dec. 16, p. 1447.

Levine, J.D., Gordon, N.C., & Fields, H.L. (1978, Sept. 23). The Mechanism of Placebo Anesthesia. *Lancet*, 654–657.

Levine, S. (1979). *A Gradual Awakening*. New York: Anchor Books.

Levine, S. (1982). *Who Dies?* New York: Anchor Books (Doubleday).

Levine, S. (1984). *Meetings at the Edge. Dialogues with the Grieving and the Dying, the Healing and the Healed*. New York: Anchor Books (Doubleday).

Levine, S. (1987). *Healing into Life and Death*. New York: Anchor Books (Doubleday).

Levine, S. (1991). *Guided Meditations, Explorations and Healings*. New York: Anchor Books (Doubleday).

Levine, S. (1997). *A Year to Live*. New York: Bell Tower (Crown Publishing).

Levine, M. (1999). From Molecules to Menus: Recommendations for Vitamin C Intake. *Journal of the American College of Nutrition 18* (5): 524.

Lewis, B.A., & Pucelik, F. (1982). *Magic Demystified: a Pragmatic Guide to Communication and Change*. Lake Oswego, OR: Metamorphous Press.

Linden, W. (1990). *Autogenic Training. A Clinical Guide*. New York: The Guildford Press.

Liptak, K. (1992). *North American Indian Medicine People*. New York: Franklin Watts.

Liu, Y.K., Varela, M., & Oswald, R. (1975). The Correspondence between some Motor Points and Acupuncture Loci. *American Journal of Chinese Medicine, 3*, 347–358.

Liu, W.H.D., Standen, P.J., & Aitkenhead, A.R. (1992). Therapeutic Suggestions during General Anesthesia in Patients Undergoing Hysterectomy. *British Journal of Anesthesia, 68*, 277–281.

Luhrs, J. (1997). *The Simple Living Guide*. New York: Broadway Books.

Luparello, T.J., Lyons, H.A., Bleecker, E.R., & McFadden, E.R. (1968). Influences of Suggestion on Airway Reactivity in Asthmatic Subjects. *Psychosomatic Medicine*, 30: 819–825.

McLauchlin, L. (1992). *Advanced Language Patterns Mastery*. Calgary, Canada: Leading Edge Communications.

Meichenbaum, D., & Turk, D.C. (1987). *Facilitating Treatment Adherence: A Practitioner's Guidebook*. New York: Plenum Press.

Melzack, R., Stillwell, D.M., & Fox, E.J. (1977). Trigger Points and Acupuncture Points for Pain: Correlations and Implications. *Pain, 3*, 3–23.

Melzack, R. & Wall, P.D. (1983). *The Challenge of Pain*. (Rev. ed.) New York: Basic Books.

Melzack, R. (1990). The Tragedy of Needless Pain. *Scientific American, 262*, 27–33. Feb.

Menahem, S. (1995). *When Therapy isn't Enough. The Healing Power of Prayer and Psychotherapy*. Winfield, IL: Relaxed Books.

Miller, S.D., & Berg, I.K. (1995). *The "Miracle" Method*. New York: W.W. Norton & Co.

Mills, J.C., & Crowley, R.J. (1986). *Therapeutic Metaphors for Children*. New York: Brunner/Mazel.

Moondance, W. (1994). *Rainbow Medicine: a Visionary Guide to Native American Shamanism*. New York: Sterling Publishing Co., Inc.

Morris, D.B. (1997). Placebo, Pain, and Belief: a Biocultural Model. In A. Harrington (Ed.), *The Placebo Effect. An Interdisciplinary Exploration*. (pp. 187–207). Cambridge, MA: Harvard University Press.

Naparstek, B. (1994). *Staying Well with Guided Imagery*. New York: Warner Books.

Neihardt, J.G. (Flaming Rainbow). (1961). *Black Elk Speaks: Being the Life of a Holy Man of the Oglala Sioux*. Lincoln, NB: University of Nebraska Press.

Native American Center. (March 1999). *Discussion*. Columbus, Ohio.

Native Peoples. (Fall, 1998) Pueblo Artists. *The Arts and Life Ways Magazine*. pp. 62–64.

O'Hanlon, W.H. (1987). *Taproots. Underlying Principles of Milton Erickson's Therapy and Hypnosis*. New York: W.W. Norton & Co.

Ornish, D. (1991). *Dr. Dean Ornish's Program for Reversing Heart Disease*. New York: Ballantine Books.

Ornish, D. (1997). *Love & Survival. The Scientific Basis for the Healing Power of Intimacy*. New York: HarperCollins Publishers.

Ottery, F.D. (1994). Rethinking Nutritional Support of the Cancer Patient: The New Field of Nutritional Oncology. *Seminars in Oncology 21* (6): 770–778.

Pauling, L. (1976). *Vitamin C, the Common Cold and the Flu*. San Francisco: W.H. Freeman and Co.

Pearson, R.E. (1961). Response to Suggestions Given under General Anesthesia. *American Journal of Clinical Hypnosis, 4,* 106–114.

Pennebaker, J.W. (1997). *Opening Up: The Healing Power of Confiding in Others*. New York: Guildford.

Perls, F.S., Hefferline, R.E., & Goodman, P. (1951). *Gestalt Therapy. Excitement and Growth in the Human Personality*. New York: A Delta Book. Dell Publishing Co.

Perls, F.S. (1969a). *Gestalt Therapy Verbatim*. Moab, UT: Real People Press.

Perls, F.S. (1969b). *In and Out of the Garbage Pail*. Lafayette, CA: Real People Press.

Perls, F.S. (1973). *The Gestalt Approach and Eye Witness to Therapy*. Palo Alto: CA: Science and Behavior Books.

Piediscalzi, N. Personal Communication, 14 October 1999.

Polster, E., & Polster, M. (1974). *Gestalt Therapy Integrated. Contours of Theory and Practice*. New York: Vintage Books (Random House).

Polster, E. (1987). *Every Person's Life is Worth a Novel. How to Cut Through Emotional Pain and Discover the Fascinating Core of Life*. New York: W.W. Norton & Co.

Price. D.D., & Fields, H.L. (1997). The Contribution of Desire and Expectation to Placebo Analgesia: Implications for New Research Strategies. In A. Harrington (Ed.), *The Placebo Effect. An Interdisciplinary Explanation*. (pp. 117–137). Cambridge, MA: Harvard University Press.

Pritikin, N. (1983). *28 Days to a Longer Healthier Life*. New York: Simon and Schuster.

Pritikin, N., & McGrady, Jr., P. (1979). *The Pritikin Program for Diet and Exercise*. New York: Grosset and Dunlap.

Rahner, K. (1985). *Dictionary of Theology*. New York: Crossroads.

Rainwater, J. (1979). *You're in Charge! A Guide to Becoming Your Own Therapist*. Los Angeles: Guild of Tutors.

Remen, R.N. (1994). *Wounded Healers*. Mill Valley, CA: Wounded Healer Press (Commonweal).

Remen, R.N. (1996). *Kitchen Table Wisdom. Stories that Heal*. New York: Riverhead Books.

Rossi, E.L., & Cheek, D.B. (1988). *Mind-body Therapy. Ideodynamic Healing in Hypnosis*. New York: W.W. Norton & Co.

Rossi, E.L., & Nimmons, D. (1991). *The 20 Minute Break*. Los Angeles: Jeremy P. Tarcher, Inc.

Rossi, E.L. (1992). Audio and videotapes of a Demonstration with a Woman who has Arthritis. Erickson Congress Dec. 1992. Available from the Milton H. Erickson Foundation, 3606 N. 24th Street, Phoenix, AZ 85016.

Rossi, E.L. (1993). *The Psychobiology of Mind-body Healing*. (2nd Ed.). New York: W.W. Norton & Co.

Rossi, E.L., & Lippincott, B. (1993). A Clinical-experimental Exploration of Erickson's Naturalistic Approach: Ultradian Time and Trance Phenomena. *Hypnos, 20,* 10–20.

Rossi, E.L. (1996). *The Symptom Path to Enlightenment. The New Dynamics of Self-organization in Hypnotherapy: An Advanced Manual for Beginners*. Pacific Palisades, CA: Palisades Gateway Publishing.

St. James, E. (1994). *Simplify Your Life. 100 Ways to Slow Down and Enjoy the Things that Really Matter*. New York: Hyperion.

Sattilaro, J., & Monte, T.J. (1982). *Recalled by Life*. New York: Avon Books.

Seligman, P.A., Fink, R., & Massey-Seligman, E.J. (1998). Approach to the Seriously Ill or Terminal Cancer Patient who has a Poor Appetite. *Seminars in Oncology 25* (2, Suppl 6): 33–34.

Shapiro, A.K., & Shapiro, E. (1997). The Placebo: is it Much Ado about Nothing? In A. Harrington (Ed.), *The Placebo Effect. An Interdisciplinary Exploration*. (pp. 12–36). Cambridge, MA: Harvard University Press.

Shapiro, A.K., & Shapiro, E. (1997). *The Powerful Placebo. From Ancient to Modern Physician*. Baltimore: The Johns Hopkins University Press.

Sharp, A.W., & Terbay, S.H. (1997). *Gifts. Two Hospice Professionals Reveal Messages from Those Passing On*. Far Hills, NJ: New Horizon Press.

Sharp, S.J., & Pocock, S.J. (1997). Time Trends in Serum Cholesterol before Cancer Death. *Epidemiology, 8* (2): 132–136.

Siegel, B. (1986). *Love, Medicine and Miracles*. New York: Harper and Row.

Siegel, B. (1989). *Peace, Love, and Healing*. New York: Harper and Row.

Siegel, B. (1993). *How to Live Between Office Visits*. New York: HarperCollins Publishers.

Siegel, B.S. (1998). *Prescriptions for Living. Inspirational Lessons from a Joyful, Loving Life*. New York: HarperCollins Publishers.

Simonian, N.A., & Coyle, J.T. (1996). Oxidative in Neurodegenerative Diseases. *Annual Review of Pharmacology and Toxicology 36*: 83–106.

Simonton, O.C., Simonton, S. & Creighton, J. (1980). *Getting Well Again*. New York: Bantam Books.

Simonton, S.M. (1984). *The Healing Family. The Simonton Approach for Families Facing Illness*. New York: Bantam Books.

Spiegel, D. (1985). The Use of Hypnosis in Controlling Cancer Pain. *CA: Cancer J. Clin., 35*, 221.

Spiegel, D., Bloom, J.R., Kraemer, H.C., & Gottheil, E. (1989). Effect of Psychosocial Treatment on Survival of Patients with Metastatic Breast Cancer. *Lancet* 2(8668): 888–91 (Oct. 14). Also, by the same author and colleagues, see: Spiegel, D. (1992). Hypnosis and Related Techniques in Pain Management. *Hospice Journal.* 8(1–2): 89–119; Kogon, M.M., Biswas, A., Pearl, D., Carlson, R.W., & Spiegel, D. (1997 July 15). Effects of Medical and Psychotherapeutic Treatment on the Survival of Women with Metastatic Breast Cancer. *Cancer. 80*(2): 225–30; Spiegel, D. (1996 June). Cancer and Depression. *British Journal of Psychiatry—Supplement. (30)*: 109–16.; Spiegel, D. (1995 July). Essentials of Psychotherapeutic Intervention for Cancer Patients. *Supportive Care in Cancer.* 3(4): 252–6; Spiegel, D. (1994 Aug. 15). Health Caring. Psychological Support for Patients with Cancer. *Cancer.* 74(4 Suppl). 1453–7; Spiegel, D. (1997 Feb.). Psychosocial Aspects of Breast Cancer Treatment. *Seminars in Oncology.* 24(1 Suppl 1): S1-36–S1-47, ; Spiegel, D., Sands, S., & Koopman, C. (1994 Nov. 1). Pain and Depression in Patients with Cancer. *Cancer.* 74(9): 2570–8.

Spindrift, Inc., PO Box 3995, Salem, OR 97302-0995.

Spiro, H.M. (1986). *Doctors, Patients, and Placebos*. New Haven: Yale University Press.

Spiro, H. (1997). Clinical Reflections on the Placebo Phenomenon. In A. Harrington (Ed.), *The Placebo Effect. An Interdisciplinary Exploration*. (pp. 37–55). Cambridge, MA: Harvard University Press.

Steiner, M. (1999). Vitamin E, a Modifier of Platelet Function: Rationale and Use in Cardiovascular and Cerebrovascular Disease. *Nutrition Reviews 57* (10): 306–309.

Suter, P.M., & Vetter, W. (1999). Alcohol and Ischemic Stroke. *Nutrition Reviews 57* (10): 310–314.

Suzuki, D.T. (1964). *An Introduction to Zen Buddhism*. New York: Grove Press.

The Alpha-tocopherol, Beta-carotene Cancer Prevention Study Group. (1994) *The New England Journal of Medicine 330* (15): 1029–1035.

Thich Nhat Hanh. (1976). *The Miracle of Mindfulness! A Manual of Meditation*. Boston: Beacon Press.

Thomas, K.B. (1987). General Practice Consultations: Is there Any Point in Being Positive? *British Medical Journal, 294,* 1200–1202.

Trichopoulou, A., & Lagiou, P. (1997). Healthy Traditional Mediterranean Diet: An Expression of Culture, History, and Lifestyle. *Nutrition Reviews 55* (11): 383–389.

Trichopoulou, A., Vasilopoulou, E., & Lagiou, A. (1999). Mediterranean Diet and Coronary Heart Disease: Are Antioxidants Critical? *Nutrition Reviews 57* (8): 253–255.

Tursky, B. (1985). Discussion. The 55% Analgesic Effect: Real or Artifact? In L. White, B. Tursky, & G.E. Schwartz (Eds.), *Placebo. Theory, Research, and Mechanisms.* (pp. 229–234). New York: The Guildford Press.

U.S. Congress Office of Technology Assessment. (1990). *Unconventional Cancer Therapies*. Washington: Government Printing Office.

Ursini, F., Tubaro, F., Rong, J., & Sevanian, A. (1999). Optimization of Nutrition: Polyphenols and Vascular Protection. *Nutrition Reviews 57* (8): 241–249.

VandeCreek, L. (Ed.). (1998). *Scientific and Pastoral Perspectives on Intercessory Prayer. An Exchange Between Larry Dossey, M.D., and Health Care Chaplains*. New York: Haworth Press.

Visioli, F.P., & Galli, C. (1998). The Effect of Minor Constituents of Olive Oil on Cardiovascular Disease: New findings. *Nutrition Reviews 56* (5): 142–147.

Wallas, L. (1985). *Stories for the Third Ear*. New York: W.W. Norton & Co.

Wallas, L. (1991). *Stories that Heal. Reparenting Adult Children of Dysfunctional Families Using Hypnotic Stories in Psychotherapy*. New York: W.W. Norton & Co.

Weil, A. (1972). *The Natural Mind. A New Way of Looking at Drugs and the Higher Consciousness*. Boston: Houghton Mifflin Company.

Weil, A. (1995a). *Spontaneous Healing. How to Discover and Enhance your Body's Natural Ability to Maintain and Heal Itself.* New York: Fawcett Columbine.

Weil, A. (1995b). *Natural Health, Natural Medicine.* Boston: Houghton Mifflin Company.

Weil, A. (1996). *Eight Weeks to Optimal Healing Power.* New York: Knopf.

White, L. Tursky, B., & Schwartz, G.E. (1985). *Placebo. Theory, Research, and Mechanisms.* New York: The Guildford Press.

White, M., & Epston, D. (1990). *Narrative Means to Therapeutic Ends.* New York: W.W. Norton & Co.

Whitney, E.N., Cataldo, C.B., & Rolfes, S.R. (1998). *Understanding Normal and Clinical Nutrition,* 5th Ed. Belmont, CA: West-Wadsworth Publishing Co.

Wilber, K. (1991). *Grace and Grit.* Boston: Shambhala.

Willett, W.C. (1994). Diet and Health: What Should We Eat? *Science* 264: 532–537.

Williams, W. (1990). *The Power Within. True Stories of Exceptional Cancer Patients Who Fought Back with Hope.* New York: A Fireside Book (Simon & Schuster).

World Cancer Research Fund in association with American Institute for Cancer Research. (1997). *Food, Nutrition and the Prevention of Cancer: A Global Perspective.* Washington, DC: World Cancer Research Fund/American Institute for Cancer Research.

Wortman, C.B., & Silver., R.C. (1989). The Myths of Coping with Loss. *Journal of Consulting and Clinical Psychology, 57,* 349–357.

Zeig, J.K. (1999). The Virtues of Our Faults: a Key Concept of Ericksonian Hypnotherapy. *Sleep and Hypnosis. 1,* 129–138.

Zureik, M., Courbon, D., & Ducimetiere, P. (1997). Decline in Serum Total Cholesterol and the Risk of Death from Cancer. *Epidemiology 8* (2): 137–143.

Index

Achterberg, J., 23, 30, 34, 78, 123, 126, 136, 351
Achterberg, Dossey, and Kolkmeier scripts, 123, 351
active imagery, 30
acupressure, 24, 256
acupuncture, 3, 10, 16, 24–25, 40, 47, 262, 359
acupuncture points, 24–25, 359
Adams, P., 267
Ader, R., 17–18, 47, 351
adherence, 238, 359
adjectives, 85, 106
adverbs, 85, 106
adverse drug reactions, 149, 258, 358
aerobic exercise, 261
Ahmad, N., 274–275, 351
Aitkenhead, A.R., 155, 359
Albano, M.C., 274, 352
alternative medicine, 8, 12, 256, 284–285, 298, 349
ambiguity, phonological, 113
ambiguity, syntactic, 114
American Cancer Society, 169, 176, 235, 256, 347, 350
American Journal of Clinical Hypnosis, 23, 353–356, 360
American Society for Clinical Hypnosis, 23, 97
Ames, B.N., 273, 351
anaerobic exercise, 260–261
analogical marking, 101
anchoring, 94–95
    anchoring, rules for, 93–95
    anchoring exercises, 94
Andreas, C., 188, 351
Andreas, S., 188, 351
Andrews, C., 266

anesthesia, hearing under, 154–155
antioxidants, 273–274, 280–281, 350–352
apposition of opposites, 112
art therapy, 32, 172, 211, 213, 215, 217, 219, 221, 223, 225, 227, 229, 231, 233
as if, 190–191
Asclepius, 40
associated state, 189–190
auditory, 29, 83–85, 92, 136, 166, 188–189
autobiographies, 225–226
autogenic training, 71, 359
awareness predicates, 106

Bailey, C., 261, 351
Baker, D.C., 61
balance, 24, 63, 271, 276, 281, 287, 290–291, 312
Baldwin, G.C., 285, 288, 352
Balentine, D.A., 274, 352
Bandler, R., 11, 99, 111, 114, 184, 188, 352, 357
Bank, W.O., 155, 247, 335, 352
Barker, P., 199, 352
Barth, T.J., 274, 352
Battino, R., xii, 1–2, 81, 97, 109, 156–157, 198–199, 279, 352
belief systems, 11, 58, 82, 95, 167, 188, 234
Belleruth Naparstek scripts, 127
Benjamin, H.H., 118, 328, 352
Benor, D.J., 58, 352
Benson, H., 38–39, 68, 71, 73–74, 352
Berg, I.K., 191, 360
Bernie Siegel imagery scripts, 130
binds, 114–115, 299

biologically correct imagery, 31
Black Elk, 300, 360
Bloch, A.S., 278, 353, 357
Block, G., 268, 273–274
bloodletting, 40
bonding, 201–205, 207
bonding anchor, 201–202
bonding for healing, 201
bone mass, 147, 262
Borysenko, J., 313–314, 353
Borysenko, J., her words, 313–314
breast cancer support groups, 170
breathing pattern, 89
Brief Family Therapy Center, 191
Brody, H., 50, 353
Brooks, A.M., 213, 265, 353, 358
Brown, G., 173
Brown, W.A., 37, 353
Byrd, R.C., 60, 353

Campbell, J., 11, 167
Campion, E.W., 284, 353
cancer as a gift, 228, 353–354, 361
cardiovascular disease, 272–273, 275–277, 279, 364
cardiovascular disease, intake of alcohol causing, 276
cardiovascular disease prevention, 275
care-givers, workbook for, 221
catharsis, 43
causal connections, 103–104
cellular imagery, 33
ceremonies, ix, 211, 213, 215, 217, 219, 221, 223, 225, 227, 229–234, 251, 265, 291, 293, 357
ceremonies, elements of, 230–231
Chalice of Repose Project, 118
changing personal history, 181–183
Charlie Brown Exceptional Patient Support Group, ix–x, 173
Cheek, D.B., 155, 194, 197, 361

chemoprevention, 273–274
Chevreul pendulum, 197
Chinese medicine, 24, 40, 43, 359
Christian Affirmation of Life, 247, 343
Christian living will, 247, 345
Cindy's story, 143, 145, 199
Clark, L.C., 274, 354
Clawson, T.A., 155
client, 7–8, 237, 239–240
client definition, 7–8
closing healing imagery script, 317
clothing decor, 244
clysterization, 41
Cohen, N., 47, 351
comatose patient, talking to, 264
Combs, G., 227, 354, 356
commentary adjectives, 106
commentary adverbs, 106
Commonweal Cancer Help Program, 22, 175, 306, 348, 361
communicating with medical personnel, 236
communicating with others, 250
complementary medicine, 172
complex equivalence, 183–184
compliance, 44, 238
Comstock, G.W., 273, 354
concrete imagery, 31
Connor, S.L., 277, 279, 354
Connor, W.E., 277, 279, 354
content reframe, 183–184
content vs process, 178
context reframing, 184
contingent suggestions, 107
control, 12–13, 19, 237, 240–241, 243–244, 277–279
controlling medication, 257
Cooper, K.H., 275–276, 354
counseling, 253–254
counselor, 250, 254
Cousins, N., 10, 17–18, 198, 240, 243–244, 265, 267, 354
Covey, P.N., 258

Hypnosis
A Comprehensive Guide
Tad James, M.S., Ph.D.
with Lorraine Flores & Jack Schober

Research shows that many people react differently to different kinds of hypnotic induction – yet many hypnotherapists are confined to using only one technique. This book makes three radically different and significant types of hypnosis easy to use in daily hypnosis work, examining in detail the techniques of Erickson, Estabrooks and Elman. Exploring methods that employ Direct Authoritarian and Indirect Permissive approaches, *Hypnosis* progresses beyond these approaches to describe a new breed of induction pioneered by Dave Elman: a technique that places responsibility for hypnosis *on the client*.

An invaluable resource for all trainers and therapists, *Hypnosis* is a comprehensive and lucid manual that incorporates:

- powerful inductions for producing deep-trance phenomena
- sections on the application of metaphor and hypnotic language patterns
- scripts for a variety of hypnotic inductions.

Tad James, M.S., Ph.D. is one of the world's most influential trainers, and a respected authority on hypnosis. He teaches and appears before audiences for over 200 days every year, and is president of The American Board of Hypnotherapy, one of the world's largest hypnotherapy organisations. Tad is also President of Advanced Neuro-Dynamics, a leading NLP firm, The American Institute of Hypnotherapy, the world's leading hypnosis institute, and American Pacific University, a Hawaii-based institution offering alternative degrees in Hypnosis, Psychology, and Esoteric Studies.

HARDBACK   240 PAGES   ISBN: 1899836454

Ericksonian Approaches
A Comprehensive Manual
Rubin Battino MS & Thomas L. South PhD

Already highly acclaimed, this is an outstanding training manual in the art of Ericksonian hypnotherapy. Designed to be easily accessible, it provides a systematic approach to learning set against a clinical background, developing the reader's learning over twenty-two chapters that include the history of hypnosis, myths and misconceptions, rapport-building skills, language forms, basic and advanced inductions, utilization of ideodynamic responses, basic and advanced metaphor, and Ericksonian approaches in medicine, dentistry, substance abuse and life-challenging diseases.

Also available: a companion audiotape – ISBN 189983642X £9.99 65 mins.

"This book should undoubtedly be read and re-read by any who consider themselves to be hypnotherapists. But it should not be limited to them. If people who are not interested in the subject of hypnotherapy are not drawn to it, this will be a loss for anyone who uses language in the course of therapeutic work.... I highly recommend this book."
– Barry Winbolt, *The New Therapist.*

Rubin Battino MS has a private practice in Yellow Springs, Ohio. He teaches courses periodically for the Department of Human Resources at Wright State University where he holds the rank of adjunct professor. He has over six years of experience as a facilitator in a Bernie Siegel style support group for people who have life-threatening diseases and those who support them. He is President of the Milton H. Erickson Society of Dayton, co-chair of an ad hoc committee to establish certification standards for training in Ericksonian hypnotherapy for the societies and institutes affiliated with the Milton H. Erickson Foundation. He has developed and teaches courses in Ericksonian hypnotherapy at Wright State University with T.L. South. He is Professor Emeritus of chemistry.

Thomas L. South PhD has his doctorate in clinical psychology from the Union Institute. He has conducted workshops for the Associate Trainers in Clinical Hypnosis, and has developed and taught courses in Ericksonian approaches at the University of Dayton and with Rubin Battino at Wright State University. He invited the faculty at the Third International Congress on Ericksonian Approaches to Hypnosis and Psychotherapy. He is the author of a chapter entitled "Hypnosis in Childbirth: A Case Study in Anesthesia." Dr. South is the founder and first president of the Milton H. Erickson Society of Dayton, and is presently a staff psychologist at the Twin Valley Psychiatric System—Dayton Forensic Unit. He has had a private practice for many years.

HARDBACK   564 PAGES   ISBN: 1899836314

Precision Therapy
A Professional Manual Of Fast And
Effective Hypnoanalysis Techniques
Duncan McColl

This publication encapsulates the work of this highly respected British therapist. *Precision Therapy* is an extremely practical book that describes how to initiate healing processes. It is eclectic in nature and free from dogma and jargon. The book is designed for the therapist-healer who does not have the need, the time or the inclination to subject clients to protracted mindgames. Its practicality is illustrated in the training material: each page is a script or a prompt-sheet that can be adapted easily to deal effectively with most problems in a matter of hours rather than weeks or months. A comprehensive manual of fast, effective hypnoanalytic techniques designed for the professional

"Duncan McColl has provided us with a fresh look at how we do our work. It is insightful and provocative. It is scholarly yet remarkably free from the language which constantly calls out for the use of a dictionary. It is fresh and invigorating."
– *The Hypnotherapist.*

Duncan McColl is a practicing member of the International Association of Precision Therapists, the International Society for Professional Hypnosis (USA) and is a biofeedback, behavioral and management science consultant. He served as a pilot in the RAF during the Second World War. He later qualified as a chartered accountant and worked as a senior financial and a marketing executive in leading British and American companies spending thirty-five years abroad, mainly in the United States, Canada, Australia, Mexico and Spain. Since 1970 he has successfully applied ancient and modern teachings, many of them not available in English, to health and business problems, to stress management, creative thinking, psychometric interviewing, and to staff motivation and development.

PAPERBACK   248 PAGES   ISBN: 1899836187

Now available in paperback

Scripts And Strategies In Hypnotherapy
Roger P. Allen

The use of scripts in induction procedures provides a framework upon which to build successful therapy sessions. Written by a practicing hypnotherapist, this is a rich, comprehensive source of scripts and strategies to be used by hypnotherapists of all levels of experience. Areas covered include inductions, deepeners and actual scripts for a wide range of problems, from nail biting to getting a good night's sleep, sports performance to past-life recall, pain management to resolving sexual problems. All scripts may be used as they stand or adapted for specific situations. A runaway bestseller.

"Imaginative, practical and essential for anyone getting started in hypnotherapy."
– Martin Roberts, Ph.D., author of *Change Management Excellence*.

PAPERBACK   180 PAGES   ISBN: 1899836462

-- ✐✐✐ --

Orders to:

The Anglo American Book Company Ltd.

FREEPOST SS1340,
Crown Buildings, Bancyfelin, Carmarthen, Wales, SA33 4ZZ, UK

Tel: 01267 211880/211886 Fax: 01267 211882
(Lines open 9am – 5.30pm Mon – Fri)

E-mail address: books@anglo-american.co.uk

Web site: anglo-american.co.uk

Or visit the
Crown House Publishing Web site at:

w w w . c r o w n h o u s e . c o . u k